They S

"I would read Wayne Coffey writing about hardwood floors. So for someone who was a diehard Mets fan in 1969, I knew *They Said It Couldn't Be Done* was a book I couldn't miss. Like *The Boys of Winter,* his brilliant book about the 1980 U.S. Olympic hockey team, this is a fantastic piece of work. Please buy it, and enjoy every page, as I did."

—TIM LAYDEN, *Sports Illustrated* senior writer and NBC Sports essayist

"Delightful . . . With Shakespearean breadth, Coffey describes the major players and also the Rosencrantzes and Guildensterns of the Amazing Mets. Yes, it was a miracle."

—GEORGE VECSEY, former *New York Times* "Sports of the Times" columnist

"*They Said It Couldn't Be Done* brilliantly brings an iconic baseball season to life. The book is a must-read for not just for Mets fans, but all baseball fans who will appreciate what indeed was the most astounding season in baseball history."

—KEN ROSENTHAL, two-time Sports Emmy winner for
Outstanding Sports Reporter

"In 1969, while much of the world was transfixed by Neil Armstrong's 'one small step,' Queens was experiencing its own giant leap—a leap of faith with its baseball orange-and-blue. Wayne Coffey has always had his finger on the pulse of New York City and its sports, and his take on the 1969 Mets proves it. If you want to know what it was like to live and witness a baseball miracle in tumultuous times, this book is for you."

—RON DARLING, former New York Mets All-Star and
bestselling author of *Game 7, 1986*

"Having lived through the Mets' 1969 World Championship in real time and re-lived it for fifty years, I thought I knew all I needed to know about my boyhood heroes, but in *They Said It Couldn't Be Done* Wayne Coffey has unearthed some fresh gems; most poignantly those involving the personal backgrounds of many of that wonderful team's players. Wayne has done a marvelous job of allowing us to relive that epochal event through a fresh prism. This is simply a great read."

—HOWIE ROSE, New York Mets broadcaster

They Said It Couldn't Be Done

THE '69 METS,

NEW YORK CITY, AND

THE MOST ASTOUNDING

SEASON IN

BASEBALL HISTORY

Wayne Coffey

B\D\W\Y
BROADWAY BOOKS
NEW YORK

2020 Broadway Books Trade Paperback Edition

Copyright © 2019 by Wayne Coffey

Published in the United States by Broadway Books, an imprint of Random House, a division of Penguin Random House LLC, New York.

BROADWAY BOOKS and its colophon are trademarks of Penguin Random House LLC.

Originally published in hardcover in the United States by Crown Archetype, an imprint of Random House, a division of Penguin Random House LLC, New York, in 2019.

Title-page spread photo by Bettmann/Getty Images

LIBRARY OF CONGRESS CATALOGING-IN-PUBLICATION DATA
Names: Coffey, Wayne R., author.
Title: They said it couldn't be done: the '69 Mets, New York City, and the most
    astounding season in baseball history / Wayne Coffey.
Description: New York: Crown Publishers, 2019.
Identifiers: LCCN 2018043635 (print) | LCCN 2019002589 (ebook) |
    ISBN 9781524760908 (ebook) | ISBN 9781524760885 (hardback) |
    ISBN 9781524760892 (trade paperback)
Subjects: LCSH: New York Mets (Baseball team)—History. | Baseball—New
    York (State)—New York—History. | World Series (Baseball) (1969) | BISAC:
    BIOGRAPHY & AUTOBIOGRAPHY / Sports. | SPORTS & RECREATION /
    Baseball / History. | HISTORY / United States / State & Local / Middle Atlantic
    (DC, DE, MD, NJ, NY, PA).
Classification: LCC GV875.N45 (ebook) | LCC GV875.N45 C63 2019 (print) |
    DDC 796.357/64097471—dc23
LC record available at https://lccn.loc.gov/2018043635

Printed in the United States of America on acid-free paper

randomhousebooks.com

9 8 7 6 5 4 3 2 1

Book design by Lauren Dong

In loving memory of Edward John Willi, Jr.

(APRIL 27, 1933–JUNE 25, 2018),

a great baseball fan and an even better person

Few things can help an individual more than to place responsibility on him, and to let him know that you trust him.

—BOOKER T. WASHINGTON

. . .

Start by doing what's necessary; then do what's possible; and suddenly you are doing the impossible.

—ST. FRANCIS OF ASSISI

CONTENTS

PROLOGUE

FORTY-ONE IS A NOTABLE NUMBER IN THE HISTORY OF FLUSHING, Queens, the biggest and easternmost borough of New York City. It's not so much because the neighborhood sits hard by the 41st latitude or because the number was once worn by men named Gordon Richardson and Jim Bethke, both of whom pitched briefly for the local baseball team, the New York Mets, in the mid-1960s. It is more because of the person to wear it after them, a rookie from Fresno, California, named George Thomas Seaver. He arrived in New York in 1967 and, unlike Richardson and Bethke, was a starting pitcher. He wore number 41 with such distinction that no Met will ever put it on again.

Tom Seaver and his contemporaries played their ball games in Shea Stadium, where the Mets took up residence in 1964 and stayed until 2008. Built on top of an ash heap, Shea opened just ahead of the 1964 World's Fair, not far from the former site of Ned's Diner on Roosevelt Avenue. In its fifth year of existence, two men walked on the moon, four hundred thousand people descended on a farm in New York's Catskill Mountains for the biggest and muddiest musical event in history, and Shea Stadium became the epicenter of the baseball world.

The last of these developments was the most unforeseen.

Shea Stadium was a bowl-shaped edifice, long on symmetry,

short on character, its most notable architectural feature the blue and orange tiles that were speckled around its perimeter like rectangular graffiti. It was located a long toss from a bay and creek that bore the name Flushing—an anglicized derivation of the Dutch town Vlissengen, given to the area by its first European settlers. In its earliest days, Flushing was the horticultural hub of New York City, a locale with rich creekside earth that spawned a wide assortment of trees and shrubs, along with the first commercial nursery in the United States. Started by a father and son, Robert and William Prince, the nursery opened for business almost forty years before the signing of the Declaration of Independence.

In Shea Stadium's formative years, it was known for neither fertile soil nor winning baseball. A four-sided clock tower with the words SERVAL ZIPPERS rose in plain view over the left-center-field fence. For decades the Serval Zipper Company helped people keep their pants and dresses on but paid scant attention to its clock, which was stuck at 10:59 for years and showed no more signs of getting unstuck than the Mets showed of ever leaving last place.

The Mets began life as an expansion team in 1962, joining the National League along with the Houston Colt .45s (renamed the Astros late in 1964, to coincide with their move into baseball's first indoor ballpark, the Astrodome). Their principal owner was Joan Whitney Payson, a scion of one of the nation's wealthiest families, a woman whose ancestry traced back to the *Mayflower*. A patron of the arts and noted philanthropist, Payson also had a deep passion for horse racing and baseball, owning a number of Thoroughbreds and a minority share in the New York Giants. When the Giants and Brooklyn Dodgers decamped for California after the 1957 season, Payson was among the appalled masses who couldn't imagine life in New York without a National League ball club. So when the league announced it was adding two franchises, Payson bought one. She thus became the first woman to purchase a club in big-league history.

Payson hired former Yankees general manager George Weiss to be the Mets' first president. Weiss, in turn, hired 71-year-old Casey

Stengel, who had led the Yankees to seven World Series titles and three American League pennants in 12 years, to be their manager. The two men had unassailable baseball credentials, but their winning pedigree did not carry over to their new enterprise.

The 1962 Mets went 40-120, losing more games than any ball club in the twentieth century and finishing 60½ games out of first place. This is not easy to do. It requires staggeringly poor results over the full six-month season, and that is precisely what the Mets achieved, with losing streaks of 9 games (to start the season), 13 games, and 17 games, along with another patch in which they lost 16 of 17. The '62 Mets made 3 errors in their first game, 3 in their last game, and 204 more errors in between. Crisp baseball was in such short supply that one player remembered a road trip in which Stengel announced the day's itinerary: "There will be two buses to the park from the hotel. The two o'clock bus is for those who need a little extra work, and then there will be an empty bus leaving at five o'clock."

The Mets' last rally of their debut season—two on and nobody out against the Cubs in the top of the eighth inning of game 160 at Wrigley Field—ended when catcher Joe Pignatano, a former Dodger and future Mets coach, came on for Clarence "Choo Choo" Coleman and hit into a triple play. It would be Pignatano's final big-league at bat, clearing his schedule to report to his off-season job in the toy department at Abraham & Straus, a Brooklyn department store.

The Mets played their first two seasons in the Polo Grounds, the former home of Payson's beloved New York Giants in upper Manhattan, just across the Harlem River from Yankee Stadium, before relocating to Shea. The move changed little beyond their mailing address. The Mets continued to lead all of baseball in futility, averaging 108 losses per season in their first half-dozen years, an avalanche of defeats that did nothing to diminish the enthusiasm of their ever-faithful fans, who kept coming through the turnstiles and kept embracing the players' earnest, if unavailing, efforts to win an occasional game.

Steve Aptheker was one of those fans, a 14-year-old kid from the Canarsie section of Brooklyn when the Mets were born who grew up to be a lawyer and eventually moved his practice (not by accident) to a few miles from the New York Mets' spring training headquarters in Port St. Lucie, Florida. To Aptheker, the indefatigable spirit of Mets fans had everything to do with the heartache that came when their National League forebears, the Brooklyn Dodgers, bolted for the West Coast after the 1957 season.

"You can't overestimate the horror of losing the Dodgers and of wandering in the wilderness for four years," Aptheker said. "The Mets were our salvation."

Indeed, the Dodgers had been as much a part of their Flatbush neighborhood as the concrete sidewalks on Bedford Avenue. Dr. Joseph Viteritti, a professor of public policy at New York's Hunter College, used to bike on those sidewalks to go to games. He and most all of the neighborhood kids would play stickball, stoopball, boxball, and punchball—every variation of baseball that their urban environment could accommodate. Baseball was their sport, and playing in Ebbets Field one day was their dream. After Dodgers games, the kids would wait on the Sullivan Street side of Ebbets, where the players would exit the park, relishing the proximity of their ball-playing heroes. The players made good money, certainly, but not so much that they lived in gated suburban mansions or Manhattan penthouses. These weren't distant, millionaire idols; they were participants in daily borough life, mostly living and raising their families in the neighborhood. Viteritti, the son of a shipfitter at the Brooklyn Navy Yard, liked that. He liked that Gil Hodges's brother-in-law owned Jack's Barber Shop on Washington Avenue and that there was a photo in the front window of Hodges stretching forward from first base to scoop up a throw. Sometimes the man himself would show up, and would always honor every autograph request. The day Viteritti got *his* Gil Hodges autograph, he tore a piece of loose-leaf paper from his school binder and was awed by the size of Hodges's forearms as he signed his name.

One of Viteritti's favorite parts of Ebbets Field was the movie-theater-style marquee atop the ballpark, between center and right field. Beneath the words NEXT GAME were white letters on a black background displaying the name of the upcoming opponent, date, and game time. The marquee always gave young Joe Viteritti something to look forward to. On the night of September 24, 1957, he and a friend biked over to Ebbets one last time. After 67 years in Brooklyn, the Dodgers were closing up shop.

The Dodgers beat the Pirates 2–0, behind Danny McDevitt. A shortstop named Don Zimmer had the last hit at Ebbets Field. Gil Hodges had an RBI single but also made the last Dodger out, striking out in the bottom of the eighth.

"We looked up at the NEXT GAME sign, and it was blank," Viteritti said. "That's when it hit us: they really were leaving. There would be no next game. It was devastating. It was like losing a member of your family."

Steve Aptheker can barely say the word *Dodgers* without gagging even now, more than six decades later. He can tell you about his first visit to Ebbets Field, sitting behind third base, rooting for his favorite player, Jackie Robinson. He can provide details of the time that Don Newcombe, a superb pitcher and powerful hitter, crushed a ball so hard it went through—not over—the Ebbets Field fence (he was awarded a home run). He can report on the night he ventured to the Polo Grounds for the first time, to see his Dodgers play the hated Giants in enemy territory. Aptheker went with his father and wore his Dodgers jacket.

"This kid has guts," the Polo Grounds ticket taker told Aptheker's father and then let the boy in for free. The date was August 31, 1956. Willie Mays homered, and the Giants went up 3–0 before Steve Ridzik, their starter, walked Robinson to lead off the fourth. Aptheker can still see Jackie Robinson dancing off first, his feet as alive as if he were on hot coals. Robinson stole second. The Dodgers went on to win behind Newcombe's twenty-second victory of the season.

When the Dodgers made their first visit back to New York to

play the Mets, there was no chance Steve Aptheker was not going to be there and even less chance he would cheer for the team that jilted him. He was now a fan of the New York Mets.

The series opened with a doubleheader on Memorial Day 1962. A crowd of almost 56,000 poured into the Polo Grounds. Aptheker and three friends—John Minichelli, Ralph Subbiondo, and Jeff Rosenberg—sat in the last row of the upper deck behind third base, along with the white bedsheet they'd brought along for the occasion.

Sandy Koufax, born and raised in Brooklyn, former baseball and basketball standout at Lafayette High School, started for the Dodgers, Jay Hook for the Mets. The Mets were down 10–0 in the top of the fourth when the kids from Canarsie unfurled the sheet and started to chant the words they'd written on it with green paint:

LET'S GO METS.

They chanted it again.

"Let's go, Mets!"

They kept chanting, over and over.

"Let's go, Mets! Let's go, Mets!"

Soon other fans joined in, and the simple, staccato chorus grew louder and louder, scoreboard be damned.

The early Mets were quintessential underdogs, largely a collection of castoffs and retreads, once stellar players who were in steep decline and whose presence might sell a few tickets. You want to take a last look at Gil Hodges or Duke Snider or Warren Spahn? Go see the New York Mets, your kindred bat-and-glove-toting souls.

"The Mets were the team from the outer boroughs, the same way the Dodgers were," Viteritti said. "They were not the Yankees, and their fans didn't want them to be the Yankees. Their fans were underdogs themselves, working-class people struggling to make a living. You sat in the bleachers once in a while or you watched the game on TV for nothing, because there was no cable. You didn't have a lot. You worked hard and hoped things would get better, and the Mets were your team."

It was a match waiting to happen.

A story about the "Let's go, Mets!" chant ran in the New York *Post* the next day. It soon became the signature chorus of Mets fans, and by 1968, it was accompanied by an actual glimmer of hope. Bolstered by a bountiful farm system presided over by general manager Johnny Murphy, a former Yankees relief star with a lantern jaw and a taste for French wine, the Mets won a franchise-record 73 games in year seven, surging into ninth place in the National League, a game ahead of their expansion bedfellows, the Astros. They still had their customary anemic offense (a league-worst .228 team batting average), but if you looked closely, you could see that as sure as the number 7 subway rattled by Shea every few minutes, the Mets were starting to make a little noise of their own.

They had one of the best young defensive catchers in baseball, a pugnacious Texan named Jerry Grote, who hit a surprising .282 in '68 and was the NL's starting catcher in the 1968 All-Star Game. They had a fast, line-drive-hitting left fielder, Cleon Jones, who, at 25, batted .297 with 14 home runs and was the best hitting prospect the Mets had ever had. Across the way in right field was Ron Swoboda, a muscular if inconsistent long-ball hitter who could look as if he belonged in double-A ball one game and in the All-Star game the next but nonetheless had significant potential. The organization's top prospect, Amos Otis, an outfielder the club hoped to convert to a third baseman, was a star in the making, according to Whitey Herzog, the Mets' director of player development. If center fielder Tommie Agee could return to form following a woeful first season after coming over in a trade with the Chicago White Sox and the sweet-fielding bantamweight at shortstop, Bud Harrelson, could recover from knee problems, well, you had the makings of a bona fide team.

But most of all, the Mets had a plethora of strong young arms. Even in 1968, the so-called Year of the Pitcher, in which Major League batters hit a collective .237, Denny McLain won 31 games for the Tigers, and the Cardinals' Bob Gibson finished the year with a preposterous 1.12 earned run average, the Mets' abundance of pitching talent was formidable. The staff was headlined by the 23-year-old Tom Seaver and 25-year-old Jerry Koosman, who combined for 35 victories, 31 complete games, and 12 shutouts. It also included Dick Selma, Nolan Ryan, and Jim McAndrew, along with a promising left-hander, Tug McGraw, who would soon be converted into a relief pitcher. All five starters—average age 23.4 years—had earned run averages well under 3.00.

Playing the Mets was no longer an occasion for opponents to rest the regulars and thank the schedule maker.

Perhaps the most important reason that the Mets changed course, though, was the man at the helm of the ship, Gilbert Ray Hodges, an original Met and beloved former All-Star for the turncoat Dodgers, an ex-Marine from Princeton, Indiana, who was renowned for his quiet strength, unimpeachable character, and hands so big they could cover a pizza pan. (The joke among the Dodgers had been that Hodges's glove was purely ornamental.)

Hodges ended his playing career as a Met, appearing in just 65 games in 1962 before accepting an offer to manage the Washington Senators. The Senators were another expansion club that specialized in losing until Hodges arrived in 1963 and began steering the club steadily, if not dramatically, upward in the American League standings. Hodges's work with the Senators was widely acclaimed, but his heart—along with his family, his home on Bedford Avenue, and his bowling alley, Gil Hodges Lanes on Ralph Avenue—remained in Brooklyn. When the Mets got rid of manager Wes Westrum near the end of the 1967 season, Hodges knew there was a job opening not even 14 miles from home. He also knew the decision to leave a fast-improving Senators team and take on the challenge of turning the Mets into winners was no less perilous than dodging cars on Grand Central Parkway. The Mets, after all, were the worst team in baseball in 1967, finishing 61-101. They cycled through so many players—54—they barely had time to learn one another's names.

A measured, thorough man, Hodges talked it over with his wife, Joan, and decided it was worth exploring. Bing Devine, the

Mets' president, and Murphy went to work to make it happen, but there was a problem: Hodges was still under contract to the Senators. George Selkirk—the Senators' general manager, a Canadian who had succeeded Babe Ruth as the Yankees' right fielder (and had even worn Ruth's number, 3)—had no interest in losing his gifted young manager but also did not want to stand in the way of Hodges's personal considerations. Selkirk and Murphy, his former Yankees teammate, dickered back and forth. On October 11, 1967, the day the Boston Red Sox beat the St. Louis Cardinals to extend the World Series to a seventh game, the Mets introduced 43-year-old Gil Hodges as their manager, in exchange for a reported $100,000 and a player to be named later.

It wasn't until after Thanksgiving, at the Winter Meetings in Mexico City, that the most important deal in the franchise's short history was finalized. Heading to Washington was Bill Denehy, a highly regarded 6-foot, 3-inch, 200-pound right-hander from Middletown, Connecticut, who may have had the strongest arm of any Mets pitching prospect this side of Nolan Ryan. Murphy tried to interest Selkirk in some other players, but Selkirk was adamant: no Denehy, no Hodges.

Denehy thus became the first player in big-league history to be traded for a manager. That the young pitcher wanted to be a Met was not a factor in the discussions. That the young pitcher had a tear in his pitching shoulder—a fact known to the Mets but apparently not to the Senators—was also not part of the discussions.

The deal was completed. Bill Denehy was nicknamed "Billy the Kid" and featured alongside Tom Seaver on a Topps All-Star Rookie Team card in 1967. Tom Seaver would wind up in the Hall of Fame. Bill Denehy would wind up winning one big-league game.

• • •

NINE DAYS INTO February 1969, right before the New York Mets were due to report to St. Petersburg, Florida, for spring training, the residents of Queens were buried beneath one of the worst snowstorms in borough history. Almost nobody saw the blizzard coming, least of all the New York City Sanitation Department, which was understaffed, underequipped, and overwhelmed.

The storm resulted in 42 deaths, more than half of them in Queens. A nurse at Creedmoor State Hospital died on the hospital grounds, buried in some 18 inches of snow. A Bronx couple was found dead in their car outside a LaGuardia airline terminal, the apparent victims of carbon monoxide poisoning. Hundreds of motorists were stranded on the New York State Thruway, and at Kennedy Airport, about four thousand snowbound travelers were entertained by Soupy Sales and Goldie Hawn, while grounded aircraft served as makeshift hotels. The entire city was virtually paralyzed but nowhere more than Queens, where the streets looked to be something out of Fairbanks, Alaska.

"We did not see a snowplow for a week," recalled Howie Rose, a 15-year-old in Bayside, Queens, who would go on to become the longtime radio voice of the Mets. "The days kept going by, and nothing changed." While Rose reveled in the rare opportunity to play midweek street hockey, others did not take so kindly to the interruption, among them Ralph J. Bunche, Nobel Prize winner and undersecretary general of the United Nations, a 17-year resident of Kew Gardens, Queens. Bunche won his Nobel Prize for the work he'd done on the Arab-Israeli conflict in the late 1940s. He was not in a diplomatic mood when he sent a blistering telegram to Mayor John V. Lindsay a few days after the storm.

"The snowstorm came on Sunday," Bunche wrote. "This message is sent Wednesday morning. In all that period no snowplow has appeared on our street or in our vicinity. There are no buses, no taxis, no mail, newspaper or other deliveries, and there have been no trash or garbage collection since last Friday. The shelves of our neighborhood grocer are empty. As far as getting to the United Nations is concerned, I may as well be in the Alps."

Early in an election year, Lindsay was already getting hammered on multiple fronts, mostly by the city's powerful labor unions. That was nothing new; at 5 a.m. on Lindsay's first day in office, January 1, 1966, New York's 33,000 transit workers walked off the job, initiating a crippling two-week strike. Rank-and-file union members across the city viewed the mayor as the enemy of the working man, and "Lindsay's Snowstorm," as his detractors called it, did nothing but reinforce the perception that he was an out-of-touch, Ivy League–educated Upper East Side liberal who championed the cause of minorities at the expense of the predominantly white working-class people of Queens. When the mayor, hoping to ease tensions, visited the borough late in the week, he was called "a bum" and "a disgrace." Those were some of the nicer comments.

"He can't even run a snowstorm, and he wants to run the country," said one citizen of Lindsay, a man with presidential aspirations.

Queens finally got dug out. Schools reopened. Trains resumed running, and Ralph J. Bunche returned to work at the U.N., just as Gil Hodges and his staff were setting up camp, minus the snowplows, at Al Lang Stadium, a quaint little park on the Gulf Coast waterfront in St. Petersburg. It wasn't the start of just any baseball season; it was the palm-lined launching of the game's centennial anniversary—a year that brought more change than the spring fashion season.

Not normally known for embracing innovation, Major League Baseball in 1969 introduced eastern and western divisions in each league; four new teams; two rounds of postseason play; a lowered mound (from 15 inches high to 10); a smaller strike zone (armpits to knees instead of shoulders to knees); and a spring training experiment called the designated pinch hitter, which would allow clubs to use an extra hitter when it was the pitcher's turn to bat. The changes aimed to inject more offense into a game that was being thoroughly dominated by pitchers, and to reverse a 9 percent decline in attendance in the previous two years, to just over 14,000 fans per game. It was the spring in which baseball said good-bye to the greatest switch-hitter in history, Mickey Mantle, who retired from the Yankees in 1968, and said hello to a new commissioner, Bowie Kuhn, who at 6 feet, 5 inches and 42 years old was both the tallest and the youngest chief executive the sport had ever had.

Kuhn was tested long before Opening Day. Many players stayed away from spring training in a dispute over increased pensions in the wake of a new Major League Baseball television contract. A portent of much more acrimonious labor relations to come, the issue was resolved before the end of February. With the assurance that the 1969 baseball season would move forward, the foremost concern in New York Mets circles was the well-being of the club's manager.

Five months earlier, on the night of September 24, 1968, Hodges had suffered a heart attack during the early innings of a game against the Braves in Atlanta. Hodges was a heavy smoker with a family history of heart trouble—his father, Charles, had had cardiac issues and had died of an embolism at age 56—and a penchant for bottling up many of the stresses that come with managing, not a good trifecta by any means. But he seemed to recover well, following doctor's orders and losing 20 pounds to get down to 205—under his playing weight. His morning routine was to walk a couple of miles from his beach hotel toward Al Lang Stadium, then get a ride from Yogi Berra and Joe Pignatano, two of his coaches. At the end of the day, Hodges and his wife, Joan, would relax by fishing off the Bayview Bridge. Besides giving up his Marlboros, Hodges was also advised to stop pitching batting practice, one of his favorite activities. With common sense and a few lifestyle changes, Hodges was convinced, he would resume his managerial duties with no problem, as he explained in a letter to Red Foley, a baseball writer for the New York *Daily News*: "[All] I can say is that I've never felt better and the doctors, who are pleased with my progress, assure me I can look forward to managing the Mets this season," he said. "And believe me that's just what I'm going to do."

• • •

FROM THE MOMENT he took over the Mets, Hodges's most daunting challenge was one his doctors could not help with. Though Wes Westrum was well meaning and mostly well liked, he instilled little discipline and wasn't so much walked on by his players as stomped on. The Mets were used to losing. For the most part, they expected to lose. Changing the culture of the organization would be about as easy as getting tar off a beach towel. When Ed Charles, the Mets' veteran third baseman and resident poet, came over from the Kansas City Athletics in a trade in May 1967, he could scarcely believe how entrenched the Mets' losing mentality was.

"We didn't have the greatest team in the world in Kansas City, but at least we were still taking the game professionally, like we were going out there to win," Charles said. "We weren't going out there saying, 'Okay, we're going to lose again.'"

After a defeat in his first year with the Mets, 1967, Charles went out for a late-night bite with Cleon Jones at a place on Astoria Boulevard called the Outfielders Lounge, an establishment Jones would later become a part owner of with Tommie Agee. When another patron saw the Mets walk in, he said in an extra-loud voice, "Ladies and gentlemen, it's the New York Mets, and I guess you know they lost again."

Normally an easygoing sort, Charles didn't appreciate being mocked.

"What the hell is that about?" Charles asked Jones. "I don't need this."

"Take it easy, man," Jones said. "The guy is just fooling with us."

"Well, I don't like the way people look at us, like we're a big joke," Charles said. And with that he departed the Outfielders Lounge.

Nobody knew more about the Mets' legacy of losing than Ed Kranepool, who, along with pitcher Al Jackson, was the lone '69 Met who had been a member of the inaugural 1962 club. In fact, Kranepool was in the Polo Grounds for the first Mets home game in history, against the Pittsburgh Pirates, on a rainy Friday the thirteenth. Sherman Jones, who would go on to a career as a Kansas City cop but at the time was just a guy nicknamed "Roadblock" with a history of arm troubles, started for the Mets. A seventeen-year-old senior at James Monroe High School in the Bronx, Kranepool played hooky that day, and you can blame the Mets, who invited Ed and his mother, Ethel, to be their guests, hoping to impress the youngster, a big, promising slugger who broke the Monroe home-run record set by the legendary Hank Greenberg, and was coveted by the Mets and almost every other club. The Kranepools sat in the owner's box with Joan Whitney Payson, and witnessed the first boos in the history of the New York Mets, after outfielders Gus Bell and Richie Ashburn let a catchable Bill Mazeroski fly ball drop for a triple. They also saw three wild pitches, which helped seal a 4–3 defeat.

About ten weeks later, the day after Kranepool became a high school graduate, Johnny Murphy and Mets scout Bubba Jonnard visited the Kranepools' Bronx residence at 847 Castle Hill Avenue. Ed was supposed to fly out the next day to work out with the White Sox. His favorite team, the Yankees, who played on the other side of the Bronx, were also keen on him. Ed's father, Edward, had died in combat in World War II, when Ethel had a young daughter and was pregnant with Ed. She was supporting the family on a pension and her secretarial work. When Murphy offered her son an $85,000 signing bonus, it was life-changing money. He took it.

Before the week was out, Kranepool went on a West Coast road trip to get a glimpse of big-league life. Wearing number 21 in a Mets road-gray uniform, he watched from the Dodger Stadium dugout as Sandy Koufax fired a no-hitter against his new club. The Mets would go on to lose 20 of their next 24 games.

Ed Kranepool was supposed to be the Mets' Lou Gehrig, the homegrown first baseman who would go on to slugging greatness, and though he grew into a respectable big-league hitter and an All-Star at age 20, the losses kept piling up like debris in a landfill.

"Winning is contagious, and so is losing," Kranepool said. "It gets tiring and frustrating. Anybody can play on a winning ball club. Being on a winning ball club is so much easier. You go to the ballpark every day with a positive attitude, and you have something to look forward to, meaningful games in August and September. When you are eliminated at the All-Star break, it makes for a long second half."

• • •

AFTER SEVEN YEARS and 737 defeats, Ed Kranepool and the Mets tried a different approach in 1969. They played meaningful games in August and September and enjoyed it so much they played eight more in October. Their victory total of 107 was more games than they'd won in their first two-plus years of existence, and if anything was more astonishing than the outcome of the season, it was the manner in which they got there, with a lineup that evoked few comparisons with the '27 Yankees. The Mets' leading run producer was their leadoff man, Tommie Agee, with 76 RBI. They didn't have a player who scored 100 runs or hit 30 home runs. They were tenth in the National League in on-base percentage (.311), next to last in slugging (.351), and had a run total (632) that was only 15 runs more than the '62 Mets had scored. The batting averages of the principal infielders in Hodges's platoon system were as follows: .248, .218, .207, .279, .252, .238, and .232.

You might think those are misprints, but as Casey Stengel said, you could look it up.

What the 1969 Mets *could* do, however, is throw the ball and catch it. Their total of 122 errors was the third fewest in baseball, trailing only the two teams the Mets would play in October, the Baltimore Orioles and the Atlanta Braves. Of the 24 clubs in the major leagues, only the St. Louis Cardinals had a better team earned run average than the Mets. The Mets' five starters—Tom Seaver, Jerry Koosman, Gary Gentry, Jim McAndrew, and Don Cardwell—combined for 48 complete games and 16 shutouts and collectively were so consistent that it made a prolonged losing streak almost unthinkable. Seaver and Koosman combined to win 18 of 19 decisions in the heat of the first pennant race either of them had ever experienced, and the one veteran of the group, the 33-year-old Cardwell, pitched the best ball of his career when it mattered most, going 5-1 with a 1.83 earned run average in August and September. All of it helped the Mets win 38 of their last 49 games. That's a pretty good way to finish a season.

It was also a good way to overcome the 10-game deficit that had even their most devoted fans thinking they were deader than the Wrigley Field ivy in winter.

• • •

THE METS' LATE-SEASON surge created all kinds of upheaval in the NL East standings, and things were no different in the place they called home. Even by the tumultuous standards of New York City, 1969 was a year that teemed with turbulence. The snowstorm helped bury Lindsay in the Republican Party primary, a stunning snub for an incumbent mayor. Shortly after 3 a.m. on June 28, a police raid of a popular gay club in the West Village, the Stonewall Inn, turned violent, triggering almost a week of clashes between city police and the gay community. In a four-month span in the summer and fall of 1969, the city was rocked by eight separate bombings, each at a major bank, business, or government office and each apparently the work of radical groups. There were no fatalities, but the detonations jolted the city with fear.

"The Establishment is in for some big surprises if it thinks that kangaroo courts and death sentences can arrest a revolution," read a letter from the bombers to the *New York Times*.

In the midst of it all, the New York Mets kept winning ball games as never before, and fans filled Shea Stadium as never before, almost 2.2 million of them. That was nearly 350,000 more than any other major league club and practically double the attendance of the vaunted New York Yankees. The Mets were the youngest team in baseball, and maybe the easiest to root for, with an overachieving cast of Everymen and four African-Americans from the Deep South who had overcome all manner of obstacles to arrive at this point, making their way in pro ball not long after Jackie Robinson had integrated the sport. During spring training, the Mets were pegged as a 100-to-1 shot to win the World Series. Even Tom Seaver, the eternal optimist, believed that if they played up to their capabilities and stayed healthy, they could make a run for second place in the Eastern Division. Seaver was wrong, and so was everyone else.

Part I

Seasoning

1

BABY STEPS

IT IS HARD TO OVERSTATE HOW MUCH GIL HODGES, A COAL MINER'S
son, was loved in his adopted city. That he excelled both at bat and
in the field in Brooklyn—he was the National League's career right-
handed home run leader with 370 at the time he retired—was a significant part of his popularity, but the Dodgers were loaded with
good players. That he drove in both runs in the decisive game seven
of the 1955 World Series to lift the Brooklyn Dodgers to their only
Series title would never be forgotten, but there were other heroic
Dodger performances in the Series as well. There was something
else about Hodges—a sincerity, a midwestern authenticity, a humility that went to his core—that endeared him to almost everybody,
making him almost immune to criticism.

"Not getting booed at Ebbets Field was an amazing thing," Clem
Labine, Hodges's longtime Dodgers teammate, once said. "Those
fans knew their baseball, and Gil was the only one who never, and I
mean never, was booed."

Even when Hodges went 0 for 21 against the Yankees in the 1952
World Series, the fans in Ebbets Field remained on his side. When
the slump continued early in the 1953 season—Hodges was hitting
.181 with one home run and five runs batted in through the first 32
games—Father Herbert Redmond of Brooklyn's St. Francis Catholic Church famously stood in the pulpit one steamy spring Sunday

and offered his parishioners one of the briefest and most memorable homilies in church annals.

"It's far too hot for a sermon. Keep the commandments, and say a prayer for Gil Hodges," he said.

In his book, *The Game of Baseball*, Hodges wrote about how he would never forget that, just as he wouldn't forget "the hundreds of people who sent me letters, telegrams and postcards during that World Series. There wasn't a single nasty message. Everybody tried to say something nice. It had a tremendous effect on my morale, if not my batting average. Remember that in 1952, the Dodgers had never won a World Series. A couple of base hits by me in the right spot might have changed all that."

The response was vintage Hodges, ever ready to accept responsibility and not at all eager to accept acclaim. He won a Bronze Star in World War II, in recognition of his "outstanding professional attainments and tireless devotion to duty" in the face of unrelenting Japanese aerial attacks in Okinawa. He never even told his parents about the honor, and whenever he was asked about it years later, he declined to discuss his service to the country. After he became only the second player in modern baseball history to hit four home runs in a game, he was inevitably compared to the first man to have done it, his fellow first baseman Lou Gehrig. "The only difference between us is he's a much better player," Hodges said.

Some 14 years later, one of Hodges's Senators players, Jim King, hit three homers in a game, and someone asked Hodges if he had ever done that.

"I'm not in the record books for three in one game," Hodges said, not wanting to intrude on King's moment.

Hodges's modesty wasn't for show, and neither was anything else about him. He was a ballplayer–cum–Boy Scout, without the oath. "Gil was the one guy I could go to for anything," Irving Rudd, the Brooklyn Dodgers' publicity director, once said. "If I needed a player to visit a blind kid in the stands, a kid in a wheelchair—Gil this, Gil that . . . he'd be there."

One night in Brooklyn, a postal worker named Alvin Miller attended a funeral for the wife of a family friend. A broad-shouldered man and a woman walked up to the door, and the man asked Miller if he was coming in. Miller said yes, and only when he got inside did he recognize the couple as Gil and Joan Hodges. The two men wound up talking about baseball and life in Brooklyn. Forty-five minutes later, Miller departed and waited for a bus to take him home to the Mill Basin section of Brooklyn. A car pulled up alongside the bus stop.

It was Hodges, who asked Alvin Miller if he'd like a ride home and went miles out of his way to take him there.

During Hodges's time with the Senators, the club acquired Ryne Duren, a four-time All-Star reliever with the Yankees who wore bottle-thick glasses and was renowned both for being the hardest thrower in baseball and for having a terrible drinking problem. It was the summer of 1965, and things weren't going well in Washington for the 36-year-old Duren, who had pitched to a 6.65 earned run average in 16 games, the last of them in Washington on August 18 in ninth-inning mop-up duty against the White Sox. Duren had faced two batters, giving up a walk and a single, before Hodges made a pitching change. Duren was completely distraught about his performance. He drank heavily after the game and made his way to the bridge over the Connecticut Avenue gorge. It was known as the "jumper's bridge." Duren climbed to the top and told police he was going to kill himself. The police called the Senators, and Hodges got word about Duren's plight. Duren had been with the Senators for only two months and by his own admission had "put poor Gil through hell." Hodges got to the bridge as fast as he could, as Duren recounted in his autobiography.

"Ryne, you're drunk," Hodges said. "Come on down. We'll get you help. You're too good to do this to yourself."

The Senators released Duren, and he never pitched in another big-league game. When Hodges met with reporters the next day and was asked about Duren, he said simply, "The decision to put Duren on waivers was something that happened overnight."

Duren eventually found sobriety and became a highly regarded drug and alcohol addiction counselor who helped countless people turn their lives around.

. . .

FROM THE TIME he arrived in 1968, Gil Hodges methodically, studiously began creating a positive clubhouse culture that allowed every individual piece of the Mets' whole to feel important. The days of the revolving-door roster and the acceptance of losing were done. This would not be achieved with verbal flourishes, hand-holding, or hearty backside slaps; that was not the Hodges way. It was done with painstaking preparation, astute strategic decisions, and an even more astute understanding of the human psyche. Nobody was an afterthought on Gil Hodges's Mets. As well as any manager in the game, Hodges understood the importance of making every player feel involved, keeping every player fresh, giving everyone on his roster a slice of ownership in what the collective team was doing. Seaver, with 25 victories, and Jones, with a .340 batting average, may have had the greatest individual seasons in club history, but players such as Bobby Pfeil, Duffy Dyer, and Cal Koonce were never made to feel as if they were any less a part of the Mets' success than anyone else. At age 25, Pfeil, a utility infielder, had already spent eight years in the minors. He was the definition of a fringe big leaguer. But he was smart, a hustler, a guy who could hit a little, play multiple positions, and was ready to do whatever he could to help the team win. On Gil Hodges's Mets, that made Pfeil a deeply appreciated asset.

"We really *were* a team," Kranepool said. "They call everyone a team, but we really were a group where everybody on the roster contributed. Sometimes you win in spite of your manager, but not with this club. Gil did everything right. He made every possible move to help our club. He never tricked you. He was so consistent. When he made out his lineup, you knew the night before you were going to play. You never showed up at the ballpark not ready. Once he said he was going to do something, he stuck with it. You were prepared when you went to the park. You got your rest. You were ready. You worked hard to stay in shape, because you knew you would be called on. He kept everybody sharp."

And he never missed a thing.

One day during batting practice Jerry Koosman was shagging fly balls. He'd done a good bit of running and felt his back tightening up. He stopped shagging briefly and squatted down in the outfield to stretch his lower back.

"All of a sudden, zoom, here comes a line drive right at me," Koosman said. "It hit right beside me. I looked up and saw Gil at home plate with a fungo bat. That's what he would do if he thought you were resting or relaxing. You don't do that. He hit a pea right at me."

Wayne Garrett was a rookie in 1969, a kid drafted out of the Braves organization who made the club and was impressed by his manager from the outset.

"The biggest difference with Gil was his planning," Garrett said. "He was always looking ahead in a game and a series. He wasn't just caught up in the now all the time. It was everything down the road. He would plan innings and innings ahead and always made sure you were ready. He was prepared all the time, and he wanted you to be prepared all the time, too."

• • •

HODGES'S FAMOUS EQUANIMITY was tested before the Mets even flew south for spring training. Koosman, his star left-hander, was in his apartment in East Elmhurst, Queens, close enough to LaGuardia Airport to smell the fumes, along with four other young Mets husbands and fathers. Their wives had gone into the city for a Broadway show, leaving the ballplayers in charge of the kids. Koosman made a batch of popcorn on the stove and was melting butter alongside it. The phone rang. Koosman answered. A minute or so later, he walked back into the kitchen to see the stove top aflame and the butter boiling over, one of the kids apparently having fooled with the gas burner. Koosman raced to the stove and grabbed the flaming pot. Kevin Collins, a 22-year-old infielder, opened the back door and Koosman flung it outside, splattering butter onto his arm and two fingers of his pitching hand in the process. He ran cold water on everything and then went to a medical clinic, where the doctor told him he had suffered third-degree burns and would require skin grafts.

Koosman reported to spring training not able to throw because of the injury, which would continue to bother him the whole year. Even by Mets standards this was not an auspicious beginning.

Things were not so hot for the front office, either. The spring was largely devoted to efforts to acquire a big hitter for the middle of the order. Frank Howard, the massive slugger whom Hodges had managed in Washington, was supposedly available, but Hodges was dubious; when a reporter asked if he'd like to have Howard in his Mets lineup, the manager said, "Yes, and Ted Williams, too." The Mets didn't get Howard, and neither did anybody else. The Mets were also interested in Donn Clendenon, a power-hitting first baseman who had just been taken from the Pirates in the expansion draft by the newly formed Montreal Expos, who had then traded him to the Astros for Rusty Staub. The deal nearly unraveled because Clendenon chose to retire rather than report to Houston, a club managed by Harry Walker, whom Clendenon had played for, and disliked, during his Pirates days. Clendenon announced he was accepting an executive position in his hometown of Atlanta, though he eventually unretired and went back to the Expos, who, at baseball's urging, sent two other players and cash to Houston to complete the transaction. That was good for the Astros but did nothing for the Mets.

Murphy, the general manager, knew whom he wanted more than anyone: Joe Torre of the Atlanta Braves. Torre was a front-line star who had grown up in Brooklyn and played third base, a position that had plagued the Mets since the glove-challenged heyday of Felix Mantilla and Rod Kanehl. Torre was a perfect fit for the Mets, and Paul Richards, the Braves' general manager, knew it, demanding the Mets include several of their most promising youngsters in return. Murphy replied that Seaver, Koosman, Otis, Ryan, and Swoboda, among others, were off-limits in any deal, even for Torre.

Koosman had forced his way onto that list on the strength of his spectacular rookie season. According to Dick Young, a columnist at the New York *Daily News* and the most plugged-in baseball writer in the city, just a year before the Mets offered Koosman straight up for Freddie Patek, the Pirates' heralded prospect who, at 5 feet, 5 inches, brought a whole new meaning to the term shortstop. The Pirates were the ones who nixed the deal, Young said. Murphy should've sent them a thank-you note. By 1969, Paul Richards had no shot at Koosman or any other of the Mets' choice prospects.

"They have given us seven untouchables," Richards said. "If they had so many untouchables, how come they didn't win the pennant?"

Torre wound up in St. Louis and the Mets stuck with what they had, at least for the time being. There was another unforeseen hiccup late in camp when Seaver slipped off a seawall while fishing, cutting his hand. It turned out to be nothing major, and Rube Walker, the pitching coach, said Seaver would be fine so long as he avoided seawalls going forward.

Seaver obliged, and after the best spring training in club history—the Mets finished 14-10—on April 8, 1969, he started the Mets' eighth Opening Day and the first international game in the annals of Major League Baseball. The Montreal Expos were visiting, which meant that "O Canada" would be sung along with the "The Star-Spangled Banner," and that Montreal mayor Jean Drapeau, who knew about power plays but probably couldn't have picked Rusty Staub out of a police lineup, would get to throw out the first pitch.

In their seven previous openers, the Mets had never managed to win a game, a circumstance that seemed to have a good chance to change against a team playing its first game ever. WELCOME EXPOS TO NATIONAL LEAGUE a message on the Shea scoreboard said. The Expos had tricolor hats that could've been designed by Barnum & Bailey. They had a left-handed reliever, Dan McGinn, who had once been a punter for Notre Dame, and a rookie third baseman, José Alberto "Coco" Laboy, who would be playing his first big-league game after 10 years in the minors.

The Mets had their own rookie sensation, Rod Gaspar, a switch-hitting outfielder from Long Beach, California, with good speed and a good glove who had just two years in the minors behind him. Drafted out of Long Beach State, Gaspar was 6 feet tall and 160 pounds, and he had the most unusual batting stance on the club—so open that he was almost facing the pitcher. Gaspar was built more like a pipe cleaner than a big-league ballplayer and was given no chance to make the team, except in the mind of Rod Gaspar. He had hit .309 in double-A ball in 1968, with 25 steals and 6 triples. It had been enough to get him an invitation to big-league camp.

"I thought I could play with these guys," Gaspar said. "That's the way you have to look at it. I don't care what profession you are in. You can't go out there thinking you're not good. If you are thinking that way, you are history."

By his own admission, Gaspar had the quintessential Napoleon complex. At 16 years old, he was 5 feet, 2 inches, and 105 pounds and just getting over an ulcer. It took him three tries to pass his driver's license test. He was a kid with major insecurities, who saw slights everywhere he looked. He didn't have a chip on his shoulder so much as a boulder.

"I don't know why I was born angry, but I was," Gaspar said. "I used to get in fights all the time. But in some ways the anger helped fuel me in baseball. When you learn to control it, it's a big plus. I was a natural—God blessed me with the ability to play the game. I would get fired up to play."

At every turn, Gaspar sought to win over all those who underestimated him. When he showed up at spring training, he was given number 57 and was sure that nobody—not Gil Hodges, Eddie Yost, Yogi Berra, Rube Walker, or Joe Pignatano—even knew his name. But when outfielder Art Shamsky hurt his back, Gaspar got a chance to play and he ran with it, hitting and fielding superbly. Gaspar found out he had made the Mets on April 3, his twenty-third birthday. When Hodges filled out his lineup card for Opening Day, Rodney Earl Gaspar was starting in right field.

Many fine things happened for the Mets in that first game. Agee had two hits and three RBI—almost 20 percent of his total for the previous year. The Mets set Opening Day club records for hits (15) and runs (10), even getting a pinch-hit, three-run homer from a rookie catcher, Duffy Dyer, in the bottom of the ninth. Unfortunately, other things happened, too. Seaver gave up two runs in the Expos' first-ever at bats. Second baseman Ken Boswell made three errors. McGinn did no punting but did manage to hit a fly ball off Seaver that landed on top of the right-field fence and bounced into the Mets bull pen. Four innings later, Coco Laboy made his long wait for the majors worth it, drilling a three-run home run of his own. The Mets lost 11–10, and after a single game the Expos were in a place in the standings—first—that the Mets had never been in.

"My God, wasn't that awful?" Seaver told reporters afterward.

The Mets made amends in game two, scoring four times in the first, Kranepool driving in two of the runs with a single. Gaspar reached base four times and scored three runs. Tug McGraw threw 6⅓ innings of sparkling relief, and with a 9–5 victory, the Mets knocked the Expos from the ranks of the undefeated.

In the series finale, Tommie Agee slugged two home runs off Larry Jaster, symbolically signaling that his disastrous 1968 was behind him. Hodges, the Mets' de facto hitting coach, had been working with Agee to get rid of a little wiggle in his swing, eliminating unnecessary movement. He'd also been working on Agee's psyche in his typical low-key fashion, assuring Agee that he considered the debacle of 1968—Agee had hit .217 with seventeen runs batted in—an aberration, that he still had total faith in him, and that he and nobody else would be his center fielder. All Agee needed to do was relax, be himself, and play ball. Here was the first payoff for both teacher and pupil.

The first of Agee's clouts came in the second inning, a 3-1 fastball that was low and in, Agee launching it into the fifth deck and a sea of empty green seats, the ball taking off like a golf ball off the tee. Not even 9,000 people were in the house. Gaspar was in the on-deck circle.

"It's the hardest-hit ball I've ever seen anyone hit," Gaspar said.

Larry Jaster wasn't in the habit of watching the trajectory of home run balls, but he watched this one because he was curious to see where it would land. When the wrecking ball reduced Shea Stadium to rubble in 2008, Agee's blast remained the only ball to have reached the fifth deck. It might've traveled over 500 feet if a seat hadn't gotten in the way. Agee hit a more modest homer off Jaster in the eighth, and for only the second time in their history, the 2-1 Mets were over .500.

• • •

THE PROSPERITY did not last. The Mets lost four in a row and six of seven, and after the Pirates shut them out 4–0 at Forbes Field, they were sitting a half game out of their accustomed last place with a record of 3-7, already 6 games behind. After his big day against the Expos, Agee had unwittingly become enamored with the long ball, and it cost him, as his average plummeted under .200. He and Gaspar soon found themselves on Hodges's bench, a temporary reprieve for their slumping bats and muddled minds.

Near the end of an inconsistent April, the Mets made their first visit to Montreal. It was a cold day. With a 2–0 lead and one gone in the fifth inning and two strikes on Expos catcher John Bateman, Koosman got the sign from catcher Jerry Grote and busted Bateman with an inside fastball. The instant Koosman released it, he felt his arm go numb. He took a little time to walk around, shake his arm, and see if the feeling came back. It didn't. He walked a little more. Grote knew something was up. Koosman normally worked very quickly. The catcher looked into the dugout, prompting Hodges and trainer Gus Mauch to head for the mound. Koosman had battled shoulder tightness through most of the spring, but this was altogether different and way more serious than flaming butter burns. He had no feeling in his arm at all. He was gone from the game, of course, but his concerns went way beyond that.

"Your career could be over just like that," he said.

The Mets flew Koosman back to New York to be examined.

Doctors found nothing structurally wrong and prescribed rest. After giving it a little time, Koosman tried to throw on the side. He couldn't even reach home plate. Koosman was terribly worried, the Mets no less so. One day in Chicago, not long after the numbness had set in, Gus Mauch was working on Koosman's shoulder on a training table when Murphy, the GM and former pitcher, came in. Koosman explained the symptoms.

"I had the same thing once," Murphy said, and then jabbed a finger into the back of Koosman's shoulder.

"I almost fell off the table," Koosman said. "I thought, 'Holy Christ, he hit the exact spot.'"

Indeed he had. It turned out that Koosman had a knot in the teres minor muscle in the back of his shoulder, which apparently was pinching a nerve, creating the numbness. He would miss almost a month, but Murphy's well-placed poke at least provided the diagnosis.

Koosman wasn't the only pitcher with health issues. Jim McAndrew had a blister on his pitching hand that kept him out for a month. Nolan Ryan strained a groin muscle right before he had to leave for army reserve duty. Things didn't look especially promising when the Mets limped into Chicago at the start of May and the first-place Cubs took the first two games to leave the Mets eight games behind at 9-14. The series concluded with a Sunday doubleheader before a standing-room-only attendance of almost 40,500 at Wrigley. Seaver pitched the opener on three days' rest because of the depleted rotation.

In the top of the second, Ron Santo, the Cubs' captain, All-Star third baseman, and emotional firebrand, led off. Santo had been on a tear against the Mets, and Seaver had seen enough of him treating Mets pitchers as if they were throwing batting practice. On an 0-2 pitch, Seaver came up and in with a fastball. He didn't hit Santo and didn't intend to. He *did* intend to send a message. Santo went sprawling. He dusted himself off, and then Seaver struck him out looking. When Seaver came up in the top of the third, Bill Hands, the Cubs' starter, drilled Seaver with a fastball. Seaver took first base and then, in the bottom of the third, returned the favor, planting a fastball in Hands's midsection.

In the dugout, Ed Charles stood and let out a modified war whoop. A bunch of other Mets did likewise. The Mets loved the way Seaver had responded to Hands's drilling him.

"I think that when Hands hit me, it helped our whole ball club," Seaver told reporters later. "The whole dugout suddenly came alive."

Seaver went the distance for a 3–2 victory in the opener, and McGraw, an emergency starter in game two, won by the same score, throwing his first complete game since 1966. Ron Swoboda scored the winning run on a wild pitch, sprinting 180 feet from second base when the Cubs left home plate uncovered. It was an exhilarating day for the Mets, but more important than the sweep was the message that Hodges's Mets were sending to the Cubs and all other opponents: we are here to play ball, and if you thought we were content to remain the league laughingstock, you didn't get the memo.

Kranepool reinforced the message in Cincinnati not even two weeks later, when the Mets rolled into Crosley Field just two games under .500. Leading early, the Mets turned what Kranepool thought was an inning-ending 5-4-3 double play. Following baseball's time-honored courtesy, Kranepool flipped the ball to the Reds' first-base coach, Jimmy Bragan, only to realize that the second-base umpire had made a delayed call, ruling the runner safe because Boswell had not touched the base. Kranepool asked Bragan for the ball back. Bragan threw it down the right-field line. Kranepool was not amused.

"I belted him, and we had a fight right there in the coach's box," Kranepool said.

The benches emptied, and one of the first to arrive was Art Shamsky, the former Red, who pulled Kranepool off of his old coach.

"I told Shamsky, 'Don't be grabbing me. Grab him. You are on our team now,'" Kranepool said. "It was a crazy play. A lot of crazy things happened that year."

Kranepool went 3 for 5 with an RBI in the game, and the Mets won 10–9. He was still annoyed by Bragan's stunt afterward. Because he'd been there from the beginning, Kranepool was more fed up with the Mets-are-a-joke leitmotif than anyone. Maybe Bragan would've done the same thing if, say, Ernie Banks, had flipped him a ball. Or maybe not. In that moment, something in Ed Kranepool said, "Enough is enough."

The Mets won again the next night, 11–3, on Cleon Jones's four runs batted in, and if the Mets' 21 runs in two games didn't draw the league's attention, their scrappiness was starting to. The Mets took their suddenly hot bats to Atlanta, home of the club with the best record in the majors. Jones, a .391 hitter, drove in two runs with a single in the first, and Bud Harrelson, a .293 hitter, tripled home three more in the eighth. Seaver shut out the Braves on three hits, and the New York Mets were 18-18, a .500 team at the latest juncture in their brief history. Their previous high-water mark had come in 1967, when they had been 4-4.

It was a sweet way to start a series, but when reporters surrounded Seaver afterward, he was quick to disabuse his visitors of the notion that it was any cause for celebration.

"What's so good about .500?" Seaver said. "That's only mediocre. We didn't come into this season to play .500. Let Rod Kanehl and Marvelous Marv laugh about the Mets. We're out here to win. You know when we'll have champagne? When we win the pennant."

2

HODGES'S LAW

THE FIRST 11 GAMES THE METS EVER PLAYED AGAINST THE LOS ANGE-les Dodgers and San Francisco Giants in 1962 resulted in 11 losses, by an aggregate score of 100–49. It launched a pattern that endured for most of the Mets' first decade, one that wasn't about the emigrant clubs teaching the upstarts a lesson but something more basic: the Dodgers and Giants were much, much better. Renowned for their Sandy Koufax/Don Drysdale/Claude Osteen–led pitching staff, the Dodgers had a record of 83-25-1 against their New York offspring in the Mets' first six years (the tie was a rain-shortened game in 1964). Renowned for their Willie Mays/Willie McCovey/Jim Ray Hart–led lineup (Juan Marichal wasn't a bad guy to send to the mound every four days, either), the Giants were not much less dominant. Year after year, the Dodgers and Giants would arrive in New York, Shea would fill up, and the Mets would mostly lose.

But the narrative was changing in Hodges's second year in charge. Though the Mets commemorated their nonmilestone of reaching .500 by losing five straight games and getting outscored 36–9, they put their faith in Koosman and his born-again shoulder to stop the skid. Koosman didn't disappoint, manhandling the Padres with a Mets-record 15 strikeouts in 10 shutout innings. Tug McGraw came on and pitched a scoreless eleventh, picking up the win when Harrelson knocked an RBI single, continuing a remarkable career rebirth that McGraw owed largely to Hodges. Signed by the Mets mostly to appease his older brother Hank, a catcher in the Mets' farm system who was then a much more highly regarded prospect, McGraw, of Vallejo, California, made his big-league debut at age 20, in 1965. He showed flashes of promise, never more so than in a late-season start, when he outpitched Sandy Koufax, who had won 13 straight games against the Mets before McGraw's 5-2 victory on the night of August 26, 1965. It was a landmark moment in Mets history, but the irrepressible, high-strung McGraw—word was that he was so excited after striking out Orlando Cepeda in his major-league debut that he needed a tranquilizer to calm down—wouldn't have many more highlights for a while.

He was 2-9 with a 5.34 ERA in 1966, hurt his arm when he tried to bulk up with weights, and spent most of 1967 and all of 1968 pitching in double-A ball in Jacksonville, his results so underwhelming in the latter year the Mets didn't even protect him in the expansion draft. McGraw was trying to perfect a new pitch—a screwball—that he learned from former Yankee Ralph Terry, who was trying to catch on with the Mets. The screwball is a difficult pitch to throw, and an even harder one to master. McGraw stayed with it and got enough results in the spring of 1969 to head north with the big club. Hodges became convinced that McGraw's temperament, and the sharp action on his screwball, which cut away from right-handed hitters and in on the hands of left-handers, made him a natural for the bull pen.

McGraw was still a spot starter early in 1969 but was seeing more and more time, with good results, in the pen and recounted to author Stanley Cohen in the book *The Magic Summer* the day in June when Hodges called him into his office.

"[Hodges] said, 'Tug, I have three pieces of advice for you'," Mc-Graw recalled. "'One, I think you should think about staying in the bull pen permanently. You could be a great reliever and at best an average starter. Two, this team needs a late-inning stopper, and I want you to be my stopper. Three, I think you'll make a lot more money as a reliever than as a starter. Now it's up to you.' I said, 'Gil, if you think that's the way for me to go, I'm there already.' The rest is history."

· · ·

THE GIANTS ARRIVED next for their first visit of the year. More than 52,000 people packed Shea Stadium. The story line looked very familiar at the start, Willie McCovey mashing an early home run off Seaver that crashed off the scoreboard in right-center. Giants left-hander Mike McCormick took a no-hitter, and a 3–0 lead, into the seventh. But on the seventh anniversary of Steve Aptheker and friends parading around the Polo Grounds with their LET's GO METS banner, with the crowd chanting those words early and often, the Mets took heed. Swoboda led off the seventh with a home run, and an inning later, Rod Gaspar surprised everyone by belting his first (and only) big-league homer to make it 3–2. Duffy Dyer, in only his fifth plate appearance of the season, delivered a pinch-hit, game-winning single. After so many years of embodying Murphy's Law, the Mets now seemed to be operating under Hodges's Law: whatever can go right will go right.

Hodges's Mets were a platoon-based team. The only true regulars for most of the year were Agee and Jones in the outfield, Harrelson at short, and Grote behind the plate. The other starters were dictated by whether the opposing pitcher was left-handed or right-handed, but even when Hodges had to depart from his platoons, things usually worked out. Ken Boswell, the left-handed-hitting second baseman, left for two weeks of military duty at the start of the Giants series, so Hodges moved Wayne Garrett to second and inserted Ed Charles at third base, even though the right-handed Charles almost never faced right-handers and the Giants were starting the notorious spitballing righty Gaylord Perry. Charles responded by driving in four runs, including a three-run home run off Perry. It was his best game of the season. Gary Gentry pitched seven strong innings and got spotless relief help from McGraw, who, still getting acclimated to pitching out of the bull pen, struck out four in two dominant innings. Here, too, Hodges's Law was at work; it was he, as much as anyone, who saw the possibilities in McGraw as a reliever, recognizing that the bull pen would be a perfect fit for his fast-twitch, high-energy disposition. McGraw wasn't sold at first, but the results were almost immediate.

After rolling the Padres and the Giants, the Mets looked to complete their West Coast run against the Dodgers. Koosman went the distance to win the first game, Seaver was almost as good the next night, and then rookie left-hander Jack DiLauro, making his first big-league start, fired two-hit ball in 9 shutout innings, matching zeroes with Dodgers starter Bill Singer before McGraw and Taylor spun six scoreless innings of relief and the Mets won another 1–0 game, this time in 15 innings.

That made it seven wins in a row, and if Hodges—deep into his one-game-at-a-time mantra—didn't want to make a big deal out of it, everybody else did. After all, the New York Mets were now a second-place team.

Second place.

For the Mets it was like a bump up to first class after years next to the bathroom in the back of coach. In the *New York Times*, Leonard Koppett wrote a column about how "the myriad members of the Celestial Chapter of the New York Mets Fan Club held this week's meeting on Cloud Nine," going on to concoct a quote from William Shakespeare: "We've all seen the tricky bounces and the friendly gusts of wind that indicate that providence is starting to smile on the legitimately splendid efforts of our improved players. It is quite possible, in short, that the Mets will win the pennant, or come close."

The Mets headed west and stretched the winning streak to a club-record 11 in San Francisco, where Don Cardwell hurled seven stout innings and went 3 for 3 at the plate, plus a sacrifice fly. Agee homered twice, Jones once. The Mets scored nine runs. Cardwell had no idea what to do with such an explosion. The Mets had been shut out in his first four starts of the year. Cardwell's luck wasn't bad. It was brutal. Everything suddenly was different.

Very different.

"When we won eleven in a row and went out on the West Coast and kept winning, that was when I knew," Kranepool said. "We beat every team. We used to lose consistently to those teams. We'd play the Giants and Dodgers and get hammered. That started the charge."

• • •

MEANWHILE, THE JUNE 15 trade deadline was approaching, and GM Johnny Murphy was busy working the phones, still on the prowl for a veteran power hitter. His leading candidate was one of his targets in the spring, Donn Clendenon, who had little to show for his time in Montreal. A month away from his thirty-fourth birthday, Clendenon was hitting just .240 with 4 home runs and 14 RBI. Murphy studied the particulars of Clendenon's situation and believed there was great value for the Mets here. Clendenon had missed all of spring training with his brief retirement. He was with a losing team that had already tried to trade him and was just a year removed from a 17-homer, 87-RBI season with the Pirates. Murphy thought the 6-foot, 4-inch Clendenon, a bright, funny fellow with a big bat and big personality, would bring not just production but a stabilizing veteran presence to the league's youngest team.

Murphy had been in regular contact with the Expos' general manager, John McHale. Now the deadline was upon them, and Murphy wanted to close the deal. Clendenon was on the road with the Expos in San Francisco, according to the account in his book, *Miracle in New York*. The phone rang in Clendenon's hotel room. He picked it up.

"I want Clendenon," a voice said. It was Murphy, who had asked to be put through to McHale but ended up being connected to the wrong room.

Clendenon didn't hesitate. "You can have him. He has a history of slavery and he can be bought, but not cheaply."

Murphy, taken aback, asked, "Who is this?"

"This is Donn Clendenon."

The sheepish Murphy collected himself and went on. An operator screwup had given him a prime opportunity to talk directly to the man he wanted to trade for, and in those innocent days before anyone had heard of tampering, the Mets' GM wasn't going to blow it.

"Donn, would you come to New York to play for us if we can make a trade for you?"

"You're damn right I would come to New York," Clendenon replied.

Clendenon had every reason to embrace the move. He would be leaving a last-place team with a 15-40 record and going to a club that looked to at least have a chance to contend. It didn't hurt that Clendenon had a very good history with Gil Hodges. In the spring of 1964, when Hodges was managing the Senators and Clendenon was trying to polish his first-base skills with the Pirates, the men intersected during the exhibition season. At the urging of his friend Jackie Robinson, Clendenon reached out to Hodges, who graciously agreed to help and spent a good amount of time teaching Clendenon the finer points of playing first base. Clendenon came away deeply impressed both by Hodges the man and Hodges the first baseman. Hodges was likewise impressed with Clendenon's intelligence and athletic ability.

All Murphy had to do now was complete the deal. He reached McHale's room, and they went back and forth. Murphy ultimately agreed to give up two well-regarded prospects, pitcher Steve Renko and infielder Kevin Collins, along with minor-league pitchers Jay Carden and David Colon. Clendenon joined the Mets in Philadelphia two days later. Hodges welcomed him and told him he was certain that he'd be a great asset, on the field and in the clubhouse. Clendenon had never played in a World Series. He thought the rest of the season had a chance to be interesting, and he found out how right he was just two games into his New York career.

The Mets were in Philadelphia for a Thursday-night game in Connie Mack Stadium, playing before a crowd so small (6,871) that the fans were almost outnumbered by vendors. Seaver wasn't sharp, giving up two homers and navigating around trouble much of the night. The Mets fell behind three times and caught up three times. Shamsky socked two home runs. Despite his struggles on the mound, Seaver was productive at the plate, drawing a walk in the seventh inning, stealing second, and then sliding headfirst into third when the ball squirted away, not necessarily a recommended activity for an ace pitcher. Down a run in the ninth, the Mets got a two-run single from Boswell, and McGraw nailed down the save for a 6–5 victory. It was a game the Mets had every right to lose and wound up winning.

Everything Clendenon took in in his first few days wearing number 22 for the Mets reenergized him. The feeling was mutual.

"It wasn't like we were trading for Henry Aaron," Johnny Murphy said later that year. "But I had a good feeling about incorporating Donn into this ball club. Sometimes you just have a feel for these things."

Clendenon started slowly with the Mets, going 2 for his first 16. But he broke out against his old club, the Pirates, knocking two hits and driving in three runs in a game at Shea at the end of June, and then blasting a three-run homer and a run-scoring double a week later in Pittsburgh, powering the Mets out of a 6–1 deficit and into an 8–7 victory—one made possible largely by four strong innings of relief work by Cal Koonce.

The least-heralded member of the Mets bull pen, Koonce, a native North Carolinian and former Chicago Cub, brought a salt-of-the-earth professionalism to the staff. Long relief, middle relief, short relief—Koonce would take the ball whenever Hodges needed him. He didn't have overpowering stuff and would fight control problems throughout his career, but few pitchers were more game than Koonce, who proved it in the finale of an eight-game road trip in early July, when the Mets rallied from six runs down and Koonce struck out six Pirates, saving a victory and extending the Mets' winning streak to five games.

The Mets flew back to Shea with a 45-34 record, and in high

spirits. A three-game series with the Cubs, who were only three games ahead of the Mets in the loss column, was next. Koosman would be on the mound for the opener. The Cubs had lost three straight against the Cardinals. It was only July, but the Mets were in the race, and when had that ever happened?

"It has taken them seven and a half years, 439 victories and 771 defeats," wrote George Vecsey in the *New York Times*, "but today the Mets finally begin an important series."

The Chicago Cubs hadn't won a World Series since 1908, and their supporters, among baseball's most passionate fans, were also the most fatalistic. This season, in which the Cubs had broken out to a 36-16 start, promised to be different. The Cubs were loaded with star players, among them Ron Santo, Billy Williams, Don Kessinger, Glenn Beckert, Randy Hundley, and 38-year-old Ernie Banks, the affable first baseman universally known as Mr. Cub. They had a workhorse of an ace, Ferguson Jenkins; two other high-quality starters, Bill Hands and Ken Holtzman, right behind him; and a seasoned pro, Phil Regan, in the bull pen. Managed by Leo Durocher, a scrappy, hard-edged underdog whose nickname—"Leo the Lip"—spoke to the fact that he never met an umpire he wouldn't abuse, the Cubs looked to be as much of a lock for the postseason as a team could be.

Mets fans could build up the importance of the series as much as they wanted to, but Durocher considered the Mets pretenders and didn't mind saying so. The polar opposite of his manager temperamentally, Ernie Banks, baseball's sunniest spirit, had a soft, welcoming face and a smile that could melt a glacier, but even he wasn't looking at the visit to Shea as packed with pressure.

"I can't think of a place I'd rather be on this glorious day than in wonderful Shea Stadium in wonderful New York," Banks said before the series began. "What a day! What a team! What a year! As I always say, the Cubs will shine in '69!"

Durocher had just the man he wanted to start the series in Jenkins, a 6-foot, 5-inch workhorse from outside Toronto, the only child of a Bahamian father and Canadian mother whose ancestors had escaped slavery in the South via the Underground Railroad. Originally signed by the Phillies, Jenkins was sent to Chicago with Adolfo Phillips and John Herrnstein in exchange for pitchers Bob Buhl and Larry Jackson early in 1966, a deal that wasn't so much a trade as a heist by the Cubs. A year later, Jenkins emerged as a full-fledged star. He had already won 11 games in 1969 and remained in peak form against the Mets, retiring the first 11 hitters and taking a no-hitter one out into the fifth, when Kranepool homered for the game's first run. Banks evened the score with a home run of his own to start the sixth, and after former Met Jim Hickman belted a homer off Koosman in the eighth, the Cubs had a 3–1 lead. There was no chance Durocher was going to the bull pen—not with his ace on the mound. When Boswell, pinch-hitting for Koosman, stepped in to start the bottom of the ninth, Jenkins had retired nine straight Mets and still had given up but a single hit.

There was nothing to suggest—even remotely—that an uprising was imminent.

The crowd of more than 55,000 was at full volume, rooting for a comeback. Boswell swung and lifted a fly to short center. Don Young, the Cubs' bespectacled 23-year-old rookie and a superb center-ter fielder, didn't get a good read on the ball, taking a step back before charging in. He sprinted hard and dived to make the play, but the ball landed safely. Boswell, running all the way, was the recipient of a gift double. After Agee fouled out, Clendenon came up and smashed a long drive toward the wall in left-center. Young raced to his right, got to the track, and reached out with his left arm, making a sweet backhand grab, only to have the ball dislodge when he hit the fence. Boswell, holding up to see if the ball was caught, advanced only to third as Clendenon cruised into second, putting the tying run in scoring position.

The Cubs had a difficult call to make. Cleon Jones, a .350 hitter, was by far the best bat in the Mets' lineup. With first base open, Jenkins could intentionally walk him to get to Shamsky, a dangerous left-handed hitter, but that would put the potential winning run on base.

Durocher decided to go after Jones.

"Battle him," Durocher told Jenkins.

Jenkins nodded and returned to work. He started Jones off with a curveball. It got more of the plate than Jenkins wanted, and Jones pounced on it, lashing a double to left to bring home both runners and tie the game. Shea Stadium exploded in a joyous roar. Shamsky was intentionally walked before Wayne Garrett advanced the runners with a groundout to second.

Up stepped Kranepool. He had already homered and Jenkins had an open base, but the Cubs elected to pitch to him. Kranepool fell behind 1-2 as Jenkins worked the outside corner with breaking pitches.

"I knew I wasn't going to see a strike," Kranepool said.

Jenkins stayed outside, with another off-speed pitch. Protecting the plate with two strikes, Kranepool reached out and served it to left, a floater over shortstop. With two outs, Jones was running on contact. Kessinger chased the ball with all he had. If he could catch up to it, the game would go to extra innings. Kessinger reached as far as he could. Kranepool's flare dropped onto the outfield grass. Jones crossed home plate, and Shea Stadium was all but quaking now. It was the biggest hit in Kranepool's life in the biggest game the Mets had ever played.

With a three-run ninth against the Cubs' best pitcher, the Mets had stolen a 4–3 victory.

After the game, Durocher's fury fell on his center fielder, Don Young. "Two little fly balls," Durocher said. "He just stands there watching one, and he gives up on the other. It's a disgrace."

Captain Ron Santo chimed in, too: "He was just thinking about himself, not the team. He had a bad day at bat, so he's got his head down. He's worrying about his batting average and not the team. It's ridiculous. There's no way the Mets beat us."

Young accepted the full brunt of the blame. "I just lost the game for us," he said. "That's all."

Young showed extraordinary guts taking the hit for the team, but the Cubs' reaction to the defeat didn't portend well for the club's long-term prospects. While Hodges would certainly take corrective action if he felt a player wasn't giving his all, he would never call one of his players a "disgrace" for not making a play he had tried his best on. Regan, the Cubs' standout relief pitcher, felt terrible for Young and was appalled by how the manager, and even more so, the captain, went after him. "Don Young was never the same after that," Regan said. "He showered and left the ballpark as soon as he could get out of there. To this day, you never hear from him. Santo was the captain and a veteran. He apologized later, but it was done. You can't do that. That hurt us."

• • •

THE NINTH-INNING RALLY against Jenkins stoked even more enthusiasm among Mets fans for the second game of the series. That Tom Seaver would be on the mound certainly didn't hurt, either. The date was July 9, a Wednesday. Seaver was 13-3 on the season and had won his last seven decisions. Midway through his third year in the big leagues, he was already a Mets superhero, the figurative S on his chest having nothing to do with his last name. At age 23, Seaver was not just one of the best young pitchers in the game. He was boyishly handsome, articulate, respectful, and the husband of beautiful, blond Nancy Seaver, his adoring college sweetheart, who could be found a dozen or so rows behind the Mets' dugout every time Tom started, fashionably turned out and seemingly hanging on every pitch. The Seavers were a real-life Barbie and Ken, almost too blessed to be true, baseball's most glamorous young couple. It was still astonishing to think about how they had come to be in Flushing.

Just over three and a half years earlier, the Atlanta Braves had selected Seaver out of the University of Southern California in the first round of the January 1966 draft. Scout Johnny Moore, a former big-league outfielder who had played for the Cubs against the Yankees in the 1932 World Series (famed for Babe Ruth's alleged "called shot"), had done a splendid piece of scouting work and found a jewel. On February 24, 1966, Seaver signed for a bonus of $50,000.

The Braves had been Seaver's favorite team growing up. Henry Aaron had been his favorite player. It was storybook stuff all the way, until Major League Baseball changed the ending. The Braves, it turned out, had broken the rules. The violation cost them the services of George Thomas Seaver.

Seaver was not considered even a low-level prospect coming out of Fresno High School. Indeed, he was still pitching on the JV in his junior year. At 5 feet, 9 inches and 145 pounds, he was undersized and didn't throw particularly hard, and though he came from excellent athletic stock—his father, Charles, was one of the top amateur golfers in the country and represented the United States in the Walker Cup—there was little to suggest that he would be a big-time pitcher.

And then everything changed. Seaver went to work for the raisin-packing plant where his father was an executive and joined the US Marine Corps Reserve. The rigors of basic training and hauling bulging sacks of raisins, along with a well-timed growth spurt, put about 4 inches and 45 pounds on his frame, as well as yards on his fastball. He enrolled in Fresno City College, a two-year school, and pitched well, and then did even better with a semipro team, the Alaska Goldpanners of Fairbanks, one of the premier summer-league teams in the country. Pitching in the most anticipated event in the Fairbanks summer—the Midnight Sun Game (11 p.m. start, no lights necessary)—Seaver shared a no-hitter with a fellow Goldpanner. His showing helped him earn a scholarship offer from Rod Dedeaux, the renowned coach at USC. Dedeaux was enamored with Seaver's stuff and his competitiveness and his pitching smarts, and soon others were, too. The Dodgers selected Seaver in the tenth round of baseball's first amateur draft in June 1965, the 190th pick overall—189 spots behind Rick Monday and 188 behind Les Rohr, the pitcher the Mets took second overall. Opting not to sign because he believed his stock would rise even more, Seaver returned to USC, and the following January the Braves drafted him at the urging of Moore, the same scout who had signed the Braves' Hall of Fame third baseman, Eddie Mathews.

Seaver and the Braves came to terms, and everything was set. Then the phone rang.

The caller was John McHale, then the Braves' general manager. McHale told Seaver that Baseball Commissioner William "Spike" Eckert had nullified the signing because USC had already played a couple of early-season games. Seaver hadn't pitched in either of them, but the rules stipulated that major league clubs could not sign amateur players after their collegiate season had begun. To make matters worse, Seaver was stripped of his amateur status by the National Collegiate Athletic Association (NCAA) because he had signed a professional contract. That he hadn't received any money and the contract had been voided was immaterial in the NCAA's view; his intent was to be a professional, so he was barred from pitching for USC.

Seaver was suddenly a pitcher non grata, a man without a mound or a team, forbidden to sign with the Braves or play college ball for USC. The predicament didn't get untangled until the 21-year-old Seaver called the commissioner's office and spoke with Lee MacPhail, Eckert's deputy, explaining that he had done nothing wrong and that it wasn't fair that he was caught in the crosshairs of Major League Baseball and NCAA fine print.

He had a point.

Eckert ultimately ruled that any big-league club (except the Braves) interested in signing Seaver for $50,000 could be a part of a special one-time lottery. Only three organizations—the Philadelphia Phillies, Cleveland Indians, and New York Mets—stepped forward. The Indians invited Seaver down to Long Beach, where he threw all of fifteen pitches, apparently the only sampling they needed. The Mets called to express their interest. Seaver never heard from the Phillies.

The big day—April 1, 1966—arrived. The Seaver Sweepstakes were all set. A studious and meticulous young man, Seaver talked it through with his father and his fiancée, Nancy McIntyre. The Indians clearly had shown the most initiative, but their pitching staff also had Sam McDowell, Sonny Siebert, Luis Tiant, and Steve

Hargan. The Mets were a last-place team, but they undeniably offered the quickest path to the big leagues. Seaver wanted no part of losing, but he *did* want a fast track to the majors.

He had no doubt: he wanted to be a New York Met.

The phone rang in the Seaver residence in Fresno. Tom picked up in the dining room. His father was on an extension. The names of the three clubs were written on slips of paper and dropped into a bowl in the commissioner's office in New York City. MacPhail was right alongside Eckert, ready to narrate the play-by-play for Seaver. Eckert stuck his hand in the bowl, picked a slip of paper and handed it to MacPhail. Seaver could hardly stand it. This was his Academy Award moment, he would say later, except that there was no envelope to open and no list of people to thank. Just a piece of paper with the name of a ball club. There would be only one winner. His whole career was at stake—or so it felt.

"The team," MacPhail said, ". . . is the New York Mets."

It was no April Fool's joke. After four woeful seasons and unending bad luck, the Mets finally had something good happen. A piece of paper pulled out of a bowl had changed everything.

• • •

HOWIE ROSE, the future Mets radio broadcaster, knew that Shea was going to be jumping the night of game two of the Cubs series. A huge Mets fan from Bayside, Queens, the 15-year-old Rose and a friend arrived later than usual because they had baseball practice, and they couldn't get their regular upper-deck seats in Section 1 behind home plate. They shoehorned into two seats down the third-base line and were lucky to do so; a Shea record crowd of 59,083—almost 4,000 over capacity—was in the house that night. About 50 of the extra fans stormed in when the bull pen gate beyond the right-field fence opened to make way for LaVonne Koosman, the wife of Jerry, as she pulled into the parking lot. The mood in the ballpark was beyond delirium; it was, Rose said, total, dizzying rapture. When Jane Jarvis, the Shea organist, played "Meet the Mets" on the Thomas organ, about 50,000 people sang along.

"It was like Woodstock a month before Woodstock," Rose said. "Every game was a party."

As he warmed up prior to the game, Seaver felt some stiffness in his right shoulder. It wasn't a huge concern. Sometimes it just took a little longer to get loose. Right behind Seaver, the Cubs' lineup on the scoreboard in right field showed an unsurprising change from the night before; Don Young was out, and a 22-year-old rookie, Jimmy Qualls, just up from the minor leagues, was in, playing center field and batting eighth.

Seaver started impressively, striking out Kessinger and Williams in the first. Agee whacked the first pitch from Cubs starter Ken Holtzman into the right-field corner for a triple and was doubled in by Bobby Pfeil. Seaver had a lead and then mowed down the Cubs in the second, striking out the side—Santo, Banks, and right fielder Al Spangler. Back-to-back errors by Santo and Kessinger got the Mets started in the second, and then Seaver, in a bunting situation, surprised the Cubs by chopping a single to right. Agee followed with a two-run double to knock out Holtzman and give Seaver a 3–0 lead.

Before Seaver was even done with the Cubs in the third, pitching coach Rube Walker was struck by how Seaver's fastball was exploding out of his hand and how he was carving up the corners with his curveball.

He has the stuff to throw a no-hitter tonight, Walker told Hodges.

Through four innings, Seaver retired every Cub he had faced. When he struck out Spangler to end the fifth, that made it 15 Cubs up, 15 Cubs down.

Seaver knew exactly what was going on as he came out for the sixth, and you could sense the buzz building in the record crowd. He faced three more Cubs and retired them all. Then came the seventh and the top of a very tough Cubs order. Kessinger hit a line drive to left. Seaver's heart sank; he thought it was a hit. But Jones got a good jump, ran toward the line, and made the grab. Beckert flied out, and left fielder Billy Williams grounded to third. Seaver walked off to a thunderous ovation, his fresh-scrubbed face down, a study in intensity.

Twenty-one Cubs had come to bat. Twenty-one Cubs had been retired.

There had been only two perfect games in the National League in the twentieth century. Jim Bunning had thrown one on Father's Day 1964 against the Mets, on this same mound. Sandy Koufax had thrown the second in 1965, against these same Cubs.

George Thomas Seaver, a 24-year-old from Fresno, California, was six outs from making it three.

Cleon Jones walloped a home run in the bottom of the seventh to make it 4–0, but nobody was thinking about the Mets' offense at the moment. This was the Tom Seaver Show.

The dangerous Santo was the first hitter due up in the top of the eighth. Hodges, seeking to tighten up the defense, brought Rod Gaspar on for Swoboda in right field and Wayne Garrett on to play second base, with Bobby Pfeil moving to third in place of Charles. Garrett took his warm-up grounders from Clendenon.

I hope nobody hits the ball to me, he thought. *I don't want to be the one to screw this up.*

Santo was one of the few National League hitters who hit Seaver well. He had four career home runs against him and hit a ball that chased Agee to the warning track in center in the fifth inning. Swinging at the first pitch, Santo made good contact again, the thwack of bat on ball resounding through Shea as the ball traveled to deep center. Agee raced back. He pounded his glove and made the catch. The huge crowd exhaled even more than it cheered. Before he threw a pitch to Ernie Banks, Seaver moved to the back of the mound and rubbed up the ball. He took a moment to survey the scene: more than 59,000 people cheering, standing, reveling. People were standing behind the last row of seats all the way down the foul lines, and they must've been ten deep by the foul poles. Seaver's father, Charles, was sitting next to Nancy in the box seats behind the Mets dugout. Seaver thought about how moments such as this were supposed to be for Sandy Koufax and Willie Mays or his hero, Henry Aaron, for baseball royalty. Not for Tom Seaver and the New York Mets.

Seaver struck Banks out swinging on a 2-2 pitch.

Four outs to go.

Al Spangler stepped in for his third trip. Seaver rung him up on three pitches, number 11 for the night.

Seaver walked off to one more standing ovation. Three outs to go.

With one out in the bottom of the eighth, Al Weis, the everyday shortstop with Bud Harrelson away on military duty, singled to left-center. The instant Weis arrived at first, a roar began to build in Shea. It was for the next hitter, Tom Seaver. As he walked to the plate, bat in hand, number 41 on his back, Seaver didn't just hear the Shea Stadium crowd cheer him; he heard them bathe him in adoration. In the upper deck, Howie Rose remembered it as "the loudest sound I ever heard in my life and the most electrifying moment I can ever remember, fifty-nine thousand people rising as one."

But it was more than that.

"My overriding emotion has always been more about what it represented than what it actually sounded like," Rose said. "The sonic roar encapsulated the realization, at least to me, that not only had the Mets at long last 'arrived' but that in Tom Seaver, we, as Mets fans, had our very own Sandy Koufax or Mickey Mantle—a transcendent star who willed his team far beyond a newfound competitiveness; who allowed us to dream that the New York Mets, in 1969, might actually be capable of something special."

Seaver bunted and barely ran to first, and nobody cared. Agee grounded out, and now it was time for the top of the ninth in Shea Stadium.

One of baseball's oldest and most sacrosanct traditions is never to talk about a perfect game or no-hitter while it is in progress. Nobody on the Mets said anything to Seaver. Randy Hundley, the Cubs' catcher, started off the ninth. Seaver delivered a high fastball, and Hundley laid down a bunt. Seaver was delighted that Hundley had done that, especially because it was a poor bunt that rolled right back to the mound. Seaver pounced on it and threw to Clendenon, his twenty-fifth consecutive retired hitter.

Two outs to go.

The crowd at Shea was standing. It felt as if the fans had been standing for an hour. The next hitter was Jimmy Qualls, the kid up from Tacoma, an infielder/outfielder whose natural position was second base. A farmer in the off-season, Qualls taught himself to hit left-handed after taking a pitch in the jaw from a right-hander shortly after he turned pro. This was Qualls's eighteenth big-league game. He was in the game because Don Young was deep in Durocher's doghouse. The Mets had no book on him, since he'd been in the Pacific Coast League for much of the year. The only Met who knew anything about him was Bobby Pfeil, who had played against him in the minors. Qualls was a solid hitter who usually made contact, Pfeil reported. In two at bats, Qualls had hit a deep line drive to right and a hard grounder to first, making better contact than any other Cubs player.

The Mets' fielders were alive, nervous, and expectant. With a left-handed hitter at the plate, Garrett was directly in the firing line. *Please, hit it somewhere else*, he thought again.

Seaver did all he could to make it business as usual, but that was almost impossible.

"In the ninth inning my heart was pounding so much," he said later. "I could just feel the adrenaline flowing in my system, and my arm felt as light as a feather. I felt like I was coming off the ground. The fans were unbelievable, overwhelming, deafening."

Since Qualls had pulled Seaver twice, Grote set up outside, calling for a fastball away. Seaver's first pitch was on the outer half but caught a good piece of the plate. Qualls got a clear look at it and hit it solidly, a line drive to left-center. Agee broke quickly but knew immediately he had no shot at it. He hoped Jones did, but it was wishful thinking.

Jimmy Qualls's line drive landed safely on the left-center field grass. Agee backhanded it on one hop. Tom Seaver's perfect game was over with two outs to go in the ninth inning.

Seaver stood on the mound with his hands on his hips, his head down.

In the Mets' broadcast booth, Bob Murphy called the play: "And it's hard hit to left field . . . It's going to be a base hit . . . A base hit by Jimmy Qualls, and it breaks up the perfect game . . . Now the applause for Tom Seaver . . . Eight and one-third innings of perfect baseball by Seaver."

The crowd gave Seaver one more standing ovation. He tried to take it in, but his emotions and thoughts might as well have been in a blender. "It was like a drain opened up under my feet," he said. "I just took a deep breath. I didn't say a word to myself. All the pressure, everything, was gone." Clendenon came in from first base, and, with deflation and disappointment running thicker in Shea than Midtown Tunnel traffic at rush hour, opted to go with humor.

"Okay, Tom, you screwed up. Now get the last two outs."

Seaver retired pinch hitter Willie Smith on a foul pop and Kessinger on a fly to left. His final pitch was his ninety-ninth. The game had taken two hours and two minutes.

The Mets swarmed Seaver when it was over, celebrating their ace and his near perfection, a victory that left them a mere three and a half games out of first place. It was, without argument, the greatest night in the history of the New York Mets. Seaver thereafter would refer to his performance on July 9, 1969, as "the imperfect game." He had been so close. He had felt so strong, so dominant. It had all been undone not by one of the Cubs' future Hall of Famers but by Jimmy Qualls, who would leave Major League Baseball with 31 hits.

"I pitched a good game, of course, but within my grasp was a perfect game. I wouldn't know how to measure the disappointment," Seaver said.

The next day, Mayor Lindsay, ever the opportunist, placed a call to Shea Stadium. Lindsay had recently lost the Republican primary and was looking at an all-but-impossible path to reelection as an independent. Politicians' greatest skill is latching onto anything—a cause, a news event, a person—that can help them. Lindsay spoke to Hodges and then had the call transferred into the clubhouse, where he got Seaver.

"I'm just sorry you lost the perfecto last night, but it was a great job," the mayor said. "Let's go all the way, the pennant, and then the Series."

There was every chance that if Lindsay had been asked the day before what a "perfecto" was, he would've said it was a Dutch Masters cigar. But no matter. Seaver thanked him for the call.

In time, Seaver's crushing disappointment abated, and he was able to take in the depth of his team's achievement in the first two games of the series against the front-running Cubs. With a half season yet to play, there was a pennant race in the National League East, and the New York Mets were in the thick of it. The Mets were hot, the Cubs were cold, and as Howie Rose and 59,082 other fans headed for home on the night of July 9, the possibilities were tantalizing to think about.

"The Mets were only eight years old, but that was the night they were Bar Mitzvahed," Rose said. In his bedroom in Bayside, Rose tried to sleep but couldn't. The jingle "Meet the Mets" played nonstop in his head, followed by "Let's Go, Mets!," the tune Jarvis played when the Mets took the field. The Mets were 47-34 exactly halfway through the season. Eighty-one games remained. Howie Rose couldn't wait to see how they would play out.

3

TEACHING MOMENTS

O F ALL THE LESSONS GIL HODGES IMPARTED TO HIS YOUNG METS, THE most important concerned staying on an even emotional keel and channeling all of their energy, mental and physical, into that day's game. It sounds simple enough, but having been through so many pennant races with the Dodgers, particularly the one in 1951 when the Dodgers lost a 13-game lead and then the pennant, after the Giants' Bobby Thomson hit the so-called Shot Heard 'Round the World, Hodges had a keener appreciation than most of the game's vicissitudes.

The baseball season lasts for six months, seven if you are doing well. It has almost twice the number of games of any other sport, a grind that doesn't deplete players physically the way, say, basketball and hockey do, but can deplete them mentally if they aren't able to rein in their emotions. Hodges wasn't the first manager to master the art of levelheadedness, but nobody was better at it—and at instilling in his team the gift of a short memory, heeding wisdom once shared by Hall of Fame pitcher Bob Feller.

"You can build on yesterday's success or put its failures behind and start over again," Feller said. "That's the way life is, with a new game every day, and that's the way baseball is."

So when the Cubs took the final game of the series and the Mets had almost as many errors (2) as hits (3), Hodges was fine with letting Durocher, his former manager in Brooklyn, take a dig about how "the real Mets" showed up today. A reporter asked Hodges how he felt about the three games. Hodges took a bite of an apple as he sat in his office chair in the corner of the Mets' clubhouse.

"It was a good series. Anytime you take two out of three, it's a good series," he said.

The clubs went their separate ways for the weekend, the Mets hosting the Expos for a series that included Old-Timers' Day. It was a sweltering afternoon, and everyone got a serious scare when Eleanor Gehrig, the widow of the Yankees' icon, fainted in the heat. She was quickly revived. In the Old-Timers' game itself, Bobby Thomson hit a homer off of Whitey Ford. Nobody called it the shot heard 'round Flushing.

The Mets took two of three from the Expos before reconvening with the Cubs on the north side of Chicago, where the home team was rooted on by the Bleacher Bums, a boisterous brigade of supporters known for their yellow construction helmets and unmerciful treatment of the opposition. The most infamous fans in baseball, the Bums typically started their day by getting fueled in a tavern known as Ray's Bleachers, then descending en masse to the left-field seats, where they carried on in broad daylight at the only big-league park without lights. With the Cubs-Mets rivalry suddenly hotter than a waffle iron, they figured to be especially vociferous. The Mets didn't appreciate Durocher's constant dismissals of their worthiness, and almost none of them had any use for Santo, who annoyed most of the league with his habit of jumping up and clicking his heels after every Cubs victory. Santo had heard about the Mets' disapproval of his heel clicking, and when he brought Durocher's lineup card out to home plate and met Hodges before a game at Wrigley, he took the opportunity to defend himself.

"The only reason I click my heels is because the fans will boo me if I don't," he told Hodges.

Replied Hodges, "You remind me of Tug McGraw. When he was young and immature and nervous, he used to jump up and down, too. He doesn't do it anymore."

New York papers were full of stories about the charging Mets and the transformation the club had undergone under Hodges, who characteristically declined to take credit.

"What turned them on?" Hodges asked, repeating a reporter's question about his players. "It's a bunch of boys who turned themselves on. Maybe for the first time they realize that it's just as easy to win as to lose—even in the major leagues."

Pitching for the first time since the Imperfect Game, Seaver began by retiring 10 straight Cubs but wound up losing a 1–0 decision, nudging the Cubs' lead back up to six games. It made the next two games of paramount importance to the Mets, who would slip back to eight games behind were the Cubs to sweep. Gary Gentry started the second game and pitched superbly to win his ninth game of the year, the decisive blow coming in the top of the fourth from the unlikeliest source imaginable: shortstop Al Weis. Cubs pitcher Dick Selma, an ex-Met (and an ex–Little League opponent of Seaver in Fresno) got ahead 1-2 and came at Weis with a fastball. Weis always looked for a fastball; if he got something else, he would adjust accordingly.

"My job was to get on base any way that I could," Weis said. "I never went to the plate in my whole career trying to hit the ball out."

Weis swung and took off running hard. He thought he had a double, at least. The ball kept going, and going. It soared over the left-field wall, the Bleacher Bums and the screen behind them, flying right out of Wrigley Field onto Waveland Avenue. Weis was as shocked as anybody.

"Don't make me out to be a home run hitter," Weis said later. "I'm not even a hitter."

It was Weis's fifth career homer, and he so enjoyed the novelty of it that he smacked number six the next day, off Ferguson Jenkins, no less, the Mets jumping out early and getting lock-down relief from Cal Koonce and Ron Taylor. When he came out of the dugout to congratulate Taylor on saving his second straight game, Seaver jumped up and clicked his heels.

The Mets moved on to Montreal but had a bit of a letdown and were in danger of losing three of four. On Sunday, July 20, not long after Apollo 11's Lunar Excursion Module *Eagle* descended onto the surface of the moon, Hodges called on Bobby Pfeil to pinch-hit. The score was 3–3 in the tenth inning of the second game of a double-header; the Mets had lost the opener. Ron Swoboda, the go-ahead run, was on third. Pfeil noticed that Montreal third baseman Coco Laboy was playing back. Acting on his own, Pfeil dropped a bunt down the third-base line.

Pfeil took off for first. Swoboda broke for home. The Expos let the ball roll. It kept rolling until it hit the third-base bag, a fair ball. The Mets had the lead, and the split, after Jack DiLauro set down the Expos in the bottom of the tenth.

Pfeil's little roller was one of the biggest hits of the Mets' season.

It was the Mets' final game before the All-Star break, a heady way to close the first half of the season. They packed up quickly and bussed to the airport, but then went nowhere fast, as their plane had mechanical difficulty. And so the Mets watched the lunar landing in a Canadian airport bar while they waited for their own aircraft to be fixed. Pfeil looked on in awe as Neil Armstrong set foot on the surface of the moon, followed by Buzz Aldrin. "I wondered what was more unusual—man walking on the moon or winning a game with a pinch-hit bunt single?" Pfeil said.

Finally landing back at LaGuardia, the Mets arrived at the All-Star break with a record of 53-39, five games back of the Cubs. They went their separate ways, except for Seaver, Koosman, and Jones, who traveled to Washington, DC, for an All-Star Game that com-memorated baseball's centennial anniversary—and another New York Mets first.

They had never had three All-Stars before.

• • •

GIL HODGES, JR., was a regular around the Mets in 1969 and a reg-ular around his father long before that. From a young age, Gil Jr. learned that his father valued trustworthiness above just about all other human qualities. If a person's word isn't his bond, if he can't be counted on to do what he says he is going to do, then he's going to have a rough go in life.

"He had a simple rule: you never lie," Gil Jr. said. "Because once you lie, people will never know when you are telling the truth again."

Gil Jr. was a 15-year-old high school student in his father's final year managing the Senators. He was on a road trip with the club when he found out from his sister that his report card had arrived and he had failed two classes.

Gil Jr. was terrified about what his father's reaction would be. Doing one's best in school was something the family put major emphasis on.

Not long after Gil Jr. learned the news, his father asked him, "Have you gotten your report card?"

"No, not yet," the son replied.

His father asked him again a day or two later.

"No. It still hasn't come," Gil Jr. said.

Another day passed. Gil Jr. was sick with worry. The Senators returned home, and Hodges, sensing that he wasn't getting the full story, summoned his son to his Washington hotel room. His father was on the phone with his school. The manager of the New York Mets found out that the report cards had, in fact, come in.

"I'm sorry, Dad," Gil Jr. said. "I was going to tell you, but I didn't know what to say."

A few moments of silence ensued. They felt like a few years to Gil Hodges Jr. He looked into his father's eyes. There were tears in them. Gil Jr. had never seen his father cry before. He'd also never seen him so disappointed.

"To see someone who put his life on the line in combat, who was a Bronze Star Marine—to see him well up that way, that was the worst punishment of all," Gil Jr. said. "It was way worse than anything that transpired afterward. It was a good lesson."

· · ·

CLEON JONES, the most trustworthy hitter Gil Hodges had, seemed to be in the middle of most everything for the Mets in 1969. He had two hits, two RBI, and a stolen base on the night in May when the Mets got to .500 against the Braves. He delivered the game-tying two-run double off of Jenkins in the opener of the Cubs series at Shea, then scored the winning run on Kranepool's hit. Right after he returned from his first All-Star Game—he started ahead of Willie Mays, Roberto Clemente, and Pete Rose and knocked two hits to help the National League to victory—he was at the epicenter of two controversies, getting ejected from two games in a week, first for arguing too strenuously with an umpire and then for getting into a scrape with Expos catcher Ron Brand after a collision at home plate.

The second series after the break brought the Houston Astros to town. This was never a good thing. In their first eight seasons, the Mets' record against the Astros was 49-87. The Astros showed up on the schedule, and invariably Mets pain and suffering would follow. Early in 1969, the Mets got swept in the Astrodome by an aggregate score of 18–4. "Something about that team brought out the worst in us," Ed Charles said.

The three-game set started with a soggy doubleheader on July 30, during a stretch of rainy weather that left the city as damp as a rain forest. In the first game, the Astros scored 11 runs in the ninth inning, getting grand slams from Denis Menke and Jimmy Wynn to win 16–3. It was the worst inning in Mets history and the first time in the 93 years of the National League that a team had hit two grand slams in the same inning. It came on Casey Stengel's seventy-ninth birthday, and few of the 43,000 fans in attendance appreciated that the Mets commemorated it by playing the way Casey's teams used to.

In the second game, Gentry was matched against Larry Dierker, the young Astros right-hander. The game was scoreless with two outs in the top of the third. Johnny Edwards, the Houston catcher, was on second base after singling. Then came a single, an error, a walk, another single, two more walks, and a bases-clearing triple by Curt Blefary that splash-landed in right-center. Six runs were in faster than you could spell *deluge*. Another single followed to make it 7–0. Hodges brought in Nolan Ryan. Edwards came up again and hit a looping fly down the left-field line for a double. Cleon Jones went after it at something short of full speed, and his throw back into third base didn't have much zip, either.

Before another Astro had a chance to get on base, Hodges came out of the dugout, hands in his back pockets. Ryan wondered why he was getting pulled after giving up one soft hit. Hodges walked right past the mound and kept going. Shortstop Bud Harrelson looked at the man heading his way and likewise wondered what his misdeed had been. Hodges kept walking, taking his small, tiptoe steps through the sodden grass until he arrived in left field. Now Gil Hodges and Cleon Jones were a few feet apart, both men with their hands on their hips. Hodges asked him what was wrong.

"What do you mean?" Jones asked.

"I don't like the way you went after that last ball," Hodges said.

Jones told him he had a tender leg and didn't want to aggravate it.

Hodges told him if his leg hurt he should come out of the game. He started walking back to the dugout with Jones, the league's leading hitter, trailing a few feet behind him.

Wayne Garrett, the rookie third baseman, watched the manager and the left fielder walk by him.

"If you told me Gil would do that to Cleon, I would've called you a liar," Garrett said. "He would never embarrass a player that way. I wouldn't have believed it if I hadn't seen it."

One of the things that Garrett, and every other Met, appreciated most about Hodges was that he would never get on you if you made a physical error. He understood that they happened to everybody. Even Hall of Fame players strike out and flub plays in the field. Mental mistakes were another matter. Hodges understood that those happen, too, but they shouldn't happen more than once. He always made it a practice to correct them, discreetly.

"He would never tell me right after I made a mental mistake. He would always wait until the next day," Garrett said. "A lot of times he would do it with a question. He wanted it to sink in. He wanted you to think about it." What's the hit-and-run sign? What were you thinking when you threw to that base? How many outs were there when you tried to stretch the double into a triple? Hodges loved the Socratic method. He would routinely pepper his bench players with questions during ball games, making sure they were totally on top of what was going on. Sometimes the questions would be straightforward—about the count or the number of outs—and other times they would be more strategic, about defensive alignment or the nuances of a pitcher's pickoff move. He was always seeking to elevate his players' baseball IQ, posing questions and letting them figure out the answers.

Like any good teacher, Hodges was methodical in his ways, as steady-going as Leo Durocher was combustible. That was what made Hodges's trip out to left field so stunning. It was so completely out of character. But if there was anything Hodges had less tolerance for than mental mistakes, it was for what he perceived as lack of effort, even if the player in question was hitting .346 and had been a starter in the All-Star Game one week earlier. To Hodges, it was a breach of trust—an offense right up there with lying.

"We were all under the same set of rules," Ed Kranepool said.

Hodges's wife, Joan, at home in Marine Park, Brooklyn, saw the Jones play on TV. "When I saw Gil leave the dugout, I said to myself, 'Oh, my God, he's not. But he did,'" she said in an interview many years later. When Hodges arrived home after the game, his wife had no intention of bringing it up, but her husband could tell something was bothering her and urged her to open up.

"Whatever possessed you to do it?" she said. She asked why he didn't talk to Jones privately, to handle it the way he always did when he had an issue with a player.

"You want the gospel truth?" her husband said. "I never realized it until I passed the pitcher's mound and I couldn't turn back."

Only Hodges knew whether his long walk was a calculated wake-up call to his team during a debacle of a doubleheader, or an impulsive reaction provoked by his profound unhappiness at a player not giving full effort. Either way, in the midst of a miserable performance by his floundering team, the stoical Hodges—

unwittingly or not—had sent his players an unmistakable message: when you step onto the field in a New York Mets uniform, you better give it your all. Ed Charles was on the bench when Hodges left the dugout.

"I thought he did what he was supposed to do," Charles said. "It was Hodges's thing, and he made it clear to all of us. If there is something wrong with you and you can't give me one hundred percent, you let me know and I will put somebody else in the lineup. There's nothing wrong with that. But when you hit that field, I want to see one hundred percent. I mean, what else can you say? He didn't see one hundred percent from Cleon on that play. So he was right in what he did."

Upon his return to the dugout, Hodges picked up the phone.

"Gil had a rule," said Matt Winick, who worked in the Mets' public relations department. "If somebody got hurt, the trainer would call up to the press box and tell us what the injury was. We were not to call down. So this time, Gil takes his stroll out to left field and gets Cleon. The phone rings in the press box. I pick it up. The person on the other end is Gil Hodges. 'He has a sore foot,'" Hodges said and hung up.

Winick then made an announcement in the press box: "The report from manager Gil Hodges is that Cleon Jones was removed from the game because he has a sore foot."

Moments later, Dierker hit a home run off of Ryan, and a 10-run inning—coming only about an hour after an 11-run inning—was complete.

The following day, Hodges and Jones had a closed-door meeting in his office. Coach Joe Pignatano, one of Hodges's closest friends, told the *New York Times* that it had taken no eavesdropping to hear Hodges holler, "Look in the mirror and tell me Cleon Jones is giving me one hundred percent!"

Jones was bitter about the incident and thought it to be needlessly humiliating. He was honest about his feelings but had the emotional maturity to let it go and not wreck the greatest year of his career.

"If I didn't respect what [Hodges] is trying to do, I could very easily hate his guts," Jones told Jack Lang of the *Sporting News*. "But I don't."

Hodges didn't hold any grudges over it, either. Jones sat for a couple of games, then got pinch hits in the next two games and was back in the lineup full-time. When he was going for the batting title at the end of the year, Hodges batted him leadoff to help him get some extra at bats.

• • •

ON THE MORNING of August 13, 1969, the three most popular men in America—Neil Armstrong, Buzz Aldrin, and Michael Collins—departed NASA headquarters in Houston and were back in a familiar place: the air. This time their vessel wasn't the Apollo 11 spaceship but a presidential jet. Twenty-four days after *Eagle* landed on Tranquility Base and men walked on the moon, the space travelers were bound for New York's John F. Kennedy International Airport, beginning a heroes' welcome that turned into a ticker-tape parade up lower Broadway, drawing hundreds of thousands of people. The confetti was so thick you could barely see the skyscrapers. Collins said he'd never been moved so much by anything in his life. The well-wishers brought signs by the thousands. Collins had a favorite. The sign read, WE LOVE THE METS. BUT WE LOVE YOU MORE. SORRY, METS.

The Apollo 11 astronauts moved on to Chicago and then Los Angeles before the day was out, the euphoria overpowering their jet lag. The Mets, meanwhile, spent the evening in Houston, experiencing no euphoria at all. In fact, they hit their bottom that night, and it was only fitting that they did it in their field of bad dreams, the Astrodome, where they went 0 for 1969. Of their 11 opponents in the National League, the Mets had a losing record against only one, their expansion partners from 1962. They were shut out on five hits in the opener and blew a 5–1 lead in the second game. In the last game the Astros went out to an 8–1 lead and coasted from there. It didn't just leave the Mets a season-high 10 games behind the Chicago Cubs; it left them in third place, a game behind the Cardinals.

The Cubs had won 10 of their last 12, the Cardinals 6 of 7. The Mets were a scuffling team, going 9-12 since the All-Star break. They had only 49 games remaining. It had been a fun four months, but the SS *Hodges* was taking on all kinds of water and sure looked ready to go under.

"The pennant race ended last night," the New York *Post* said.

In the New York *Daily News*, the famed cartoonist Bill Gallo had his iconic character Basement Bertha, a hefty washerwoman and Mets diehard, looking crestfallen. Bertha said, "Hey, Gillie—Don't tell me that kid on Apollo '69 is comin' back to earth!"

4

GOOD-BYE, LEO

STEVE ZELKOWITZ SPENT THE SUMMER OF 1969 MAKING $2.10 PER hour in the shipping room of a nuts and bolts wholesaler near Manhattan's Union Square. He was 21, a student at NYU, and had been a Mets fan since the beginning.

"A friend and I went to the Polo Grounds in 1962," Zelkowitz said. "They were playing the Phillies and losing 11–1, and they got it to 11–9. Don Zimmer was in the midst of his legendary 0-for-34 slump. How could you not love this?

"It was crazy. They had Casey Stengel. There were no expectations. The whole thing was fun. You are thirteen years old. Puberty is starting. You have the insecurity of the teenage years. The Yankees won every year. What's the fun in that?"

Zelkowitz's family moved from Washington Heights in northern Manhattan to Rego Park, Queens, in 1963, and the Mets followed him to the borough a year later. He became a Shea Stadium regular. Zelkowitz was at Jim Bunning's perfect game on Father's Day in 1964. He was at Opening Day in 1968, when rookie left-hander Jerry Koosman loaded the bases with nobody out against the Giants in the top of the first, then struck out Willie Mays, got Jim Ray Hart on a foul pop, and struck out Jack Hiatt.

I think we may have something here, Zelkowitz told himself.

Zelkowitz never imagined that that *something* would materialize so quickly in 1969. He went to as many games as the nuts and bolts would allow and was as disappointed as anyone when the Mets fell into third place after being swept by the Astros. Figuring it was a good time to get away before school started back up, he and a few friends headed upstate to an alfalfa field in the tiny farming community of Bethel, New York, in the Catskill Mountains, the site of a musical event known as the Woodstock Music & Art Fair. Zelkowitz bought a ticket for $18 for all three days. He loved Jane Jarvis but was looking forward to hearing other musicians.

As his reeling Mets prepared to play the San Diego Padres, Zelkowitz and four hundred thousand of his close friends camped out in a natural amphitheater, near a pond on the property of a local dairy farmer, Max Yasgur. Creedence Clearwater Revival was the first big-name band to sign on to perform. Soon almost every artist and/or rock band in the country—including Jimi Hendrix, the Grateful Dead, the Who, Arlo Guthrie, Jefferson Airplane, Crosby, Stills & Nash, Joan Baez, Janis Joplin, and a few dozen others—were booked, mostly through the connections of Artie Kornfeld, a 26-year-old songwriter, musician, and VP at Capitol Records. The son of a New York City policeman and union organizer, Kornfeld cowrote such songs as "Dead Man's Curve" for Jan and Dean and "The Rain, the Park and Other Things" for the Cowsills and traveled with his band, Changin' Times, as the warm-up to Sonny and Cher for their "I Got You Babe" tour in 1965. Kornfeld was born in Brooklyn, but spent most of his youth in Levittown, Long Island. He was a high school pitching star who threw a fastball and a knuckleball. In his senior year, then pitching for Hauppauge High School farther east on Long Island, he took the mound against Bridgehampton High School and its touted star, Carl Yastrzemski.

"Yaz hit a home run that went about twice the distance of the outfield fence," Kornfeld said.

He went on to pitch for Adelphi University, throwing seven perfect innings in an upset over West Point, but his deepest passions were music, peace, and social justice.

"To me, Woodstock was about uniting a generation and giving people hope," he said.

Days before Richie Havens opened the show on Friday afternoon, it was clear the size of the turnout had been massively underestimated. By Wednesday, roads all over western Sullivan County were choked with cars, and by Thursday, the nearest major road, Route 17, was backed up for miles. The group Iron Butterfly landed at LaGuardia Airport and never got any closer because the promoters refused to send a helicopter to get them.

It took Steve Zelkowitz and his friends 10 hours to make a two-hour trip. They got within a mile of the site, parked their car, and walked. Other motorists, by the thousands, did the same thing. Tents were pitched on every available patch of land. The crowds were so huge and arrived so early that the entrance gates and fencing were not completed. The promoters of Woodstock Venture—Kornfeld, Michael Lang, Joel Rosenman, and John Roberts—gave up all hope of revenue from walk-up sales. The virtual tidal wave of humanity had effectively made Woodstock a free event.

"Nobody ever took my ticket," Zelkowitz said.

The size of the turnout overwhelmed everyone and everything. The shelves of local grocery stores were bare almost before the weekend started. The lines to use the porta potties stretched for an hour. Zelkowitz and his friends had plenty of food, and in the spirit of the event, shared it with people who didn't. Water was scarce. Marijuana was not. It started to rain Friday and continued into Saturday, and the field turned into a muddy, music-filled mosh pit, a sloping pasture overrun with hundreds of thousands of music-loving, peace-loving, tie-dye-wearing young people, a weekend during which sleep and clothing were entirely optional.

"It was the most people I've ever seen in my life," Zelkowitz said. "We were all wet and smelly. It was nuts. Nobody slept on Saturday night. The Jefferson Airplane, the Dead, and Creedence played. The Who played 'Tommy' as the sun came up. I remember some people jimmied into an ice cream truck and started throwing out Dixie cups. They were flying all over the place. I caught a whole carton. As I walked away, some guy tapped me on the shoulder and said, 'Hey man, can I have a Dixie cup?'

"I said, 'Sure.' All of a sudden I heard a roar, 'Ice cream!' I was throwing people Dixie cups like they toss T-shirts at the ballpark."

Woodstock wound up spilling into a fourth day, with Hendrix the thirty-second and closing act. By then the Zelkowitz party was long gone, somehow finding their car on a Sullivan County roadside and making the 110-mile trip back to Queens on Sunday. Zelkowitz's return to the real world featured a long, hot shower and a resurgent baseball team.

• • •

AFTER THE METS hightailed it home from Houston, Seaver stopped the bleeding against the Padres, combining with Ron Taylor on a two-hit shutout and launching a four-game sweep over the Woodstock weekend. The Mets' pitching, which wobbled badly against the Astros, yielded only five runs in the four games.

Then the Giants came to town, starting their ace, Juan Marichal, in the first game. Marichal pitched scoreless baseball into the fourteenth inning. Gary Gentry and Tug McGraw matched him 0 for 0, Gentry for the first 10, McGraw for the last 4. The Giants thought they had the lead in top of the thirteenth, when Willie McCovey, their slugging first baseman, belted a ball to the top of the wall at the 371 mark in left-center. But Hodges had opted to go with a strategy he employed against the league's best power hitters: a four-man outfield. He moved Bobby Pfeil, the third baseman, into the left-field corner and Cleon Jones into left-center. Jones made a leaping catch of McCovey's drive, holding on as he tumbled to the warning track.

With one out in the bottom of the fourteenth, Tommie Agee came up. He had struck out three times and had yet to hit a ball out of the infield. Marichal threw a ball on his 150th pitch of the night. His next pitch was over the plate, and Agee lined it over the left-field fence. The winning streak stood at five, and one night later, the oft-overlooked Jim McAndrew pitched a two-hit shutout as the Mets got a home run and four RBI from Art Shamsky in a 6–0 victory.

The Giants took the final game of the series, but then the Mets ran off six more victories to make it 12 of 13. McAndrew threw another shutout, this one a five-hitter over the Padres. That made it three victories in a 10-game span for McAndrew, doubling his season total. In a stretch of nine late-season starts, McAndrew pitched to a 1.60 earned run average. His timing was impeccable.

A 25-year-old from Lost Nation, Iowa, a speck of a farming town on the eastern edge of the state, McAndrew was a thoughtful young man who had majored in psychology in college and was perhaps prone to being *too* thoughtful and demanding about his own performances. He didn't have the arsenal, or the raw power, that Seaver, Koosman, and Gentry had, and at times it was easy to feel insecure about that. Hodges urged him to trust his ability and reminded him that Whitey Ford was the toughest pitcher he had ever faced, and Ford didn't throw as hard as McAndrew did.

Much of the '69 season had been a study in exasperation for McAndrew, who got a flu shot in spring training and promptly came down with the flu. He started the second game of the year, against the Montreal Expos, but suffered a deep bruise on the middle finger of his pitching hand when outfielder (and future Met) Don Hahn slammed a single up the middle in the second inning. McAndrew tried to pitch through it but had to leave the game and then spent so much time soaking the finger in the whirlpool that it got tender and he developed a nasty blister. In and out of the rotation, he finally got rid of the blister, but then his shoulder started acting up. He insisted it was fine and again he tried to pitch through it, but his string of performances, ranging from poor to disastrous, blew his cover, prompting a stern talking-to from Hodges.

"It was shoulder to shoulder," McAndrew told reporters in the Mets' clubhouse. "You might call it father to son. He asked me what I was doing right and what I was doing wrong. He asked me why I was not contributing to the club. I wanted to pitch, but by me pitching, I hurt the club. Maybe it was selfish on my part, but I wanted to be out there."

McAndrew took a couple of weeks off, and his shoulder responded. He won four games in August, pitching as well as anyone on the staff. In 11 second-half starts, his ERA—2.12—was three and a half runs better than it had been in the first half. Backup catcher Duffy Dyer, who was behind the plate for every one of McAndrew's dominant starts, saw a striking difference in both McAndrew's location and his self-belief.

"Jim wasn't as sure of himself as the other guys," Dyer said. "Seaver knew how good he was. He was one of the smartest pitchers I ever caught, if not the smartest. If you put down a sign and he shook you off, you went to something else. With other guys you might stick with it, but not with Tom. When he shook you off, you usually went with what he wanted to throw.

"Jim McAndrew was a very smart pitcher, like Seaver. We worked well together. You just needed to talk to him a little more—give him [some nurturing and reassurance], tell him, 'We need to get the ball down a little bit, and hit our spots.' One of the things Gil always stressed was that you should call a game according to a pitcher's strength on that particular day. You don't pitch to a hitter's weaknesses. You always go with your pitcher's strength. He emphasized that a lot. Our coaching staff—Rube Walker, Joe Pignatano, Yogi Berra—were all former catchers, but Gil taught me more about calling a game than anyone. He taught me how important it was to know your pitchers, know their personalities—who you had to get on, who you had to give a pat on the back to, and how to help smooth things over."

Koosman followed a McAndrew shutout with a two-hitter against the Padres to get the Mets within two and a half games. The Cubs, meanwhile, were in free fall, losing seven of nine in an eight-day span, including four straight at Wrigley Field. The confines suddenly were not feeling all that friendly. For weeks, a Chicago newspaper had been running a cartoon showing Durocher with a crown on his head, along with the Cubs' magic number to clinch the division. The number had stopped going down.

Steve Zelkowitz returned to NYU uplifted by an almost unfathomable thought: his baseball team was in a pennant race after all.

The Cubs' lead was still two and a half games when they came to Shea for the last time in 1969, a two-game series on September 8 and 9. They had been in first place from day one of the season, and though they tried to downplay the pressure they felt, they were as tight as a vacuum seal. Durocher had played his regulars game after game in the stifling heat of the Chicago summer. Randy Hundley, the Cubs' All-Star catcher, played in 151 games that season, more than any other big-league catcher. Thirty-eight-year-old Ernie Banks played 155 games. Phil Regan, the star reliever, pitched in 71 games. Game after game, Durocher passed over other solid bull pen options, such as Hank Aguirre and Ted Abernathy. It became a running joke in the Cubs' pen: the phone would ring, and the guys would say, "Get up, Regan."

In an interview years later with the *Chicago Tribune*, Cubs reliever Rich Nye said, "Sometimes Don Nottebart and I would start warming up on our own, just to get mentioned in the press box."

"We were all tired," Regan said. "At the end we couldn't catch a ground ball. We couldn't catch a fly ball. We couldn't do anything. The pressure . . . we had never been there. We didn't make the plays, and that was pretty much it.

"Leo kept charging all the time. That was Leo. We had a game that we won, and after he called a meeting and said to Santo, 'That's going to cost you two hundred dollars. You loped down to first.' He never backed off."

Bill Hands, a 16-game winner, started the first game of the series for the Cubs, Jerry Koosman for the Mets. On the first pitch of the game, Hands knocked Agee down. On the third pitch of the game, Hands knocked Agee down again. Hands, a first-rate pitcher and even better competitor, had engaged in a knockdown battle with

Seaver early in the year and was eager to send a fresh message to the Mets. The Cubs were ready to play some serious hardball to protect their tenuous lead.

Koosman took note.

Santo, the Cubs' captain and All-Star third baseman, led off the top of the second. Koosman's first pitch was a fastball, and it rocketed toward Santo's midsection. Santo instinctively covered up. The ball drilled him in the forearm. Santo clutched it in pain and headed shakily to first. Koosman's control suddenly returned and he struck out the side. Battle lines had been drawn.

Agee got the sweetest possible payback in his second at bat against Hands, socking a two-run homer in the bottom of the third. The Cubs evened the score in the sixth before Agee struck again, hitting a double and coming home on Wayne Garrett's single, getting a controversial safe call as Hundley applied his one-hand slap tag after taking a strong throw from Jim Hickman. Koosman pitched out of trouble in the eighth, getting Santo to hit into a double play and then striking out Ernie Banks before coming up to hit to lead off the bottom of the eighth.

Hands fired a fastball right above Koosman's blue helmet.

"You don't throw hard enough to hurt anybody!" Koosman hollered at him.

Taking the mound for the top of the ninth, Koosman was done with the trash talk. He had a 3–2 lead to protect. Koosman struck out Hickman to start the inning. After Hundley singled, Durocher sent up a pinch hitter, Ken Rudolph. Koosman whiffed him, too.

One out remained. Hands was due up. Durocher again called for a pinch hitter, this time Randy Bobb, a reserve catcher. It was Bobb's first at bat of the year. Koosman came at him hard and set him down on strikes—his third K of the inning and thirteenth of the night. It was as if Koosman had unilaterally decided the Mets were not going to lose the game.

The Mets were a game and a half out of first place and had Seaver going for them Tuesday night. It was the most important game of the Cubs' season. If they didn't arrest the Mets' momentum and their own travails here, who knew where they would end up? Seaver's mound opponent was supposed to be Ken Holtzman, but Durocher switched to Fergie Jenkins at the last minute, starting him on two days' rest. Jenkins was the unquestioned ace, but the move reeked of panic. Durocher said that if Holtzman started, his next turn would fall on Rosh Hashanah, a holy day that Holtzman had requested off. So Jenkins it was.

Jenkins walked Agee to lead off the game and walked Jones one batter later. Boswell smoked a two-out, two-run double to right-center, giving Seaver an early two-run cushion. In the fourth, the normally sure-handed Glenn Beckert dropped the ball in a rundown (one of the 17 errors the Cubs had in a nine-game stretch) and Clendenon crushed a two-run homer to make it 4–0.

With one out in the top of the fourth, Beckert doubled, bringing up Billy Williams. Santo moved into the on-deck circle. He had just started to loosen up when a black cat came out of somewhere—a lot of cats lived in Shea Stadium—and crossed right in front of Santo and scurried toward the dugout, directly in line with Durocher. The crowd howled in delight.

"I saw that cat come out of the stands, and I knew right away we were in trouble. I just wanted to run and hide," Santo told a reporter. The cat went back under the stands, and Santo knocked an RBI single, but that was it for the Cubs' offense. The Mets tacked on three more runs, including an Art Shamsky home run, and the crowd grew more gleeful by the inning, serenading Durocher with chants of "Good-bye, Leo," sung to the tune of "Good Night, Ladies." Seaver finished with a five-hitter and a 7–1 triumph.

The two-game sweep left the New York Mets a half game out with a record of 82-57. Mrs. Payson was so delirious that she made an impromptu decision to visit the clubhouse. The Mets scrambled to put their clothes back on.

"This is just so wonderful," she told Hodges. "When I got the Mets, I never dreamed we'd be so good so soon. Can I kiss you?" Accompanying Payson was her friend Jerold Hoffberger, the beer baron who owned the Baltimore Orioles. Hoffberger said that if he tried to kiss his manager, Earl Weaver, he would get punched in the nose.

Hodges removed his cap, and his owner stepped forward and kissed him on the cheek.

"It's too soon to think we'll be champions," Payson said. "But we're challenging for the championship, and that's really great after all our years as the poor little clowns."

One night later, the Cubs lost to the Phillies in Philadelphia, and the Mets were locked in a 2–2 tie in extra innings in the first game of a doubleheader against the Expos. McAndrew pitched 11 stellar innings, and Taylor set the Expos down in the twelfth. With two outs and nobody on in the Mets' half of the inning, Jones singled to center. The crowd came to life and made even more noise when Rod Gaspar walked, pushing Jones into scoring position. Ken Boswell hit a single up the middle and Jones turned third and raced home. The Mets had a 3–2 victory, and the Shea crowd went berserk.

For the first time in 156 days the Cubs were not in first place.

For the first time in their history, the New York Mets *were* in first place.

At day's end, the Mets were 84-57, the Cubs 84-59. Hodges stayed as steady as ever at the wheel. The Mets had 19 games yet to play. A one-game lead was nothing. There was no room for letup or reason for self-congratulation. The Mets just needed to keep it going. They traveled to Forbes Field in Pittsburgh for a Friday-night double-header. Koosman pitched brilliantly in the opener and knocked in the winning run in a three-hit, 1–0 shutout. In the second game, Cardwell pitched shutout ball for eight innings and got relief help in the ninth from McGraw. Cardwell also drove in the only run in another 1–0 victory. It is the only time that two pitchers drove in the winning run in 1–0 doubleheader victories in the almost 100 years that RBI have been a recorded statistic, according to the Elias Sports Bureau.

"When we heard that the Mets won two 1–0 games in Pittsburgh and the runs were driven in by the pitchers, we were thinking 'What the hell is going on?'" said the Cubs' Phil Regan.

Back in Chicago, the newspaper stopped running the Durocher cartoon with the magic number.

The Mets moved on to St. Louis, and more improbability accompanied them. Left-hander Steve Carlton struck out a record 19 hitters but lost a 4–3 decision because Ron Swoboda paired two strikeouts with two, two-run homers. By then the Mets' lead was four and a half games, and the Cubs were on their way to an 8-18 record over the final month. Now the magic number belonged to the Mets, and it stood at one on September 24, the 1,128th game in Mets history. The Cardinals, in the final days of their reign as world champions, were in town. Summer had turned to fall. It was the last home game of the season. A total of 54,928 fans were stuffed into a ballpark built on an ash heap.

The first-place Mets had a record of 95-61. The second-place Cubs were 90-67, having won that afternoon to keep a pulse, however faint. It was a year to the day that Gil Hodges had had his heart attack in Atlanta. The Cardinals went with Carlton against Gary Gentry, an Arizonan who favored western wear and had a large poster of Raquel Welch in a small bikini in his locker. The Mets had been winning since the poster went up, so why mess with karma?

Carlton struck out Cleon Jones in the bottom of the first, the only out he recorded. The next hitter, Donn Clendenon, hit a three-run shot over the center-field fence, and Ed Charles followed with a two-run homer to right-center. Clendenon would add another home run to make it 6–0. Gentry threw a four-hit shutout, getting the final two outs when Joe Torre, the Brooklyn-born slugger the Mets had spent much of the off-season trying to acquire from the Braves, hit into a 6-4-3 double play. Clendenon closed his glove around Al Weis's throw, and at 9:07 p.m. the New York Mets were not a punch line anymore.

They were National League East champions.

Instantly the merriment began, fans pouring onto the field, and the Mets, racing to the safety of their clubhouse beneath the first-base stands, pouring champagne all over one another. The field was as crowded and chaotic as Times Square at rush hour, but a lot happier. A string of fans perched on top of the outfield fence like crows on a clothesline. One believer, seeking greater heights, climbed the scoreboard in right-center, only to fall off and break his leg. Fans dug up the pitching rubber, home plate, and chunks of sod. The Shea infield looked as though it had been the scene of a riot, and for good reason: it had.

In the clubhouse, the Mets spent nearly an hour spraying champagne, shaving cream, and any other product they could find. For nearly an hour the mayhem was carried on the Mets' television network, with Seaver, 25-game winner and chief champagne sprayer, dousing Hodges and announcer Ralph Kiner as they did an interview. M. Donald Grant, the team chairman, also got drenched.

"Our team finally caught up to our fans. Our fans were winners long ago," Grant said. The Mets got drunker and happier as the minutes passed. The dousing went on and on. There wasn't a dry Met or visitor in the room.

"We're just a bunch of young kids who love to play the game," Seaver said.

"When I first started [with the Mets], I didn't think we'd ever make it," Cleon Jones said.

• • •

AS HE WATCHED the division-clinching game on TV in his parents' apartment in Rego Park, four miles south of Shea Stadium, Steve Zelkowitz found himself in a state of suspended disbelief. Was this really happening? Was this the same team that just 42 days earlier had fallen into third place, 10 games back, right before he had taken off for Woodstock? The same team that had looked hopelessly out of it?

Zelkowitz took it all in: Clendenon's two homers and Charles's homer in between, and the masterful pitching performance by the rookie Gary Gentry. He could feel the fans' crescendo of emotion building as the game moved into the late innings, and Gentry kept on mowing down Cardinals, getting Vada Pinson, Tim McCarver, and Torre in order in the seventh, then striking out pinch hitter Ted Simmons to end the eighth.

When the Mets turned the game-ending double play on Torre and the fans stormed the field, Zelkowitz had almost no words to describe his joy. He was watching the game with his father, a Holocaust survivor from Poland.

"In Poland when your team wins, people go out with their friends to celebrate. Are you going to go out?" his father asked him.

"I'm not sure," Steve said. He decided to stay home. He wanted to savor every moment of it without distractions, no matter what happened from here on in the playoffs.

"I just shook my head at the wonderment of it all," he said.

• • •

THIRTY-SIX-YEAR-OLD ED CHARLES was the oldest Met and the one who had had the hardest journey to get to this point, not receiving a call-up to the big leagues until he was almost 29, about six years later than it should've happened. His home run off of Carlton would be the eighty-sixth and last of his career. No 360-foot tour of the bases was ever sweeter for Charles, who clapped his hands emphatically as he went.

"It's a beautiful feeling," Charles told Ralph Kiner.

The clinching game was the first of four straight shutouts by the Mets in the final week of September. They finished the year with nine consecutive victories before a meaningless loss to the Cubs in their season finale, going 38-11 from the day they hit their bottom in Houston. Their record stood at 100-62. Only the Baltimore Orioles, with 109 victories, won more games in 1969. The Mets and Orioles were joined by the Atlanta Braves and Minnesota Twins in baseball's first two-tiered postseason, Mets versus Braves for the National League pennant, Orioles versus Twins for the American League pennant, the winners advancing to the World Series. Winning it all would require seven more victories. Gil Hodges had his pitching rotation set to go. It began with Tom Seaver, number 41, who was heading into his first October along with 24 teammates, every one of them a key contributor in his own way, each man holding hard to the belief that the New York Mets—rated a 100-to-1 shot six months earlier—had as good a chance as anyone to become World Series champions.

Part II

Brave New World

5

OCTOBER SURPRISE

LOU NISS WAS A BALD, BESPECTACLED MAN WHOSE JOB WAS TO GET the New York Mets—players, coaches, staff, and equipment—wherever they needed to go. His title was traveling secretary, baseball's benign and utterly misleading occupational label for detail-driven work typically long on logistics and short on appreciation—the sort of labor, not unlike umpiring, that nobody notices until something goes wrong. Niss, one of the first hires the Mets made after they opened for business, handled it all with aplomb and humor. Born in the city of Minsk 14 years before the Russian Revolution, he emigrated to the United States as a young boy with his family, settled in Queens, and found work as a teenage sports reporter in Brooklyn. He wound up as sports editor of the Brooklyn *Eagle* and a friend of Branch Rickey, Casey Stengel, and Gil Hodges. After the paper folded, Niss worked as the publicity man for Rickey's Continental League—a new baseball enterprise that aimed to fill the void left behind by the Dodgers and Giants—and subsequently joined Joan Whitney Payson's Mets.

After the Mets clinched and were about to embark on their final road trip of the regular season, Niss gave the new National League East champions their itinerary, telling them where they needed to be and when, right down to October 2, the day of their final regular-season game in Chicago. The Mets' opponent in the first NLCS still hadn't been determined when Niss circulated the information, a fact he allowed for in his final entry for the day:

> *6:30 p.m. United Airlines Charter 5000 leaves O'Hare*
> *Destination Paradise—Site unknown.*

Just to be sure that the youthful Mets—the youngest team in the big leagues—didn't get carried away with their newfound status as divisional champions, Niss added an admonition at the bottom of the itinerary, as reported by Joseph Durso in the *New York Times*:

"Only those who have paid their incidentals in the hotel will be permitted aboard."

• • •

PARADISE, IT TURNED OUT, was Atlanta, Georgia, land of the Braves, a club that had to survive a much more harrowing pennant race than the Mets' to make it to the postseason. One of five teams in the NL West within two games of first place with three weeks left in the season, the Braves won 10 games in a row and 17 of their last 21, finally outdistancing the San Francisco Giants in the final weekend. With a formidable lineup that included Henry Aaron, Rico Carty, and Orlando Cepeda, they were a fitting opponent for the Mets, since the clubs' general managers, Johnny Murphy and Paul Richards, had spent much of the previous winter and spring wrangling over the never-to-happen Joe Torre trade. Even in the face of Aaron's 44 homers and Carty's .342 batting average, Murphy wasn't backing off his faith in the young pitchers he'd refused Richards.

"Good pitching stops good hitting, [and] we've got good pitching," Murphy said. "They could lower the mound all the way to the ground, and pitching still stops hitting."

Born in Boston, the Braves relocated to Milwaukee in 1953 and then again, to Atlanta, in 1966. They weren't much more popular a pick than the Mets to be in the postseason, rated a 50-to-1 shot in the Vegas books after finishing at .500 (81-81) in 1968, but they started hot and finished hot, getting surprisingly effective starting pitching to complement their long line of hitters. The Mets had dominated the Braves during the season, winning 8 of their 12 meetings—a result, of course, that would have no more bearing on the forthcoming series than General Sherman's March to the Sea 105 years earlier.

The Mets encountered an unforeseen complication before they got anywhere near Atlanta Stadium for the 4 p.m. start. Leaving the team hotel, the bus driver, perhaps new on the job, took the club on a circuitous route, meandering through downtown Atlanta. The trip took twice as long as it should have. In the front seat, alongside Hodges, was a special passenger, Casey Stengel, who had come all the way from Glendale, California, for the occasion.

"I think it's Casey's fault," Seaver said of the long ride to the park.

"That's right," Stengel said. "I left my ticket at home and asked the driver if he could swing by so I could get it."

• • •

GAME ONE BROUGHT abundant sunshine, 86 degrees, and the traditional postseason pageantry to Atlanta, a burgeoning metropolis that for decades had been known mostly for being the home of the world's most famous soft drink, Coca-Cola, but was now emerging as an economic powerhouse in the New South. Inhabited for most of its history by Native Americans—predominantly the Creeks and Cherokees—Atlanta wasn't even a street corner until 1837, when railroad engineers made it the terminus of a new rail line that would connect Georgia with Chattanooga, Tennessee. Other rail lines followed. A rail hub grew, and even the city's near-total razing near the end of the Civil War didn't stop Atlanta from rising again.

By the 1960s, the city had three new sports franchises—the Braves, Hawks, and Falcons—to further burnish its civic pride, and now the first NLCS was coming to town, with the hometown team made a slight favorite. Bill Bartholomay, the Braves' owner, wanted to commemorate Atlanta's postseason debut in style, so he invited his friend Robert Merrill, the Metropolitan Opera star, down to sing the national anthem. With the Met on strike, Merrill had a free

Saturday, so he accepted the offer. Merrill was no stranger to ball fields: he had played semipro ball before taking his talents to the opera world. Merrill had kicked off the season singing the anthem on Opening Day in Yankee Stadium and now was closing it with the Mets in Atlanta.

Atlanta mayor Ivan Allen, Jr., threw out the ceremonial first pitch, an apt choice for the first postseason game played by Major League Baseball's first southern ball club. A grandson of a Confederate cavalryman, Allen had evolved from avowed segregationist into an ardent advocate of integration who championed the cause of racial healing in his city, never more than in the aftermath of the assassination of Atlanta's most famous son, Martin Luther King, Jr., the year before. Allen's healing message was particularly important given that Lester Maddox, Georgia's governor, didn't even want flags to be flown at half-staff. The Braves were in Savannah, playing their top farm club, on the April Thursday when King was gunned down on a Memphis motel balcony. The club canceled one of the three exhibition games they had scheduled for the weekend against the Baltimore Orioles in Atlanta Stadium, but kept the other two.

"The only reason we didn't cancel all of the games is that we didn't want people to think we were panicking," said Dick Cecil, a longtime Braves executive who was one of the visionaries who made the club a model of progressiveness from the moment the franchise arrived in town, even as the civil rights movement wheeled into high gear. The Braves had perhaps the most integrated front office in American sports. They unabashedly made Henry Aaron, an African-American from Mobile, Alabama, the face of their franchise. The club had close ties with Andrew Young and the leadership of the Southern Christian Leadership Conference, and a number of Braves players and officials were among the estimated 200,000 people who turned out to honor Dr. King as his coffin passed through the streets of Atlanta on a wooden cart powered by two mules. Once the 1968 season got under way, Martin Luther King, Sr.—or "Daddy King," as he was universally known—showed up for almost every Braves home game, as he had since the team arrived in Atlanta.

"We had a standing order," Cecil said. "If Daddy King came to the ballpark, we let him in. He'd come to the [office], and we'd give him a ticket, and he'd sit in the same seat, in the same section, at the club level."

Back in New York on the day of game one, the Mets were literally front-page news, the biggest story in town by tape-measure distance. The *Daily News* had a page-one photo of a smiling Gil Hodges and Tom Seaver, along with a prediction by correspondent Casey Stengel: "The Mets will play all the way to the end of the World Series because they have more pitchers and they throw lightning. And you can look it up, that's best for a short series." Hodges's humility and restraint would never allow for something as unseemly as a boast, but he was certain his team would not be overwhelmed by the occasion or by the fact that most people favored the Braves.

"These boys have been underdogs all year. They've been underdogs since 1962," he said.

By the evidence of the Mets' workout the day before, nerves were not a significant concern. Noticing that an NBC-TV technician had exited his golf cart, Rod Gaspar hopped in and sped off into the outfield, shouting to Yogi Berra to hit him a fungo. Berra complied, and Gaspar made a nice motorized catch.

Game one started at 4 p.m. to allow viewers to watch the ALCS between the Orioles and Minnesota Twins first. The bunting was hung, the players were announced, and Robert Merrill sang. Mayor Allen made his toss and then left the mound to the professionals, a matchup of the top two winning pitchers in the National League, Seaver, with a record of 25-7, against Phil Niekro, with a record of 23-13. Seaver had already beaten the Braves three times without a defeat in the regular year; Niekro had done exactly the opposite against the Mets, going 0-3.

Seaver fully appreciated the irony of the matchup, going up against the team of his youth, the club that signed him to his first big-league contract, albeit illicitly, about three and a half years before. Had the Braves gotten his contract done before USC played those two games at the start of the 1966 college season, Seaver might well have been getting the game one ball not from Hodges but from Luman Harris. That Seaver had thoroughly dominated the Braves in his three years in the league, with a 10-2 record and a 1.92 ERA, ensured that the wound remained fresh.

It would be hard to find pitchers of more contrasting approaches, Seaver bringing power and precision with his muscular, drop-and-drive delivery, Niekro relying almost wholly on the whimsical, spinless flights of one of baseball's best knuckleballs. Niekro's windup started deliberately, and then he'd come forward as if somebody told him to hurry up, springing toward the plate, releasing the ball with fingers extended, waiting for the seams and the air currents to do their thing and send the ball on its untrackable flight. The Mets were as well prepared to face Niekro as a team could be; they had seen him four times during the season, and Hodges had counseled his hitters to be patient, hoping Niekro would fall behind and have to throw a fastball. When they did have to swing at a knuckler, they knew they would need to shorten their stroke and not try to crush the ball. The Mets also had a secret advantage: a noted knuckleball authority, catcher J. C. Martin, was among their ranks, wearing number 9. During his years with the White Sox, Martin had caught Hoyt Wilhelm, Wilbur Wood, and Eddie Fisher. He knew as much about the quirks of the game's most confounding pitch as anyone.

Niekro cruised through an easy first inning. Seaver had an easy first inning of his own, and then his teammates went to work. Art Shamsky, the Mets' only .300 hitter besides Cleon Jones, had had a highly productive season, belting 14 home runs and driving in 47 runs in only 100 games, and he kept it up by starting the second with a long single to right. After Ken Boswell took four straight balls, Jerry Grote punched a single to right to score Shamsky and send Boswell to third.

Niekro struck out Bud Harrelson, but Harrelson wasn't the only one who missed the pitch; Bob Didier, the Braves' 20-year-old catcher, did, too, the ball rolling almost to the temporary box where Mrs. Payson, M. Donald Grant, and other Mets dignitaries were sitting, allowing Boswell to score to give the Mets a 2–0 lead. Like most every catcher tasked with trying to corral knuckleballs, Didier used an oversized glove to better his odds, but it didn't help.

Seaver had his own challenges, though, dealing with enough nervous energy in his first October start to launch a rocket, and struggling to modulate it all day. Nerves were with him before every outing, but typically they would subside after a pitch or two, and then he would settle into his rhythm. In game one, that rhythm proved elusive. Rico Carty, a Dominican strongman who had had a remarkable comeback season following a year's absence due to tuberculosis, ripped a long double to lead off the Braves' second. Boswell, not the most sure-handed of Mets defenders, muffed a grounder, which advanced Carty to third. Then Braves third baseman Clete Boyer, a former Yankee, hit a sacrifice fly to cut the Mets' lead in half.

An inning later, Felix Millan, Tony Gonzalez, and Henry Aaron, Seaver's boyhood hero, pounded consecutive doubles off Seaver, all of them to right.

Rushing his delivery, trying to throw too hard, Seaver was laboring to hit his spots. Grote saw the problem: Seaver's overamped delivery was causing his hips to open and his arm to drop a bit. That was all it took to throw off his command. Grote went to the mound to try to get him to slow down, but Seaver couldn't get himself locked in. A man who had been as mechanically flawless as a metronome for six months was suddenly out of kilter.

One of the things that separate great pitchers from everybody else is the ability to find a way out of the woods even when they are off the path. With two outs and the bases loaded, Seaver muscled up by striking out Didier, escaping with only two runs across. It was a solid piece of damage control from a man who specialized in it. Seaver had faced 14 hitters in bases-loaded situations in 1969 and had not yielded a single hit. The Mets rewarded him forthwith in the top of the fourth, when Harrelson bounced a chopper just beyond the glove of the leaping Cepeda at first. The ball rolled down the right-field line, and the speedy Harrelson wound up at third with a two-run triple, putting the Mets back up 4–3.

"A real seeing-eye job," Harrelson would call it later.

Seaver's struggles continued, however. Tony Gonzalez, the Braves' center fielder, playing because of an injury to regular Felipe Alou, hooked a ball inside the right-field foul pole to tie the game in the fifth inning. Two innings later, Aaron guessed curveball and got it, driving it almost 400 feet to left, the ball landing near the teepee of Levi Walker, Jr., aka Chief Noc-A-Homa, the Braves' mascot, lifting the Braves into a 5–4 lead.

Niekro, on the other hand, was knuckling away impressively, retiring 9 of the last 10 Met hitters as the game moved to the eighth. The Braves were six outs away from beating the league's number one pitcher and grabbing the series lead.

Wayne Garrett, 21, a red-haired, freckle-faced rookie and the youngest of the Mets, led things off. Garrett was another Met very familiar to the Braves; the Mets had selected him off of the Braves' roster in December 1968, after the Braves did not protect him. At the start of camp Garrett got noticed mostly for being a Huckleberry Finn look-alike, but he had a superb spring training and earned the left-handed half of the third-base platoon spot opposite Ed Charles. Though nobody was ready to compare him to Torre, Garrett had a strong first half before fatigue set in and National League pitchers began feeding him a steady diet of breaking balls. His average after the All-Star break was .163. Still, Hodges believed Garrett would turn it around, and didn't want to send the kid a message that he didn't believe in him, so he gave him the start in game one.

Despite his youth, Garrett, the kid brother in a baseball family, had a good grasp of the situation. He had gone 0-2 with a walk against Niekro and knew that he had one job leading off the eighth inning: to get on base. It didn't matter how. He was determined not to chase Niekro's knuckler. He was going to make him throw strikes. He would shorten his swing and follow the pitch all the way in.

He would do whatever he had to.

Garrett protected the plate well, and when Niekro floated in a knuckler on the outer half of the zone, Garrett liked it and took a swing. He poked a spinning cue shot down the third-base line.

Boyer, the Braves' third baseman, was well off the bag. With a slow-tossing knuckleball pitcher and a left-handed hitter, guarding the line made little sense.

Garrett's ball squirted past Boyer, into left field, for a leadoff double. The next hitter was Jones, a hitter skilled at going the other way. Jones figured to hit the ball to right to advance Garrett to third, where he could score on a sacrifice fly, but Jones got out front of Niekro's knuckler and looped a short ball to left, not well struck but providentially placed. The ball dropped safely for a single. Garrett read the ball well, racing home to tie the game at 5–5.

Shamsky kept it going with a single to right, his third knock of the day. Jones, the go-ahead run, stopped at second. Hodges brought Al Weis in to run for Shamsky, knowing he was going to be using Weis as a defensive replacement for Boswell the following inning, anyway. Boswell came up to bunt and squared around. Eager to get a good jump to beat the throw to third, Jones moved well off second, a good twenty or twenty-five feet. Boswell missed the bunt.

Behind the plate, Didier saw how far off second Jones was. He knew he had him with any kind of decent throw. Jones knew it, too, so he took a half step toward second, hoping to draw a throw instead of having Didier run at him.

Didier sprang from his crouch. He gunned a throw to second, and the instant he did, Jones took off for third.

I can beat this, Jones thought.

Gil Garrido, the shortstop, caught Didier's throw at second and quickly whipped the ball to Boyer. The ball got there fast. Jones got there first.

"If Didier had run at me instead of throwing, I'm [out]," Jones said afterward. "He would've made me commit myself."

Boswell bounced a grounder back to Niekro, who checked Jones before throwing to second for the force on Weis. Jones wasn't going anywhere this time, but he wanted to give Boswell a little more time to beat out a potential double-play ball, so he faked toward home to occupy a moment or two of Niekro's attention. It worked; Niekro got Weis at second, but Boswell beat the relay to first.

With one out and the slow-footed Kranepool coming up to bat, a double play remained a strong possibility on any ground ball. Mets third-base coach Eddie Yost made sure Jones knew to hold the bag on anything in the air and to run on contact as soon as it was clear the ball was on the ground. On the mound, Niekro's mission was to keep the ball out of the air at all costs. Kranepool got set. Niekro came forward and delivered a diving knuckler—just what he wanted. Kranepool swung and tapped it toward first. Orlando Cepeda moved in and gloved it. Jones broke for the plate. Cepeda had enough time to leaf through a magazine before he threw. Knowing how much he would be out by if he kept going, Jones ran only half-speed, hoping to get into a rundown that would allow the other two base runners to advance.

Cepeda had made only three errors in the second half of the season. *Make sure it's a good throw*, he told himself. *Don't rush it.*

Fielders will tell you that sometimes the hardest plays are the ones when you have time to think. All the mind does is gum up the natural process of catching and throwing. On one of his more routine plays of the season, Cepeda, a future Hall of Famer, thought way too much, and threw way too low, the ball skipping past Didier.

Jones scored. The Mets had a 6–5 lead. In the jubilant, freshly installed owners' box, Joan Whitney Payson led the cheers.

After Grote grounded out, the Braves intentionally walked Harrelson so Niekro could face Seaver instead. The bases were loaded. Seaver had thrown 123 pitches and given up five runs, and Hodges saw no reason to push him further. So the manager made another move, based on a strong hunch: Why not pinch-hit with J. C. Martin, the man with an unofficial doctorate in knuckleballs? Who would know better than Martin what to expect from Niekro?

Martin was a tall, handsome man, almost courtly in his bearing, Gary Cooper with a mask and chest protector. In so many ways, he was the quintessential Met, a player whose stat line for the season—.209 average, 4 home runs, and 21 runs batted in in 66 games—belied his importance to the club and his ability to deliver when it mattered most. This would be his first at bat in the postseason after a decade in the major leagues. His recent history was not encouraging: he had hit .071 in the final month of the season and .106 (5 for 47) over the final two months. Hodges was not exactly going with a hot hitter. He *was* going with his baseball instincts.

Martin grabbed a bat and got his head into knuckleball mode. "It really is a tough pitch to learn to hit," he said. "You can put away all the ideas you have in your head about going up there and swinging hard. The ball is not going to be where you think it is. You have to cut down your swing sixty-five or seventy percent. You've got to manipulate that bat and try to put the bat on the ball and not be swinging for the fences."

Before Martin headed to the plate, Tommie Agee, the next hitter, stopped him in the on-deck circle. Agee had already had three at bats against Niekro and came with fresh data.

"J, look for a pitch that looks just like a changeup," advised Agee. "Let the ball come to you. Don't be anxious."

Martin nodded and got into the box with Agee's words in mind.

"It helped settle my mind and prepare for the at bat," Martin said. "It was a wonderful gesture on Tommie's part to tell me what to expect."

Niekro delivered a knuckleball, and Martin spanked his first pitch into right-center. Boswell scored. Kranepool scored. And when the ball skipped by Gonzalez in center, Harrelson scored. The Braves cut down Martin as he tried to get to third, but the damage was done, and so was a five-run eighth inning.

Mets 9, Braves 5.

With three hits, two of them pillow soft, some savvy baserunning by Jones, an error, a walk, and a huge pinch hit by Martin, the Mets had seized control of the game, running around the bases as if they were conducting a fire drill. Atlanta Stadium was suddenly as quiet as a library.

Ron Taylor, a Canadian and the only pitcher in baseball with a degree in electrical engineering, came on in relief. A stalwart all year in the Mets' pen, Taylor cruised through a 1-2-3 eighth before the Braves got two hits and put men on second and third with two outs in the ninth. Cepeda stepped in, with a prime chance to atone for his errant throw. Taylor came at him with hard stuff. Cepeda swung and hit a pop-up to second. Weis called for it and made the catch.

The Mets' postseason record moved to 1-0.

They still had to win two more games, of course, but to come from behind on the road and steal a game when their ace was surprisingly vulnerable made it an especially exhilarating outcome for the Mets and equally deflating for the Braves. Cepeda called it "the worst game we've played in a long time." Harris, the Braves' manager, said, not incorrectly, that the Braves had "hit Seaver a hell of a lot harder than they hit Niekro." The great Henry Aaron and his teammates were unanimous in their belief that if they got five runs off Tom Seaver, they should win the game every time.

Nobody was offering those things up as excuses. There would be another game tomorrow. In the Mets' clubhouse, Seaver wore long white underwear as he spoke to the press. The eight hits and five runs amounted to his worst start since the All-Star break. His postseason record nonetheless was perfect, the same as his team's.

"God is alive and living in New York," Seaver said, "and I know who's paying his rent."

6

HIT MEN

NOT UNLIKE TOM SEAVER, JERRY KOOSMAN HAD HIS OWN ATLANTA connection. After his second year in pro ball, working his way up through the Mets' farm system, Koosman took an off-season job as a UPS deliveryman. Once the Christmas rush ended, he got laid off and found himself looking for work again. A friend and teammate of Koosman, a pitching prospect named Jerry Wild, had a job in the Atlanta area and suggested Koosman come down, too. Koosman liked the sound of Wild's idea, so he hopped in his new Pontiac Catalina, a V-8 with four on the floor, making the 1,200-mile trip from the family farm in Appleton, Minnesota.

Koosman heard that Georgia Power, a huge utility company, was hiring. He interviewed, took a written exam, and got a call to come in the next day.

"You're hired," a company official told him. "Let me show you your office."

Koosman looked at the man, perplexed. "Whoa, whoa, I don't want an office," he said. "I didn't come down here to be in an office. I want a labor job—to be out in the field. What's the toughest job you have?"

"Well, I guess that would be lineman's helper."

"Fine. That's the job I want," Koosman said.

A lineman's helper hauled transformers and huge spools of cable and got everything together for the lineman, who then took it up the pole. Koosman didn't just want income; he wanted to get in shape for spring training, to lift and sweat and put his rugged farm boy body to work.

Koosman got a $90 apartment on Peachtree Street, ate a lot of bologna sandwiches, and worked hard. He spent close to two months helping the Atlanta metro area stay plugged in, and made a little money. It was all good.

When the gig was over, Koosman, Wild, and another young player piled into the Catalina and headed for Florida. They got as far as Athens, Georgia, where a woman slammed into them at a traffic light, spinning them into a utility pole that fortunately did not have a lineman or his helper working on it. The impact totaled Koosman's Catalina. Nobody was hurt, but they still had to get to Homestead, Florida, the site of the Mets' minor-league camp. Together the three ballplayers didn't have much more than loose change in their pockets.

Koosman called Joe McDonald, the Mets' farm director. McDonald, who had started with the Mets as a statistician in 1962, said he would wire him $50 to get them down to camp.

The trio made it to Homestead, but Koosman's spring showing wasn't much better than the condition of his Catalina. He had a strong arm but was inconsistent and largely unimpressive. At the end of the spring, the Mets' player-personnel men met to decide whom to cut and whom to keep. The Mets were on the verge of releasing Koosman.

Then McDonald remembered the loan.

"I gave him $50 of Mrs. Payson's money," said McDonald, who didn't want an accountant chasing him down later in the season. McDonald decided to give Koosman and his gifted left arm another shot. Clyde McCullough, the manager of the Auburn Mets in the Class A New York–Penn League, said he would take the pitcher.

The night before the team broke camp, some older players invited Koosman out to celebrate. "I got hammered," Koosman said. He missed the bus to Auburn the next morning and then scrambled to get on the bus to the Mets' double-A affiliate in Williamsport, Pennsylvania. From there he bussed to Syracuse and got a cab to Auburn, about 20 miles away. McCullough was irate.

"He didn't pitch me for a month," Koosman said. "He made me run thirty-six wind sprints every day. That's why I chose number 36 [when I got to the Mets]." Producing is the fastest way out of a manager's doghouse, and Koosman produced, going 12-7 with a 2.38 earned run average, emerging as perhaps the most dominant pitcher in the league. He was on his way to Flushing.

• • •

KOOSMAN'S OPPONENT in game two was Ron Reed, who held the distinction of being the best rebounder in all of Major League Baseball. That could not even be argued. At 6 feet, 6 inches, lanky and athletic, Reed had spent two years in the mid-'60s with the Detroit Pistons, learning the NBA ropes from his coach, Dave DeBusschere, another man who pitched during baseball season and rebounded during basketball season. An Indiana native, Reed had starred at Notre Dame, setting a school rebounding record—17.7 per game— that still stands. Despite playing only one year of collegiate baseball, Reed signed with the Braves for $500 a month in 1965 and made a rapid climb up the organizational ladder, starting 1966 in single-A ball and finishing the year in Atlanta. Along the way that year, Reed pitched for Austin, the Braves' double-A club in the Texas League, starting the second game of a June doubleheader against El Paso that will forever be remembered for one of the shortest-lived trials in the annals of professional sport. In the opener of the doubleheader, the Austin players wore red shorts instead of heavy flannels, the thinking being that shorts made much more sense in the withering heat of the Texas summer. When the Austin players, predictably, finished the game with an assortment of strawberries on their knees and shins, the shorts were jettisoned. Reed pitched the second game wearing long pants.

Nineteen sixty-nine was a career year for Reed. He finished the regular season 18-10, the Braves' best pitcher in the heat of the fierce

NL West pennant race. Like many tall pitchers, Reed seemed to unfold like a beach chair as he delivered to the plate, a tangle of long limbs and sharp angles. The unfolding in game two against the Mets came after Coretta Scott King, the widow of Martin Luther King, Jr., threw out the ceremonial first pitch. She was warmly received in her home city. Things did not proceed as smoothly for Reed.

Agee led off with a single to right. Garrett walked on four pitches. Harris, the Braves' manager, immediately made a call to the bull pen and had Paul Doyle, a sidearming left-hander, start warming up. There is no more dispiriting sight for a starting pitcher than to see the bull pen stirring when the game is two batters old, but Harris felt he had no choice. Already down a game in a best-of-five series, he considered this all but an elimination game.

Reed fell behind Cleon Jones, 2-0. He came to the set position, and when he looked toward second, he saw Agee stepping out to a bold lead. Reed thought he had a great shot at picking him off. With the way things were going, an easy out via a pickoff would be a godsend.

Agee edged out farther from the base. Reed waited another moment, then whirled and fired. He was certain he had Agee nailed, but as he let the ball go, Agee took off for third, the same way Jones had in game one. Agee beat the relay to third with room to spare.

· · ·

MAYBE THE LEAST surprised man in America to see Tommie Agee do this was his big brother, Joe. Joe Agee had played a lot of baseball with Tommie while growing up in Whistler, Alabama, just outside Mobile, the only boys in a family of eleven children. He had seen Tommie's heroics for Mobile County Training School, the all-black high school Tommie had attended with his friend in left field, Cleon Jones. He had seen Tommie become a sprint sensation for the school and a star receiver on the football team. Joe Agee was an inspector at the Pontiac automobile plant just outside Detroit. He watched the NLCS on a small black-and-white TV in the little home he'd just bought in Pontiac, where he lived with his wife and two small children, and to see his brother back at the top of his game was a joy. The previous season—Agee's first with the Mets—had been an unmitigated disaster, beginning with a spring training beaning by Bob Gibson in his first at bat in a Mets uniform. A former American League rookie of the year with the White Sox, Agee had wound up hitting .217 with 5 home runs and 17 runs batted in. Hodges never lost his belief in Agee, who was one of the Mets' best players from beginning to end in 1969.

Before the Braves series began, Joe Agee asked his brother what he thought of the Mets' chances.

"We're going to win," Tommie said.

"How can you be so sure?" Joe asked.

"Three reasons," Tommie said. "Tom Seaver, Jerry Koosman, and Gary Gentry."

Joe Agee watched his kid brother dancing off third, doing all he could to get the Mets off to another fast start in game two. His heart filled up.

"It was something. Really something," he said.

• • •

CLEON JONES WALKED, pushing Garrett to second, loading the bases with nobody out. The angst in the big crowd was as thick as the Georgia humidity. Reed stood on the rubber, towering, as he looked in for the sign. Art Shamsky, the Mets' cleanup hitter against right-handed pitchers, fresh off his three-hit effort in game one, stood in. Reed reconnected with the strike zone and got Shamsky to swing through a 1-2 pitch for the first out. Next up was Boswell. Reed again got ahead and struck Boswell out, too. He was one out away from escaping a bases-loaded, nobody-out mess.

Now it was Kranepool's turn. He had had two hits off Reed the last time the Mets had seen him, in August, when Reed had fired a five-hit, 10-inning shutout. He was also a .342 hitter that season with two outs and runners in scoring position. Kranepool hit a chopper to Felix Millan, the Braves' Gold Glove second baseman. Playing

deep with two out, Millan didn't have to move far. He crouched and
was ready to make the play when the ball kicked up above his chest
on its last hop, glancing off his glove. Millan bent down to grab it
and fired across his body to Orlando Cepeda. Not a man who would
ever be compared to Lou Brock on the basepaths, Kranepool busted
it out of the box and beat the throw to first. Agee crossed the plate.
The official scorer generously gave Kranepool a hit, and the hit gave
the Mets a 1–0 lead.

For the second game in a row, the Mets had jumped out front
early.

With one out in the second, Koosman, a .048 hitter (4 for 84)
who had drawn one walk all season, took a 3-2 pitch for ball four. It
was Reed's third walk in less than two innings. In his previous 32
starts, he had walked more than three batters only once. This was
the worst possible time for Reed to lose the strike zone. On a 1-1
pitch to Agee, he threw a changeup. Agee hit it 405 feet into the left-
field seats, another shot that touched down near Noc-A-Homa land.
In Pontiac, Michigan, Joe Agee's heart filled up some more.

The Mets led 3–0, and two batters later, Jones pounded a double
to left and never thought about stopping at first, not with Carty the
Brave in charge of stopping him. Rico Carty was one of the premier
hitters in the game, but a series of shoulder dislocations left him
barely able to reach the infield with his throws. The Mets' game plan
was to run on Carty's arm and to be aggressive on the bases against
all the Braves, forcing them to make plays. A year earlier, Hodges
had been in the same city, but in a quite different place, recovering
from his heart attack and under strict instructions to take it easy in
Crawford W. Long Memorial Hospital. Now that he was back where
he belonged, in the Atlanta Stadium visitors' dugout, Hodges had
no thought of his team taking it easy.

Shamsky followed with a single to right. The great Henry Aaron
charged the ball hard. With one of the best arms in the game, Aaron
thought he had a shot to cut down Jones at home, but his throw
sailed into empty space between home and third. Jones scored, and
Reed's day was done. The Mets were running around the bases as if

they were on a carousel. For a supposedly anemic offensive team, it was huge fun.

Doyle replaced Reed and gave up two more runs in the third before giving way to Milt Pappas. It didn't matter whom the Braves sent out there; the Mets kept pounding hits. In the fourth inning, Boswell belted a two-run homer—his first since July—to make it 8–0, and in the Mets' owners box, Mrs. Payson was whooping it up in a gray checked suit and fur beret. She had never envisioned this when she had received a friendly, pregame greeting from one of her employees, Ron Swoboda.

"Did they brief you on how to duck those line drives that might come over here? Or how to catch them?" Swoboda had asked.

Mrs. Payson's previous trip to Atlanta had been almost 30 years earlier, to see the premiere of a film she had invested in, *Gone With the Wind*. Frankly, her baseball investment was suddenly giving returns that were just as generous.

A game and a half into the NLCS, Mrs. Payson's players were schooling the Atlanta Braves. They had scored in every inning of game two, with ample help from Atlanta fielders, who looked so asleep they could've been playing in their pajamas. Backed by 11 hits and the owner of a 9–1 lead, Koosman, the winner of eight of his previous nine decisions, looked to have a stress-free day of pitching ahead of him.

• • •

HENRY AARON HAD waited 11 years to get back to the postseason. He had been the breakout star for the Milwaukee Braves in 1957, hitting .393 with three home runs and seven RBI in a seven-game upset over the Yankees. At age 35, he knew he might not pass this way again. Before game two Aaron sat at his locker, beneath a picture of the pope, and listened to the music of one of his favorite singers, Lou Rawls, a smooth-singing baritone whose big hit then was "Love Is a Hurtin' Thing." Aaron had his own trademark, two of the strongest and quickest wrists in the game. He was undeniably the Braves hitter the Mets feared the most.

Koosman got Gil Garrido on a fly to center to start the bottom of the fifth, Agee flipping down his glasses to track the ball in the slanting late-afternoon sun. Pinch hitter Tommie Aaron, five years younger than his brother Henry, tapped a ball back to the mound for the second out. Felix Millan hit a nubber to Kranepool, wide of the first-base bag. Koosman was late in getting over, and Millan won the footrace for an infield hit. Koosman walked Gonzalez on four pitches, bringing up Henry Aaron with two on.

Koosman missed low with a breaking pitch. Aaron socked his next pitch far over the left-field wall to make it a 9–4 game.

Just an out away from getting through five innings to secure what seemed to be a certain victory, Koosman tried to settle himself, but he issued another four-pitch walk, this time to Carty. Orlando Cepeda pounded a high curveball on one hop to the left-field wall to put runners on second and third. Behind the plate, Jerry Grote got a sign from Hodges to go out and talk to Koosman, to give Ron Taylor and Nolan Ryan more time to warm up. Kranepool came over from first and joined the conversation. Koosman wasn't much in the mood for small talk. He just wanted to get an out. Clete Boyer came up next and stung a single to center to make it 9–6.

Hodges had seen enough. He headed to the mound and signaled for Taylor. Koosman departed in disgust and embarrassment, the unhappiest former lineman's helper in the building.

"I never cared to pitch with a big lead," Koosman said. "I usually didn't have to worry about it, because we never got big leads." With the eight-run cushion, Koosman started throwing more fastballs, just wanting to get ahead and make hitters swing at the first pitch or two. He was nobody's excuse maker. His team had given him a big lead, and he failed to protect it.

"I had good stuff but poor location," he said. "I just couldn't make a pitch when I had to."

Rushed into the game following Koosman's implosion, Ron Taylor retired Didier on a liner to center to get out of the inning. When the Mets came up for the sixth, Taylor marched right back to the bull pen to throw more warm-up tosses. He had never done that before. This was new territory for all of the Mets.

Agee walked to start the seventh against Cecil Upshaw, the Braves' fifth pitcher, getting on base for the fourth time. He stole second and took third on Garrett's long fly to center. Up stepped Jones, who already had two hits. A sidewinder and the Braves' top reliever with 27 saves, Upshaw missed inside to fall behind, 2-1.

Agee eyed Upshaw carefully with every pitch. Upshaw was all but ignoring him. The Mets already had four steals in the game. With each pitch, Agee edged a little farther off third. Two men were out. There was no call from the dugout. This was all on Tommie Agee. Upshaw looked in for the sign, pitching from a full windup. Agee crept out a little more, the gangly Upshaw started his motion, and Agee took off for home.

The Atlanta crowd was watching an attempt at a true rarity; no player had stolen home in a postseason game since 1955, when Jackie Robinson had done it against Whitey Ford in the eighth inning of game one of the World Series. Jones, Agee's best friend on the Mets, had no idea he was coming. Nobody else did, either. In midwindup, Upshaw suddenly realized that Agee, a man with sprinter's speed, was heading full throttle toward the plate. Agee had gotten a great jump. Upshaw sped up his delivery. Behind the plate, Didier sprang out of his crouch. Agee was closing in on home. Spotting Agee from the corner of his eye, Jones sought to protect him and keep Didier from catching the pitch unimpeded and applying the tag.

So he swung.

Jones's intent was to miss.

He did not miss.

He drilled a line drive right toward Agee's head, and the bat followed in the same direction. Both ball and bat landed in foul territory, missing Agee by inches.

"Ooooh-eeeee," Bob Murphy said on the Mets' radio broadcast. "Cleon did not see his pal, Tommie Agee."

In the moments after the most shocking play of the game,

everything seemed to stop. Agee wobbled back to third, practically staggering. Jones stood at the plate and stared at him for a few seconds, then slowly made his way down the third-base line to make sure Agee was okay.

"If he had hit me, it might've been all over," Agee said later.

"What are you trying to do, cheat me out of an RBI?" Jones teased.

"Get a hit this time!" Agee yelled back.

• • •

CLEON JONES AND Tommie Agee were born five days apart in 1942. They had an easy, playful rapport, the kind you have when you are lifelong friends and you've been prep baseball and football stars together. At Mobile County Training School, Agee was a swift, sure-handed receiver and Jones a swift, punishing running back. Jones had 26 touchdowns his senior year, and Agee had a bunch of his own, most of them coming on their favorite play. The team called it 49-option. Jones would get a handoff from the quarterback and roll out. Agee would fake a block, then release and run downfield for a pass. It was good for seven or eight touchdowns that season, Jones recalled.

Jones was routinely identified as a resident of Mobile, but his actual hometown was Plateau, Alabama, a tiny, depleted enclave near the Mobile River on the Gulf Coast, a community composed mostly of sad shacks, weed-choked lots, and rutted roads, along with the powerful pull of history. For years the air over Plateau was thick with the acrid spew that belched from the smokestacks of the nearby paper mills rising like concrete sentinels over the flatness. The community, three miles north of downtown Mobile, is more accurately known as Africatown.

Africatown was settled by a small group of West Africans who were among the 110 enslaved people brought to Alabama in 1860 on a two-masted schooner named the *Clotilda*. An estimated 12.5 million African people were stolen from their homeland and brought to the United States in the history of the slave trade. The United

States banned the practice in 1808, but the human trafficking continued for decades more. The people on the *Clotilda*, from a tribe in the West African country now known as Benin, were the last reported slaves to be smuggled into the United States.

A prominent plantation owner and shipping magnate named Timothy Meaher was the force behind the enterprise, which reportedly began with a barroom wager, Meaher boasting that he could successfully bring a shipload of slaves into Mobile. Meaher enlisted the help of Captain William Foster, who built the ship as a schooner so it wouldn't resemble the cargo ships that were the standard slave-trade vessels. Foster reached the so-called Slave Coast of West Africa (in the region that is now Benin) in March 1860, picked out his human cargo from the barracoon, or slave pen, and began the long journey back to the Gulf Coast. He made sure to arrive under cover of night, and made elaborate arrangements to avoid getting caught, having a tugboat lead the *Clotilda* to a secluded spot a few miles upriver. The *Clotilda* was burned to destroy the evidence, and the human cargo was dispersed onto smaller boats and taken to the various plantations and businesses, where enslavement waited.

After spending five years in servitude, the West Africans were freed, along with all the other American slaves, at the end of the Civil War. Many of the passengers on the *Clotilda* stayed in touch and made plans to return to Africa, but the cost and logistical obstacles made that all but impossible. In her brilliant and exhaustively researched book about the *Clotilda* and its passengers, *Dreams of Africa in Alabama*, author Sylviane A. Diouf explained what happened next: "When their plan failed, they decided to do the next best thing: re-create Africa where they were. They shared all they had, saved money, built each other's houses, and solved problems collectively. Despite the hardships, their sense of unity and kinship made their 'African Town' a success. . . . Within this African enclave, they raised their children, teaching them the languages and values they had learned from their families and brought from the homelands they cherished."

The most notable citizen of Africatown was Cudjo Lewis, who

was 19 years old when he was captured and sold to Foster. His African name was Oluale Kossola, but his master had trouble pronouncing it, so he became known as Cudjo. Cudjo was among the strongest advocates among the *Clotilda* captives for returning to Africa and was instrumental in the group purchasing a parcel of land along the Mobile River and Chicasaw Creek that would become Africatown. When Cudjo Lewis died in 1935 at the age of 94, he was believed to be the last surviving former slave in the United States.

Cleon Jones grew up in a shotgun house with no running water, where he and his brother, Tommie Lee, were raised by a grandmother he knew as Mama Myrt. Jones's father had fled for the north when Cleon was a toddler after an altercation in downtown Mobile one day while he and Cleon's mother were waiting for a bus. A white man objected to Jones's mother standing in front of a white woman on the line for the bus. The man used the N-word and told her to go to the back of the line. The Joneses knew they would have to sit in the back of the bus once they boarded, but they weren't aware of any protocol for standing on line. Jones's mother didn't move, so the man yelled at her, used the N-word again, and pulled her ponytail. Jones's father had seen enough. He beat the guy up, and then they ran off.

Jones's father didn't stop running until he was in Chicago. His mother left a few years later after finding work in Philadelphia. That left Cleon and Tommie Lee Jones in the care of their grandmother. She worked as a cook at Mobile County Training School and was the only mother the boys truly knew. Cleon grew into a stellar, two-sport athlete and wound up signing a pro contract with the Mets. His pro baseball travels took him all over the country, but home always remained Africatown. With some of his baseball earnings, he built a brick home on the same lot as his old shotgun house, "I can't imagine being anyplace else," he said.

• • •

ONCE EVERYBODY HAD decompressed after Agee's near-calamitous steal attempt, Jones settled back into the batter's box and Upshaw went back to work. Agee took a good-sized lead, but he wasn't going to try another straight steal of home. The Braves were alert to Agee now, so the element of surprise was gone.

Jones worked the count full. A tough assignment for right-handed hitters, Upshaw delivered the payoff pitch via third base, a curveball he thought was in a good spot. Jones stayed in, and timed his swing perfectly. He drove the ball over the left-field wall, the Mets' third two-run homer of the day. Their lead was now back to five, 11–6.

Tug McGraw, starter turned relief ace, pitched two scoreless innings in the seventh and eighth and was trying to lock up a 2-0 NLCS lead in the bottom of the ninth. Millan led off and worked out a walk. Tony Gonzalez followed with a single to center, and suddenly the Braves were cooking. The middle of their order was coming up, led by Henry Aaron, who not only had hit the three-run homer off Koosman but had smoked a ball off McGraw in the seventh. One swing could change the whole narrative.

McGraw got two strikes on Aaron and threw his best pitch, a screwball, on the outside corner. Augie Donatelli, the plate umpire, came up with his right arm.

McGraw had caught the great Henry Aaron looking.

Rico Carty stepped in. McGraw stayed on the outside of the plate and got Carty to rap a ground ball to second. Al Weis, who had come on for Boswell, fielded it cleanly and threw to Harrelson, who fired to Kranepool, a crisp 4-6-3 double play that left the Mets in a fine mood.

Across two games and 18 innings in Atlanta, the Mets not only came away with two victories, they put up 20 runs and 23 hits and debunked the idea that all they could do was pitch. Shamsky had six hits in two games and was hitting .667. Garrett had four hits in two games. Jones was hitting .400. Two of the Mets' top sluggers, Donn Clendenon and Ron Swoboda, hadn't even gotten onto the field. That Seaver had tweaked a leg muscle shagging flies in the outfield before the game was a concern, but the Mets, overall, were not in a worrying place.

Three hours and 15 minutes after Coretta Scott King made her first pitch, the New York Mets were leaving Atlanta one game from the World Series. In the owners' box, Rhett Butler and Scarlett O'Hara were old news. Joan Whitney Payson was much more interested in discussing the heroics of Shamsky and Garrett, Jones and Agee, Taylor and McGraw.

"If you'd told me in April that we'd almost have a National League pennant on October 5, I would've told you you were crazy," she said.

7

BRING ON THE BIRDS

WITH THE METS' OFFENSIVE ONSLAUGHT IN ATLANTA COMPLETE, Nick Torman, the team's equipment manager, packed up their smoking bats and loaded them on the plane for the trip back to LaGuardia Sunday night. Game three would be the next afternoon. The Mets and Braves didn't get a day off, and the Mets didn't want one.

Eleven-year-old Gary Cohen was good with that. Cohen lived with his family in Parkway Village, a 675-unit brick apartment complex in Jamaica, tucked between Union Turnpike and Grand Central Parkway, about five miles south of Shea Stadium. He skipped a day of seventh grade at the United Nations International School on October 6, 1969, and did so for both personal and historical reasons.

There was no chance he was going to miss the first postseason baseball game at Shea Stadium.

Shortly after the Mets clinched the division on September 24, Cohen learned that NLCS tickets would go on sale at Shea the next morning. He didn't know how long the supply would last, so it was imperative that he get a good spot in line. The youngster went to bed and set his alarm for midnight. When the alarm rang, Cohen stirred but was in no rush to get up. His mother, Joyce, the big Mets fan in the family, nudged him awake. Cohen left Parkway Village in the dead of night and rode the Q44A bus to the Union Turnpike subway station, where he transferred to an E train. He took the E train to Roosevelt Avenue, where he transferred to the 7 train. He took the 7 to the Willets Point stop, walked down the steps, and staked out his spot by the advance ticket sales window. There were maybe a hundred other people ahead of him. Cohen had no food or drink, nor any qualms about spending the night outside Shea Stadium as a seventh grader. All he had was enough cash to buy two tickets for game three.

Dawn broke over Flushing. When the ticket window opened, the orderly line morphed into Grand Central at rush hour, a crush of people storming the booth. Cohen was all but stampeded but finally arrived at the window. He bought two upper reserved tickets at $5 apiece.

On a sunny, windswept Monday morning in Queens 10 days later, Gary Cohen and his father, Shel, made their way to Shea Stadium. They headed out toward left field and kept going until the stadium ended, Section 48. They climbed up to Row R, the last two seats on the right, so far up in the upper deck they all but had to dodge air traffic coming out of LaGuardia.

"We had a great view of the visitors' bull pen," Cohen said.

The city was in a state of near hysteria. The Mets commanded the front and back pages of the tabloids and regular editorials in the *New York Times*. On page one of the October 6 edition of the *Times*, Leonard Koppett wrote about how the Mets had transcended the adjectives "amazing" and "unbelievable" and entered the realm of the "supernatural." This was no longer a cute, cuddly underdog story. The New York Mets were a game away from the World Series.

Eight months after terribly mismanaging a snowstorm, Mayor John V. Lindsay threw out the first pitch at Shea and was booed longer and louder than any of the Braves. You got the feeling the fans would've thrown snowballs at him had they been available. A month away from Election Day, Lindsay was well aware that constituencies that had previously supported him—notably Italian Americans—had turned against him. His opponents, Mario Procaccino and John Marchi, the Democratic and Republican candidates for mayor, respectively, were solidifying their electoral bases. Lindsay had a perilous path ahead of him toward reelection, but if one variable worked in his favor, it was the New York Mets. The Mets made people feel good, and Lindsay was doing all he could to ally himself with them.

The Braves entrusted their season to Pat Jarvis, a squatty right-hander who was nicknamed "Little Bulldog" and would do everything but bite a hitter to get him out. A former minor-league roommate of Denny McLain—they had combined for 27 victories for the Duluth-Superior Dukes, the Detroit Tigers' class-A club in 1963—Jarvis's trademark was a quirky, short-legged motion. His opponent in game three would be Gary Gentry, the hard-throwing rookie and a 13-game winner. Gentry was celebrating his twenty-third birthday. His catcher, Jerry Grote, was celebrating his twenty-seventh birthday. Gentry was as skinny as a chopstick but had a seriously strong arm; batters underestimated him at their peril. He had fired nine shutout innings against the Braves in August, so they knew what he had in him.

Gentry hoped to restore some order to the Mets' rotation, after the vaunted Seaver and Koosman had gotten roughed up. With his hat pulled down low over his angular face, Gentry looked in for Grote's first sign and saw Ed Sudol, the home-plate umpire, looming right behind him. A more superstitious pitcher might have seen this as a bad omen. Sudol, a big, beefy former minor-league first baseman, had a knack for being behind the plate for big, unhappy Mets moments. When the Mets lost to the Houston Astros 1–0 in 24 innings in the Astrodome on April 15, 1968—the longest shutout in big-league history—Sudol was the man in the mask. Four seasons earlier, in the newly opened Shea Stadium, Sudol was behind the plate for the Mets' 8–6 loss to the Giants in 23 innings, the 7-hour, 23-minute nightcap of a Memorial Day doubleheader. Sudol had a much shorter workday at Shea three Sundays later, when he called Jim Bunning's perfect game on Father's Day.

Gentry was unconcerned with Sudol's history. His task was to put zeroes on the board.

It didn't go well from the outset. The second batter of the game, Tony Gonzalez, stroked a single to left. That brought up Aaron, the Braves' hottest hitter. He took his usual slow walk to the plate. He slid one foot lightly over the dirt, then the other, and settled into his stance, taking two slow, looping practice swings, then a quicker, more compact third one. At 6 feet and 180 pounds, Aaron wasn't an especially large man, but he was a marvel of biomechanical efficiency, generating astonishing power with his rippling forearms and quick hands, especially the left one.

"My power hand," he called it.

Aaron liked thick-handled bats. He kept his left hand loose on the bat until the pitch came in, then would tighten it up a bit and draw both hands back to generate more power when he swung.

Gentry got ahead 1-2, Aaron swinging through a curveball. Gentry had been working away, but his next delivery, another breaking pitch, got more of the plate. Aaron's hands edged back, and then he came forward, his weight shifting, his hips opening, the bat a blur through the zone, connecting with a sonorous sound that filled the ballpark and sent the ball rocketing to center. Agee ran back as if he might have a play on it. He finally ran out of room, the ball smacking into the flagpole and caroming right back into center field. It was Aaron's third homer in three games.

In Section 48, young Gary Cohen, future Mets broadcaster, was in disbelief. *What are the odds of a man hitting a ball 420 feet squarely into a pole?* he wondered. "I'll never forget the sight of that," he said.

One out later, Cepeda drilled a double down the left-field line. Gentry got out with no further damage, but three hard-hit balls and two runs wasn't an auspicious beginning.

Jarvis had his own bumpiness in the first, Agee lashing a lead-off double into the left-field corner, Wayne Garrett following with a smoked line drive right at Jarvis's head. Somehow Jarvis got his glove up, snared the liner, and fired to second to double up Agee. The Braves had played a brutal series, no doubt, and deserved to be two games down, but they had also had terrible luck: Soft Mets pops dropped for base hits. Routine Mets grounders took bad hops. Well-struck Braves hits found Mets gloves. Jarvis's play, which could well have saved him a trip to the hospital, if not the cemetery, may have been their first bit of good fortune in three games.

Gentry righted himself in the second, but Tony Gonzalez greeted him in the third with another roped single, this one down the right-field line, and Aaron followed with a laser to left-center for a double. Young Gary Cohen didn't like the way this was going.

When Aaron arrived at second, Ken Boswell, the young second baseman, chatted him up.

"Henry, we're trying to win this thing. Let up on us, will you?" he said.

Aaron wasn't letting up, and neither were the Braves. They hadn't gone 20-5 in September by being timid. It was a pivotal moment in the series, and everybody in the park knew it. The Braves had men on second and third with nobody out, a prime opportunity to put Gentry in serious trouble, and they had the right man, Rico Carty, to do it. A strapping right-handed cleanup hitter, the 6-foot, 3-inch Carty was from the coastal city of San Pedro de Macoris, Dominican Republic, a region as famous for exporting baseball players as Hawaii is for exporting pineapples. He had grown up in a family of 16 children and become a feared amateur boxer under the tutelage of a couple of uncles before switching to baseball. Carty hit right-handers better than left-handers and was the Braves' most dangerous hitter down the stretch, hitting .376 with 25 RBI in 25 games after September 1.

Rube Walker, the pitching coach, went out to talk to Gentry. Jim McAndrew and Nolan Ryan were warming up in the pen. Gentry got ahead 1-2 and came inside, Carty fouling the ball off. Grote set up inside again. He wanted to tie up the muscular Carty, to avoid giving him a chance to extend his arms. Gentry took a long look at the sign. Carty, tired of waiting, stepped out. Gentry finally was ready and delivered. Carty launched a missile down the left-field line that didn't miss being a three-run homer by much. In Section 48, Row R, a young fan sighed in relief. On the mound, a young pitcher did the same thing. There was an audible gasp all over the ballpark.

Gentry got a new ball from Ed Sudol and paused for a moment to look at where Carty's shot had landed when he saw Gil Hodges climb the dugout steps and head toward the mound, in the same manner as always, jacket on, hands in his jacket pockets, taking tippy-toe steps as if he didn't want to hurt the grass. Hodges's tippy-toes meant only one thing: Gentry's afternoon was over after two-plus innings.

Gentry was not happy to see Hodges and didn't pretend to be. In his mind, Seaver and Koosman were always given preferential treatment and much more proverbial rope when they struggled. Gentry, on the other hand, felt he needed to prove himself on every pitch. It was not an easy way to work. Seaver and Koosman had been hit hard in Atlanta, and the Mets had still found a way to win both games. To Gentry, this was his chance to make a statement—to work out of a jam and go deep into the game to lock up the pennant. He had pitched brilliantly in shutting out the Cardinals to clinch the pennant just 12 days earlier.

Had his manager forgotten that?

As he handed the ball to Hodges, Gentry's body language was fairly screaming "The score is only 2–0, and I am ahead 1-2 on the hitter. Are you really going to pull me after a foul ball in the third inning?"

That was exactly what Gil Hodges was doing.

Hodges didn't expect Gentry to be happy, but his job was to manage the club, not take account of Gary Gentry's feelings. Hodges was an astute baseball man and an excellent reader of pitchers. Gentry was a tremendous young talent with star potential, but everything Hodges had seen during Gentry's brief outing had told him that a complete unraveling was imminent. The Braves were pounding the ball. Carty, one of the most dangerous hitters in the game, had just missed making the score 5–0. Hodges needed one strike to get Carty out, and in the bull pen he had one of the hardest throwers on Earth to get it.

• • •

A 22-YEAR-OLD TEXAN, Nolan Ryan had a right arm that was already part of Mets lore. One day when he first came up, late in 1966, he was warming up in the bull pen, throwing to a young catcher named John Stephenson. This was in the Astrodome, just 30 miles north of Alvin, Texas, Ryan's hometown. When a pitcher warms up, he lets the catcher know what pitch he's going to throw. Ryan got loose and started throwing curveballs. Stephenson was catching them, throwing them back. It was a routine warm-up session until Ryan, apparently tired of throwing curveballs, decided to go back to his fastball. The only trouble was that he forgot to tell Stephenson that it was coming.

"John held up his glove, expecting the ball to break, and the ball hit him right in the heart," Ed Kranepool said. "He went over on his back like he'd been shot. We thought, 'Holy shit, he's dead.' It was one of Nolan's rising fastballs, and it never touched his glove. He could've died, no question about it. We carried him to the trainer's room. He had a welt on his chest for weeks."

Red Murff, the Mets' Texas-based scout who signed Koosman and Boswell, saw Ryan when he was in high school and said on his scouting report that the kid had "the BEST arm I ever saw ANYWHERE in my whole life." Murff had scouted Jim Maloney and Turk Farrell, men he believed had the best fastballs in the National League at the time, and said the 17-year-old Ryan threw harder than either of them. Murff wasn't overhyping his prospect; in Ryan's first full year in the minors he had 307 strikeouts in 202 innings.

Ryan made it to New York for good by 1968, showing great promise in 18 starts, but 1969 was marked more by interruptions than by steady progress. Between military duty and assorted injuries, he appeared in only 25 games, starting 10, alternately overpowering and inconsistent.

Carty had faced Ryan only once, three years earlier. This was a big plus in Hodges's mind. People could try to prepare you for Ryan's fastball, but until you were in the batter's box with a bat, you couldn't fully appreciate how quickly the ball got on you. Ryan also had a curveball that would become so lethal later in his career it was hard to hit even if he told you it was coming. He was by far the Mets' best strikeout pitcher and wild enough to make hitters very uncomfortable in the batter's box.

Needing a strikeout and reasoning that even if Ryan got a little wild, the count was 1-2 and first base was open, Hodges saw no downside. With his tight, high-kicking windup, Ryan fired his first pitch, a fastball.

Carty swung right through it.

One out. The crowd erupted.

After an intentional walk to Cepeda, Boyer came up with the bases loaded. The Mets' infield was at double-play depth. Boyer swung through a fastball for one strike and fouled off another fastball for 0-2. The count went to 1-2 when Ryan missed with a high fastball. Grote called for another fastball, the only pitch Ryan had thrown since coming into the game. The pitch blazed to the plate. Boyer didn't budge. Sudol jerked up his right hand. Ryan had his second strikeout, and the crowd roared again.

Bob Didier, the 20-year-old switch-hitting catcher, fought off a couple of 2-2 pitches, fouling them away. Ryan came at him with more heat. Didier flied harmlessly to left, Jones catching the ball by the foul line.

Ryan walked off the mound to a thunderous ovation. The score remained 2–0.

• • •

AFTER RYAN'S escape act, Tommie Agee came up with one out in the bottom of the third. Agee may have been the Met who scared opponents the most. Cleon Jones was a better pure hitter. Donn Clendenon had more power. The 27-year-old Agee had major holes in his swing and struck out far more than any other Met, but he was nonetheless a player who could beat you with his bat, glove, and legs. In game two of the NLCS alone, he had homered, scored three runs, and might've stolen home if his buddy Cleon hadn't almost decapitated him. He was bold on the bases and had few peers in the field. This was no departure from his performance in the regular season, when Agee showed not just the form that helped him win the AL Rookie of the Year trophy in 1966 but also why Hodges was so eager to acquire him from the White Sox. Hodges knew Agee could be a difference-maker for the Mets, but Agee's passage to stardom in New York was not easy.

The Agee home in Whistler, Alabama, was a tiny, two-bedroom place that was more shack than house, Joe and Tommie in one bedroom and the nine sisters crammed into the other. The parents were Joseph Agee, a minister, and Carrie, who wanted Tommie to become a clergyman as well. The Agee kids were all born at home, delivered by a midwife. They lived on a dirt road named Railroad Street, next to a humble white clapboard house of worship, the Church of God and Christ. There was an outhouse in the backyard, surrounded by clucking chickens. The chicken population would decline by one when it was time for a special family dinner. Tommie and Joe's favorite activity was to play stickball with a Spaldeen and one of their mother's old broomsticks. That was how Tommie Agee learned to play baseball.

The Agees were originally from Magnolia, Alabama, about 135 miles to the north, but Joe Sr. moved the family when he got work and housing for his family as a plantation caretaker. It looked to be a good opportunity, but it did not last long. Several white youngsters in the area picked grapes one day, right off the vines that were climbing up the Agees' home. Four of Joe and Tommie's sisters took exception to that and got into a fight with the boys. The white youngsters went home and told their father, who showed up a short time later with a shotgun, proclaiming that he was going to kill the entire Agee family. The situation was dangerous enough that the plantation owners allowed the Agees into their home.

That same night, Joe Sr. borrowed a truck from his brother and moved the family to the Whistler area.

"He wasn't fooling. My sisters saw the guy with the gun," Joe Agee, Jr., said. "You do what you have to do."

The family settled into life on Railroad Street. Years after the Supreme Court's landmark ruling in *Brown v. Board of Education of Topeka* made segregation in public schools unconstitutional, schools on the Gulf Coast of Alabama remained very much separate and unequal. The Agee children were bussed for miles to attend all-black schools, passing well-appointed, well-equipped white schools en route. Nobody complained, because that's the way it was. When Tommie reached high school age, he enrolled in Mobile County Training School, emerging as a four-sport star. Able to run the 100-yard dash in under 10 seconds, Tommie's speed made him a wicked wide receiver to cover on the football field. County never played against the local white schools; its biggest football game was played every year on Thanksgiving Day against Mobile Central High School, another all-black school. The contest would draw thousands of fans. Central's star players included Willie McCovey and Henry Aaron.

With a fleet of fast backs and ends, County defeated Central three straight years during Agee's career, and he and Cleon Jones were a major part of that. Agee liked football, but baseball was his best sport—and his favorite—reinforced by his memory of seeing Jackie Robinson playing big-league baseball on television in the early 1950s. Agee wasn't even 5 when Robinson broke baseball's undeclared ban of players of color. Only a few people in Whistler had TV sets then, so people in the neighborhood would gather every time Robinson and the Dodgers were on TV.

Agee's segregated world in Whistler offered no chance to shatter any racial barriers, but his athletic gifts enabled him to earn a scholarship to Grambling State University. At Grambling, an industrial and agricultural school in northern Louisiana that provided higher education for thousands of young African-Americans over the decades, Agee was focused only on baseball, and that was fine with Dr. Ralph Waldo Emerson Jones. The grandson of a slave, Jones was the president of Grambling and also the baseball coach. Everybody called him "Prez." In Agee's first game for Grambling, he homered over the left-field fence in his first at bat, homered over the center-field fence in his second at bat, and homered over the right-field fence in his third at bat. He must've gotten tired of trotting, because in his fourth at bat, he walloped the ball over the center fielder's head and sprinted around the bases for an inside-the-park home run.

Prez had a good idea that he would not have Tommie Agee for long. And indeed he did not.

Soon after his freshman year, Agee signed with the Cleveland Indians for a bonus of $65,000 and showed immediate promise, hitting .261 with 15 home runs in just 64 games at Dubuque, Iowa, in the Class D Midwest League. The next year he moved up to class-B ball in Burlington, North Carolina, hitting .258 with 7 homers and 25 stolen bases without being caught once. Joe Jr. went up to Burlington to see Tommie play in a game in 1962. The stands were completely segregated, whites on one side and a handful of blacks on another. Tommie had been warned that Burlington had a fan who would stand behind the plate and shout the N-word and all sorts of racist bile. He was also told that if he responded in any way he would be sent back to Whistler and it would be a one-way ticket.

Sure enough, when Tommie overthrew third base as he tried to cut down a runner, the guy started in on him. "Hey, nigger, you're supposed to be the next Willie Mays?" he hollered. "You ain't nothin'. They should've left you in Alabama."

The fan kept up the hateful spew for the whole game. Tommie Agee never responded.

The next night, the team had a game 60 miles to the east in Raleigh. The stands were fully integrated. There were no incidents.

"It was amazing to see the difference," Joe Agee, Jr., recalled.

The Agee family was not easy to scare off. Autherine Lucy, Tommie's cousin from Shiloh, Alabama, was the first African-American to enroll at the University of Alabama, in 1956. She had originally been accepted in 1952, but when the university discovered she wasn't white, she was denied enrollment. A subsequent lawsuit, filed with the help of NAACP lawyer Thurgood Marshall, overturned the university's decision. Autherine Lucy started classes in early February 1956, but days later a hostile mob confronted her and forced her to seek safety in an empty classroom. The university board voted to expel her out of purported concern for her own safety. Decades later, the expulsion was overturned, and she received her master's degree in education from the University of Alabama in 1992.

"My response to fear is: do it anyway," Lucy said. "Let nothing stop you. You have to push forward."

Cousin Tommie, meanwhile, was on a fast track to the big leagues, getting a late-season call-up to the Indians in 1962 at age 20. The Indians thought he'd benefit by playing winter ball, so they sent him to Venezuela, a country famous for its passionate, and sometimes unruly, fans. In one game, Agee let a ball go through his legs. When Agee went to the wall to retrieve it, someone launched a Coke bottle at him. It hit Agee in the forehead and knocked him out cold.

"I didn't let no more ground balls go through my legs after that," Agee told his brother.

Agee had two more short stays with the Indians the next two years, but after a big year in Portland, Oregon, in triple-A ball, the highest level of the minors, he was traded to the Chicago White Sox in a three-team deal with the Kansas City A's that sent Rocky Colavito to Cleveland. Agee struggled through a year of injuries and slumps at Indianapolis, the Sox' triple-A affiliate, and was immensely frustrated by his lack of progress, believing he still hadn't gotten what he considered a full shot to make the majors.

He called home to talk to brother Joe.

"I think I'm just going to pack it up and come home," Tommie said. "This isn't going anywhere."

"Why would you do that?" Joe asked.

"I'm tired of it. I'm tired of getting close and dropping back again. I don't think I'm getting a fair shake."

Joe let Tommie vent a little longer. "Let me ask you a question," Joe said. "Has the team asked you to pack up and leave?"

"No."

"Is the team still paying you?" Joe asked.

"Yes," Tommie said.

Joe Agee was working as an upholsterer's apprentice then, making $32 per week.

"If they are still paying you and haven't asked you to leave, you should just stay there and finish out the year," Joe said. "Your time will come."

The following year, 1966, Tommie Agee made the White Sox and was voted Rookie of the Year after hitting .273 with 22 home runs, 8 triples, 86 runs batted in, and 44 stolen bases. He was named to the All-Star team and earned a Gold Glove for his work in center field.

Agee was an All-Star again in 1967 but fell off in the second half, hitting .234 overall and only .199 against right-handers, prompting the White Sox to wonder if he would be better off as a platoon player. The White Sox might've been wary, but the Mets, who had already cycled through a squadron of center fielders in their first six years, were not. At Hodges's urging they parted with their best hitter, Tommy Davis, and a workhorse of a starter in Jack Fisher.

Agee's fresh start in a new league, alongside Cleon Jones, began in the first game of spring training, against the St. Louis Cardinals. Agee batted third in Hodges's lineup. On the mound was the Cardinals' ace, Bob Gibson. Jones warned Agee about what to expect.

"When Tommie came over, I told him there is one guy who's going to find out whether you're a man or a mouse, and it's Gibson," Jones said. "He did it to me. He did it to everyone who he thought was a good player coming into the league. He wanted to know if you could beat him a tough situation. I told him he's going to throw at you. You just weather the storm and get out of the way, and get back in there and have your good at bat. Once he knows he can't rattle you, he'll leave you alone."

Agee dismissed Jones's warning.

"I ain't worried. I've faced plenty of guys like that who throw hard," Agee said.

Said Jones, "You never faced a Gibson, take my word for it."

One of the hardest throwers in the game, Gibson's first pitch to Agee was a ball, up and in. The next pitch came in head high, slightly behind Agee. He froze for an instant, then reeled backward.

The ball crashed into the back of his helmet with a sickening crack. Agee went down instantly, collapsing in the dirt. He was taken away by stretcher and rushed to the hospital for X-rays.

Bob Gibson knew that intimidating hitters would work to his advantage. He never denied that he wanted to send Agee a message.

"It's very easy to hit a batter in the body with a pitch," Gibson told Roger Angell of *The New Yorker*. "There's nothing to it. It's a lot harder to hit him in the head. Anytime you hit him in the head, it's really his own fault. Anyway, that was just spring training."

Jones said that Agee's terrible struggles in his first year in the National League had much more to do with learning new pitchers and probably pressing than with Gibson's beanball. Still, Gibson's welcome didn't help, and Agee didn't forget it.

"Tommie never wanted to have much of anything to do with Gibson after that," Jones said. "If he ever saw him, he just didn't care to talk to him. I don't think Tommie ever forgave him for what he did."

Agee's initiation to New York was just beginning. His car was stolen the first time he drove it into Manhattan. He got off to a rousing start to the year with two hits, two runs, and a stolen base in the Mets' opener, but four games later he went 0 for 10 in the 24-inning loss to the Houston Astros. The slump extended to 0 for 34, tying Don Zimmer for the club record, and Agee never really found his footing after that, despite an uptick the final month of the season. It was almost unimaginable to see his season-ending stats—the .217 average and the 17 RBI—alongside his name.

"I can't describe how I felt that year," Agee told a reporter. "Sometimes it was so bad I felt like I was numb. I didn't know what to do, didn't know where to turn."

The Mets sent Agee to Florida for extra work after the season, but after a week he headed back to Whistler, needing to clear his head and not think about baseball for a while. He and Jones would go out fishing almost every morning. They baited their hooks, put their lines into the water. They waited for nibbles and talked about hitting, about mechanics. In the afternoon, Tommie Aaron would join them, and they'd go to a field and have batting practice. Agee didn't want to overthink things anymore. He just wanted to get back to swinging at good pitches, seeing the ball and hitting the ball—trying to keep it simple.

It would've been easy for Hodges to bail on Agee after the disastrous '68 season, but Hodges remained staunchly in his corner, knowing that the biggest problem was that Agee was trying too hard. Agee spent more time in Hodges's office than any other Met. It was a relief to know that Hodges still saw him as his everyday center fielder.

Agee got off to a fast start in 1969—highlighted by the tape-measure shot off Larry Jaster in the third game of the season—but he went into a slump in late April, prompting Hodges to give him about 10 days off before he broke out with a four-hit game against the Cubs. The center fielder the Mets had coveted had returned to form, playing better than he ever had. It didn't change for the rest of the year.

• • •

WITH ONE OUT in the bottom of the third, Agee came up to face Jarvis. Agee had doubled in the first, and came up a confident hitter. Jarvis had fallen behind Agee the first time and didn't want to make the same mistake. His first pitch was a breaking ball, out over the plate. Agee swung and drilled it straight toward center, the ball soaring far over the wall to give him his second homer in as many days and make it a 2–1 ball game.

An inning later, the torrid Art Shamsky got another hit, his seventh of the series, bringing up Boswell. At third base, Boyer crept in, playing for a possible sacrifice. Boswell showed no bunt and was ahead in the count 2-1 when Jarvis put a fastball on the outside corner. Ed Sudol took a minute to brush off the plate. Boswell double-checked the count with him. On Jarvis' 2-2 pitch, Boswell swung and launched it deep to right, the crowd rising with the ball.

It landed in the Mets' bull pen, where Joe Pignatano tried to catch it but dropped it and suffered a bruise in the process. Later Boswell teased Pignatano that the coach's hands were worse than his were.

The Mets had their first lead of the day, 3–2, and Boswell had his second homer in two days, not bad power production for a man who had hit three homers all season.

The Braves' Cepeda answered emphatically, though, spanking a two-run homer over the 396 sign in left-center in the top of the fifth. It was the first hit off Ryan and put the Braves back in the lead. The Braves felt better than they had the whole series.

"After I hit that home run, I really thought we had them," Cepeda said. "We showed them that we weren't going away."

Minutes later, with one out and one on in the bottom of the fifth, Wayne Garrett, the former Atlanta farmhand, came to the plate. Garrett had two older brothers, Adrian and Jim, who had also played in the Atlanta organization. To Wayne's thinking, his brothers had never gotten a fair shot to make the big club, especially Adrian, who had had some big years in triple-A and double-A, only to be continually overlooked.

Wayne Garrett played for Charlie Lau and the Braves' double-A affiliate in the Texas League in 1968. He had started out in the Braves system as a shortstop, but Lau was convinced he didn't have the range or athleticism to be a big-league shortstop.

"You need to play third base. That's your best route to the majors," Lau told him.

After the 1968 season, the Braves sent Garrett to the Arizona Fall League. It was in Arizona that he caught the eye of Bob Scheffing, the Mets' director of player development. Scheffing liked Garrett's instincts, the way he carried himself, prompting the team to grab him in the Rule 5 draft. Nobody ever told Garrett. He went home to Florida. As far as he knew, he was still with the Atlanta Braves.

Adrian, who was five years older than Wayne and would wind up hitting 398 home runs in 19 years in pro baseball, clued him in.

"Have you seen *The Sporting News*?" he asked.

"No."

"You've been drafted by the Mets, and you are going to the big leagues with them next year," Adrian said.

Wayne Garrett had no idea about the minutiae of baseball contracts, but Adrian was all over it. He knew that if Wayne didn't make the Mets' 25-man roster in 1969, he would be returned to the Braves and the Mets would be out half of the $25,000 they had spent to draft him. Adrian Garrett also knew that chances to make the big leagues do not come around often. Adrian hit 24 homers and drove in 75 runs in the Texas League during his kid brother's rookie year in 1969. He wound up playing parts of eight seasons in the majors.

"He was a better ballplayer than I was," Wayne said. "There's no doubt about that."

Hodges's decision to start Garrett in the NLCS, notwithstanding his second-half slump, was based on Hodges's belief in Garrett's makeup and in the approach he would bring against the Braves' right-handers. The manager wasn't one for hand-holding, but he made sure that everybody on the roster felt valued, even when a guy wasn't doing well.

"It was one of Gil's strongest traits," Duffy Dyer said. "He made everybody feel a part of it. He made a point to come around and say something to you every day, even a small thing. 'How are you doing today?' He'd check in with you. He knew you were there. He made you feel part of the team."

Garrett stepped in against Jarvis. By his own admission, he was "a dead-red hitter," a guy who would jump on fastballs but struggled against breaking stuff. Jarvis, ever the bulldog, came right at him with a fastball. The pitch came in over the plate and looked the size of a cantaloupe. Garrett drilled a deep line drive to right. Aaron gave chase. The ball had some hook on it, but Garrett had hit it so hard it didn't have time to curve foul. It landed just inside the right-field foul pole, allowing the Mets to reclaim the lead at 5–4. The Shea crowd, temporarily dispirited by Cepeda's blast, erupted once more.

It was Garrett's first home run in five months.

• • •

THE METS TACKED on two more runs on RBI singles by Boswell and Agee to extend their lead to 7–4, and Ryan seemed to be getting stronger as the game went on, retiring seven straight Braves, closing the top of the seventh by blowing a fastball by Gonzalez and getting Aaron on a pop to short. In the eighth, after Carty singled, Ryan pitched carefully to Cepeda, who had homered off him three innings earlier. More than any other Brave, Cepeda seemed to be right on Ryan's fastball. With the count 2-2, Grote called for a curveball. Ryan delivered a sweeping, fast-spinning breaking pitch for a strike. Cepeda never budged.

Ryan caught Boyer looking at a fastball for the second out, his seventh strikeout, but pinch hitter Mike Lum lined a single to left and Ryan quickly found himself in a jam. The dangerous Felipe Alou came up to pinch-hit for Gil Garrido, tying run at the plate. A .317 hitter with 210 hits the year before, Alou would've been in the lineup had it not been for a leg injury. Hodges got the bull pen going, Ron Taylor and left-hander Jack DiLauro. Alou settled into his stance. Ryan delivered. Alou was right on it and drilled a line drive that was speared by Bud Harrelson at shortstop. The packed house at Shea let out a roar of relief.

The first two Mets went down in the bottom of the eighth, bringing up Ryan. The Shea crowd gave him a standing ovation. Ryan singled through the middle for his second hit, and the Mets probably wished he hadn't. Agee struck out, ensuring that Ryan would not have to do any additional running, and out came Ryan for the top of the ninth—his seventh inning of relief work.

The National League pennant was three outs away.

Pinch hitter Bob Aspromonte, a native of Brooklyn whose own father was swept up in Mets hysteria, stepped in, hitting a liner to center that was nabbed by Agee. Millan, the leadoff man and the most patient hitter in the Braves' lineup, hadn't swung at the first pitch in three games. He kept the streak intact. On a 1-1 pitch, Ryan got him to hit a grounder to Harrelson, who charged it and fired to Kranepool for the second out. Ryan needed only four pitches in the top of the ninth to put the Mets on the precipice of the unthinkable after seven years of haplessness.

A "Let's go, Mets" chant began to rock the ballpark. The crowd in the box seats started surging forward, a human tsunami about to flood the field for the second time in twelve days. Gary Cohen, who had camped out all night at Shea to ensure that he wouldn't miss this experience, was already hustling down to field level from Row R of Section 48. Cohen had listened to game one on a transistor radio in the back of his grandfather's dry cleaning store, where he worked every Saturday. He had been thrilled when they had come back to win, swept the two games in Atlanta, but nothing could beat this.

Tony Gonzalez, a left-handed hitter, stepped to the plate. Ryan wound and delivered. Gonzalez swung and missed a letter-high fastball for strike one. Grote knew that Gonzalez would be looking for more heat. He called for a curve, and Ryan spun it hard, on the outer half of the plate. Gonzalez swung and rolled it out toward third.

Gary Cohen could hardly fathom what was about to happen.

Wayne Garrett fielded the ball cleanly. He threw to first. Kranepool stretched to meet it and clamped his big mitt around the ball. Ed Vargo, the first-base umpire, brought up his right hand.

The Mets were National League champions.

Kranepool ran toward the mound to congratulate Ryan and had plenty of company. The party was on. Gary Cohen jumped the railing along the left-field line, landed on the warning track, and took off. He ran around left field, which had been manned by Cleon Jones just moments before, zigging here and zagging there, no particular destination in mind.

Was this really happening? Were his Mets really the champions of the National League? He had no idea what to do or how to express his joy, so he just ran, stopping only when he decided it was time to grab a chunk of Shea sod—National League pennant–winning sod—to take home to Parkway Village.

The Mets celebrated briefly around Ryan and then ran for the cover of their clubhouse. Champagne flowed like the fountains at the Unisphere. Sportscaster Lindsey Nelson, who along with colleagues Ralph Kiner and Bob Murphy had been with the Mets from the beginning, corralled Hodges and asked how it felt compared to all the other pennants he'd won in Brooklyn.

"This is beautiful," Hodges said. "This is the greatest pennant I've ever been in, and I've been in a few. Nothing can compare to the feeling of this right now." He talked about how, as much as he'd believed his club could win, he was stunned that they'd scored 27 runs and knocked in 37 hits in the first three postseason games in its history.

"I just don't know how to explain it, Lindsey," the manager said. "Except that these boys are great individuals and they have so much confidence that they can't lose and they're not going to lose."

Nolan Ryan, of course, had played a bigger role in the outcome than anyone. He had pitched three-hit baseball over seven innings to help obliterate the frustrations of a scattered, uneven season. No less a source than Henry Aaron said that Ryan "did a hell of a job today." Ryan wasn't given to self-congratulation or revelry. He was a kid from Texas in New York City, and his manager had given him the ball in the most important game of the season. He wiped the sting of champagne from his eyes.

"When I came in the game, I hadn't had a lot of time to warm up," he said. "All I knew is I had a good fastball. I wasn't able to throw any curveballs in the bull pen. So I just knew I had to throw strikes. I had a real good fastball today and was able to get my curveball over when I needed to. This is the greatest day of my life."

Ed Sudol, the umpire who had been there for so many Mets ordeals, also took it in. "I've seen the Mets go from the depths of despair to the celestial heights," he said. "I took literature in school, as you can tell."

Clubhouse celebrations are, by nature, events of excess, the combination of euphoria and alcohol tending to make inhibitions shrink and emotions surge like a Ryan fastball. So it was in Flushing, Queens, on October 6, 1969, when the most gushing sentiments came from a non-Met, Mayor John V. Lindsay, who said to Gil Hodges, "You are the most beautiful man I've ever seen in my life. I love you."

Joan Whitney Payson, the principal owner, stepped toward Lindsey Nelson's microphone. Seaver poured her a cup of champagne. There was much to celebrate. One minute and 43 seconds before the Mets won the pennant, Mr. University, one of Payson's Thoroughbreds, had won the $22,950 first division of the Long Island Handicap at Belmont Park, about 10 miles from Shea, with Angel Cordero up.

Nelson asked Mrs. Payson about the prospect of playing the mighty Baltimore Orioles, who were on their way to their own sweep in the American League Championship Series. She took a sip of the champagne Tom Seaver had given her.

"Bring 'em on," she said.

Part III

There Are No Words

8

MISPLACED ACE

World Series Game One
Baltimore, Maryland

THAT A CLUB FROM NEW YORK CITY WOULD BE IN THE WORLD SERIES
was hardly a new development. The Series had been played more
often in New York than anyplace else. Among the Yankees, the New
York Giants, the Brooklyn Dodgers, and the Dodgers' predecessors,
the Brooklyn Robins, New York clubs had made a total of 52 Series
appearances in the twentieth century. Fourteen times, both participants in the Series had been from New York. If citizens of the five
boroughs had come to regard the World Series almost as much a rite
of autumn as fall foliage and Halloween, you couldn't really blame
them.

But there was nothing remotely routine about the 1969 World
Series, because the local representative was the New York Mets, the
erstwhile laughingstock of the sport. From subways to street corners, high-rises to high schools, Broadway to the Bowery, the civic
discourse focused on little else. The Mets were the lead item on the
evening news and in the morning papers. Mayor Lindsay, continuing to ride the best story in years like a jockey (albeit a 6-foot, 4-inch
one) aboard one of Mrs. Payson's horses, was in the middle of the
festive sendoff at LaGuardia Airport before the Mets departed for
Baltimore, wearing an oversized WE'RE NO. 1 button. Nearby was
a six-piece jazz band in candy-striped jackets, which played a rol-
licking rendition of "Take Me Out to the Ball Game." Lindsay even

wrote a poem he called "Ode to the Mets," a takeoff on "Casey at the Bat" that was published in the *New York Times* and the *Daily News*.

Arthur Daley, sports columnist for the *Times*, called the outpouring "Metsomania"—a peculiar kind of lunacy unmatched anywhere else. "For the better part of a century," he wrote, "New York prided itself on being a city of sophisticates, accepting with blasé restraint the continuing successes of the old Yankees and the occasional successes of the departed Giants and Dodgers.

"But the current Mets have transformed the city into a provincial village of wild-eyed, vociferous and partisan rooters. The beauty of it is that nobody is embarrassed by it. It is quite wonderful."

Indeed, there was no precedent for what was happening. The day before the Series began, the *Daily News*' lead editorial ran beneath a headline:

CLOBBER 'EM, METS

Maybe the only other place in the country where there was as much excitement over the Mets was in the African-American precincts of greater Mobile, Alabama. Two-thirds of the Mets outfield had played for coach Curtis Horton on the Mobile County Training School Whippets, after all. A banner in front of the school read, HOME OF CLEON JONES AND TOMMIE AGEE—FROM A WHIPPET TO THE WORLD CHAMPION NEW YORK METS.

Horton arranged to have students at the school get out of class and gather in the gym to watch the World Series games that would be played during the week.

"There are not too many coaches who had two boys on a major-league club period," Horton told the *New York Times*. "And it's really something when you have two on the same team in the World Series."

Not all of Mobile was so enthused. The newspaper in town, the Mobile *Press-Register*, mostly ignored the exploits of the African-American athletes in the community. When a New York reporter reached out to Mobile city offices before the Series began and asked about Cleon Jones and Tommie Agee, the employee asked, "What's his name—Leon?"

"No, Cleon. C-L-E-O-N," she was told.

"And what's his last name?" she asked.

"Jones."

She said she had never heard of him.

. . .

THE BIGGEST STAR in the 1969 World Series wore number 20, but not for the New York Mets. Frank Robinson had won a Most Valuable Player Award in the National League in 1961, duplicated the feat in the American League five years later, and remains the only man in the history of baseball to win MVPs in both leagues. When he had last seen the Mets on a ball field, as a Cincinnati Red in 1965, he had had two homers, a double, and five RBI in a 13–6 Reds victory. The Mets were then on their way to a record of 50-112, leaving them 47 games out of first place. That made them the worst Mets team ever, other than the 1962 edition, which almost doesn't count. The '65 Mets had two 20-game losers, Jack Fisher and Al Jackson, who pitched for an infield that treated the ball as if it were coated in oil and deserved way better. Their leading hitter, the already long-suffering 20-year-old Ed Kranepool, hit .253.

Frank Robinson knew that much had changed about the Mets in the intervening four years. He knew about the arrival of Gil Hodges, about the young arms of Seaver, Koosman, Gentry, McAndrew, and McGraw, and about the 100 victories and the sweep of the hard-hitting Atlanta Braves. Still, he wasn't terribly concerned. His Baltimore Orioles had finished off their own championship series sweep of the Minnesota Twins. In fact, the Orioles had never lost a postseason game, taking out the favored Dodgers in four straight in the 1966 World Series. They had superb pitching, even better defense, and a dangerous lineup that produced 175 home runs, helping the Orioles outscore their opponents by 262 runs for the season and win more games than any American League team since the

Cleveland Indians in 1954. In the ALCS, they held the Twins, the league's most explosive offensive club, to five runs in three games and kept slugger Harmon Killebrew without a home run or an RBI.

Robinson was the ultimate baseball hard-ass. He stood over the plate and dared pitchers to hit him. He would slide into second as if he were a rolling tank. You could ask Al Weis about that; the last time Weis played in Memorial Stadium in Baltimore, his season, and his Chicago White Sox career, ended with knee surgery after Robinson charged into him to break up a double play. Weis held no ill feelings toward Robinson. "He plays the game hard, and so do I," Weis said. "He did what he was supposed to do." Robinson hadn't come through the play too well, either, suffering double vision and a concussion. Robinson's belief, and his playing MO, was that the team that played the hardest and wanted it the most would win.

Robinson's intensity hadn't won him many popularity contests early in his career, but he was now widely seen as not only a superstar but a man of both intelligence and integrity—and a strong candidate to become baseball's most important pioneer since Jackie Robinson. His stated goal was to become the first African-American manager in baseball history. Few discounted his chances, and his goal would come to fruition in 1975, when he was named player-manager for the Cleveland Indians.

In the fall of 1969, though, Robinson's agenda was strictly to beat the Mets four times and earn his second World Series ring in four years.

"We're going to whip the Amazin' Mets," Robinson said in the Orioles' clubhouse after the ALCS. "The World Series might go five, or it just might go four. . . . The Birds haven't decided yet."

"We're here to prove there's no Santa Claus," added Brooks Robinson, the Orioles' other Hall of Fame–bound Robby.

All that squishy nonsense about the so-called Amazin' Mets being a team of destiny, a charmed club in the midst of a magic carpet ride of a season, was seen as just that—nonsense. The notion that the Mets were going to do to the Orioles what their Shea Stadium cotenants, the New York Jets, had done to the Baltimore Colts nine months earlier in Super Bowl III?

Please.

Have a crab cake and calm down.

The Orioles were so confident that they had a motorcade through downtown Baltimore the day before the World Series started. Usually such an event is held *after* a team wins.

"If somebody upstairs is guiding the Mets, as we're told," Earl Weaver, the Orioles' crusty manager, said, "then all I can say is He is guiding us better because we won 109 games to their 100."

Even Gil Hodges, Jr., thought the Orioles looked close to unbeatable. He was 19 in 1969 and spent a good amount of time around the club throughout the season. A few days before the Series started, he was in his father's office, on the other side of the desk, studying the stat sheets for the two teams, first the Mets, then the Orioles. He put the sheets down.

"Can I ask you a question?" he asked his father.

"Sure. What?"

"How are you even on the same field with this team? These guys are incredible."

Gil Sr. stood up, walked around his desk, and closed the door to his office. He looked squarely at his son and spoke in a low but emphatic voice.

"I don't ever want to hear you say that again," he said. "There are twenty-five guys out there who think they can win. That's what matters. The numbers have no bearing on it. Boog Powell has thirty-seven home runs? That doesn't matter. We have to win four games. That's it. If you believe in yourself and compete and you catch a break and take advantage of it, that's how you win."

This wasn't to say that Hodges didn't have profound respect for the Orioles. He had seen them for five years in the American League when he managed the Senators, just 50 miles away. There was nothing not to be impressed by. Baltimore was a club constructed on the so-called Oriole Way—an organizationwide commitment to fundamentals and rigorous teaching of young players of what they should, and should not, do—thoughtfully assembled by such smart baseball people as general manager Harry Dalton and his assistant, Frank Cashen, who would later be the architect of the world-champion 1986 Mets. Star players such as Brooks Robinson and Boog Powell had come up through the farm system, as had a bevy of gifted young pitchers, including Dave McNally, Jim Palmer, Tom Phoebus, and Eddie Watt. Cuban left-hander Miguel Cuellar, who set a club record with 23 victories in 1969, had been all but pilfered from the Astros in a deal for Curt Blefary. Center fielder Paul Blair, who would go on to win eight Gold Gloves, had been snatched out of the Mets organization in 1962. After leaving Blair unprotected, the Mets sent him to the Florida Instructional League to work on his hitting. He did so well that the club was afraid other teams would notice and sat him down with a nonexistent ankle injury.

The Orioles noticed, selected Blair in the first-year draft, and soon had the best ball chaser in the American League.

Baltimore's most important acquisition of all, though, was Frank Robinson, who had come over from the Reds late in 1965 in exchange for pitchers Milt Pappas and Jack Baldschun and outfielder Dick Simpson. Bill DeWitt, the Reds' general manager, hailed it as a "million-dollar deal." The only trouble was that the millions flowed in one direction, toward Baltimore. Ten months after the deal was consummated, Robinson, a player DeWitt believed was on the downside of his career, won the American League Triple Crown, the MVP, and the World Series MVP. Before the 1968 season was two months old, Pappas, Baldschun, and Simpson were no longer members of the Cincinnati Reds.

• • •

MIGUEL (MIKE) CUELLAR, the Orioles' starter in game one, was a 32-year-old left-hander whose work life might well have been spent alongside his three brothers in the sugar mills of his native Cuba if not for his gift for throwing a baseball. Cuellar was a teenager when he joined the Cuban army of dictator Fulgencio Batista because it came with an opportunity to pitch for the army's baseball team. He threw a no-hitter and quickly attracted the attention of scouts, ultimately signing with the Cincinnati Reds. Just two years later, as Batista's regime was being overthrown by Fidel Castro, Cuellar made his big-league debut, beginning a circuitous path to stardom that would result in four 20-victory seasons and the distinction of being the first Latino pitcher to win a Cy Young Award.

It was a sun-splashed Saturday in Baltimore—October 10—as the sixty-sixth World Series began in Memorial Stadium, a ballpark that had a grove of trees just beyond center field and took its name seriously; engraved over the main entrance were the words TIME WILL NOT DIM THE GLORY OF THEIR DEEDS. Cuellar headed from the Orioles' dugout to the mound, taking exactly the same number of steps he always did. He was as superstitious as any player in baseball. He sat on the lucky end of the training table when he got his pregame arm rubdown, ate Chinese food the night before he pitched, and would never stop warming up before the game until the opposing pitcher did. Once when the team was on the road in Milwaukee, he left his lucky hat behind. The Orioles had to have it shipped to him.

Cuellar's idiosyncrasies earned him the nickname "Crazy Horse" from his teammates, and it seemed fitting that his best weapon was a screwball, a pitch that dived away from right-handed hitters, the yin to his curveball's yang. Listed at 6 feet and 165 pounds, Cuellar didn't overpower hitters, but he was a master at keeping them off balance.

The Mets' assault on the Braves had been led by their left-handed swingers—Art Shamsky, Wayne Garrett, and Ken Boswell—so there was much speculation that Hodges might keep the hot hitters in his lineup, all the more because Cuellar's screwball was typically more effective against right-handed hitters. The right-handed platoon players—Ed Charles, Donn Clendenon, Al Weis, and Ron Swoboda—hadn't played in more than a week, another reason to consider staying with the lefties.

But Hodges stuck with the platoon approach. He wasn't being

stubborn, but strategic. The Orioles were starting another left-hander, Dave McNally, in game two and would almost surely be coming back with Cuellar and McNally in games four and five. Hodges knew the Mets would need contributions from everybody to defeat the mighty Orioles and saw no reason to send a message to his right-handed hitters that he didn't have full faith in them to deliver the way they had all season. Despite having been a star player himself, Hodges had an uncanny ability as a manager to connect with reserve players. He appreciated their value and excelled in finding ways to maximize that value, nobody more than Bobby Pfeil, the career minor leaguer who had been called up early in the year and had filled in superbly all over the infield. Pfeil hit just .232, but the Mets were 33-17 in games he started. He also batted .556 (5 for 9) as a pinch hitter. Hodges would've loved to have had Pfeil on the postseason roster, but the Mets wanted to have a second left-hander in the bull pen and assigned the twenty-fifth spot to Jack DiLauro. Hodges did the next best thing: he got permission from Major League Baseball for Pfeil to be on the bench and in uniform.

Cuellar had his screwball working well as his first World Series start got under way, dropping it on the outside corner, then mixing in his curve on the inner half. He got the first two hitters, Tommie Agee and Bud Harrelson, on grounders to Brooks Robinson at third, and after Cleon Jones singled, he struck out Donn Clendenon.

Out came Tom Seaver for his World Series debut. Jim Russo, the Orioles advance scout, had written a thorough report on the Mets, telling Orioles hitters that Seaver had superb control and usually got ahead in the count, so it would be best to come up ready to swing. The Orioles' leadoff hitter was Don Buford, their 5-foot, 7-inch left-fielder who, like Seaver, was a USC man. Buford took a fastball inside on Seaver's first pitch of the game. Seaver's next pitch was another fastball, this one over the plate, and Buford, a switch-hitter batting left, hit a long fly to right. Swoboda retreated tentatively, not quite getting back to the fence in time. He jumped, but his glove was not in the right spot. Buford's ball fell a few inches beyond the wall as Swoboda slumped to the warning track.

Two pitches into the game, the Orioles were on the board.

Seaver's day had been out of kilter from the start. He had gone down to get breakfast at the team hotel at 9:30 a.m. only to find the restaurant overcrowded and understaffed. He waited 15 or 20 minutes, never saw a waitperson, and gave up, getting on the team bus to head to the park. Equipment manager Nick Torman got him a roast beef sandwich for his pregame meal.

Seaver, in so many ways, was the polar opposite of Cuellar. He was young. He was right-handed. For all his extraordinary polish and poise at age 24, he was fundamentally a power pitcher, relying on two different fastballs—one rising, the other sinking, along with a hard slider and curveball. While Cuellar specialized in fooling hitters and fouling up their timing, Seaver, as often as not, got his results with exploding fastballs and plate-carving curveballs. He had won his last ten decisions of the year and thrown complete games in his final nine starts, three of them shutouts. He had gotten cuffed around a bit by the Braves in the NLCS, when he had trouble quieting his nerves, and though he said that wasn't a problem in the World Series, the start wasn't close to what he had envisioned. After Buford's homer, Seaver struck out Paul Blair and Frank Robinson with high, riding fastballs, but Powell pounded a fastball to right for a hard-hit single, and Brooks Robinson hit a long drive to center that Tommie Agee caught up to just a few feet from the center-field wall.

Even with his uneven first inning, Seaver's mechanics looked as flawless as ever in his road grays. He rested his glove in its usual spot, against his left thigh, as he looked in for Jerry Grote's sign and then stepped into his compact windup, his left leg powering up like a piston before he planted it and came forward, so low to the ground he'd often scrape his right knee into the dirt. He cruised through the next two innings and looked in complete control in the fourth, getting Powell on a checked-swing bouncer to short and Brooks Robinson on a pop to second. Seaver fell behind 3-0 to Elrod Hendricks, the Orioles' catcher, who singled sharply to right on a 3-1 pitch. He walked second baseman Dave Johnson, and then shortstop Mark Belanger punched an outside pitch for a single to right. Swoboda charged the ball hard but made an errant throw home, allowing Hendricks to score on the play. Seaver suddenly was laboring. In short order, Cuellar dunked a looper into short center for another run and Buford turned on another fastball, smoking it into the right-field corner to make it 4–0.

Five straight Orioles had reached base. One more hit would just about lock up game one for the Orioles. It was time for an intermission.

Clendenon came over from first to visit Seaver. Seaver took off his hat and wiped his forehead. He removed his glove, tucked it under his arm, and rubbed up the ball vigorously with both hands. Rube Walker came out, giving Ron Taylor, who had just gotten up, a little more warm-up time in the bull pen.

Seaver got out of it when Ed Charles made a nice play on an in-between hop to throw out Paul Blair, but he still seemed to be fighting himself. Though he retired two Robinsons and one Powell in the bottom of the fifth, all of them hit the ball hard. A week earlier, Seaver had been shagging fly balls in batting practice when he slightly strained a calf muscle. It was more of a low-grade tweak than anything, but it curtailed his running regimen for four days, and without his customary conditioning work, he could feel his legs—his power base—tiring.

"I had warmed up for eighteen minutes before the game, had really good stuff and threw well for three and two-thirds innings," Seaver said afterward. "But then I started to drop out of the strike zone."

Hodges decided it was time for a pitching change, and in the top of the sixth he lifted Seaver for a pinch hitter, Duffy Dyer. It was Seaver's shortest outing in more than two months. He was replaced by Don Cardwell, who at 33 years old was a veteran of 13 big-league seasons and the oldest pitcher on the Mets' staff.

A lifelong resident of North Carolina, the 6-foot, 4-inch, 220-pound Cardwell was a southerner to the core, a low-key, amiable fellow with a pronounced drawl who pitched for five National

League clubs and whose teammates, wherever he went, invariably called him "Big Man." Cardwell wasn't easily riled, but he was nobody to mess with. During the 1968 season, he had managed to get into two skirmishes in one three-day span. The first was with the Astros' Doug Rader after Rader had cleared both dugouts with a nasty slide into Kevin Collins, the Mets' rookie third baseman. The second was with teammate Ron Swoboda on a commercial team flight from Los Angeles. Swoboda was wearing a necklace of wooden love beads that had been given to him by some fans. Cardwell, a conservative man who didn't much care for antiwar protests or the peace-and-love set, wasn't a fan of love beads and said something. Swoboda said something back. Cardwell snatched the beads off of Swoboda's neck, and two of the biggest, strongest Mets had to be separated.

Cardwell had come to the Mets in the winter of 1966, along with center fielder Don Bosch, in exchange for Dennis Ribant and Gary Kolb. He pitched well for the club in 1967 and 1968 but had a record of 2-8 in late June of '69, with an earned run average of 3.23, which tells you that his biggest problem was lack of run support. Cardwell pitched superbly down the stretch, though, going 5-2 with a 2.18 ERA in the second half of the season. Hodges trusted him totally. In fact, he told Cardwell before the Series that although he was going to give Seaver, Koosman, and Gentry the first three starts, Cardwell would be used in long relief and would be starting game seven if necessary.

Cardwell took over in the bottom of the sixth. He was by far the most seasoned Mets pitcher but was scared in his World Series debut.

"I don't remember when I was more scared," Cardwell told *Newsday*'s Steve Jacobsen.

His warm-up pitches were all over the place. He threw a fastball to start off Hendricks, well off the plate and high. He missed almost as badly with another fastball. He was all keyed up and having a very hard time getting unkeyed.

Cardwell stood in the center of Memorial Stadium and pawed

at the rubber a few times. He had a talk with himself. He reminded himself he'd been pitching all his life, and that he knew what to do and how to do it, and needed to get out of his own way. This was no time to be messing up. That was for sure. He just needed to trust himself, the process of winding up and throwing the ball for a strike. How many times had he done that in his life? Thousands?

He got the 2-0 pitch over the plate and Hendricks hit a harmless bouncer to Clendenon at first. Johnson grounded to third on the next pitch, and then Belanger fouled out.

Cardwell's self-talk had done just what he'd hoped it would do.

Cuellar had an unusual custom on the mound, stooping toward home plate before delivering a pitch, bending at the waist, looking as if he were almost bowing. His deliveries in the seventh inning abruptly began missing their target. Clendenon whacked a 2-2 curveball for a single to center. Swoboda got ahead 3-0 and walked on a fastball that was high and outside. With one out, Grote took two high fastballs to get ahead 2-0, then spanked a single to left, Clendenon stopping at third.

The Mets had the bases loaded and the tying run at the plate. Next up was Weis. He reminded himself not to chase the screwball. He wasn't looking to tie the game up with one swing; he just wanted to have a good at bat and make solid contact. Weis worked the count full. Cuellar came with the payoff pitch, and Weis ripped it on a line to left. Don Buford tracked it well and caught the ball with a little leap. Clendenon, waiting on the catch, tagged up and scored. Had the ball been a foot higher, it would've gone to the wall. Weis and the Mets had to settle for a sacrifice fly. It was the first run Orioles pitchers had allowed in World Series play in 39 innings, dating back to game one in 1966.

With men on first and second, Hodges elected to have Rod Gaspar, the rookie outfielder who hadn't even been expected to make the club, pinch-hit for Cardwell. Gaspar had unwittingly been in the headlines before the Series began, after he had predicted that the Mets would beat the Orioles in four straight. When Frank Robinson heard the boast, he said, "Who the hell is Ron Gaspar?"

Blair corrected his teammate. "It's not Ron. It's Rod, stupid."

To which Robinson replied, "Who the hell is Rod Stupid?"

A switch-hitter, Gaspar settled into the right-handed batters' box, trying to calm himself down. Before the first pitch, Hendricks asked, "You nervous, Rod?"

Gaspar said, no, he wasn't nervous.

"Then how come your knees are shaking?"

Ahead 1-2, Cuellar threw his screwball on the outer half. Gaspar, with his open stance and hands held low and close to his body, topped the ball toward third. Gaspar had good speed. It looked as if it would be a certain infield hit, loading the bases for Agee. Gaspar stumbled getting out of the box. Robinson and his famous glove—a Rawlings XPG-3H model with an Edge-u-cated heel—charged the ball hard, but there was no time for leather now, Robinson scooping the ball up bare-handed, making sure his left foot was forward. It was one of his trade secrets for fielding a swinging bunt; by having your left forward, you could get much more on the throw. He always tried to make the throw across the seams, and with an overhand motion if time allowed.

Robinson's throw was straight and strong. It beat Gaspar easily.

This exact play had become Robinson's signature, just one reason why he would win a Gold Glove 17 years in a row. Robinson ran off the field to the Orioles' dugout, where he got backslaps all around. Cuellar and the Orioles had seen him make the play dozens of times but never appreciated it more than they did now.

. . .

THE GAME WENT to the ninth, the Mets' last shot at Cuellar. Swoboda hit an infield single, and Weis drew a four-pitch walk. With two outs, the tying run was at the plate in the person of pinch hitter Art Shamsky.

Lean and long-limbed, Shamsky had the club's best mutton-chop sideburns and its most potent power bat. He didn't have the muscular physique of most long-ball hitters, but he had once hit four home runs in four at bats over two games for the Cincinnati

Reds, and hit 14 homers in 1969 in part-time duty. He was also the Mets' hottest hitter after mashing the ball for three straight games against the Braves. Orioles pitching coach George Bamberger went out to talk to Cuellar and Hendricks. Eddie Watt and Pete Richert were warm and ready to go to in the Orioles' bull pen. Cuellar told Bamberger he had plenty left to get Shamsky, and whether it was true, the pitcher convinced him. Bamberger returned to the dugout. Weaver stuck with Cuellar. He had thrown 290⅔ innings for the year and 18 complete games, both team highs. Cuellar liked to finish what he started, and he was going to get the chance to.

Shamsky grabbed both ends of the bat, lifted it overhead, and brought it down behind his neck, toward his shoulders, stretching his upper body. He did it twice. He took one full practice swing and was ready for business. He was a pull hitter, and you knew he would be looking to turn on a ball. With the Memorial Stadium wall only 309 feet away down the line, he had an inviting target. In center field, Paul Blair moved over into right-center.

Cuellar started Shamsky off with a curveball away that had him way in front. On the 0-1 pitch, Cuellar stayed away again. Shamsky tried to pull it. He made decent contact, but his two-hopper went straight to second baseman Dave Johnson, who threw to Powell to end the rally, and game one.

The final score was 4-1. The Orioles were pleased not only with the outcome but with the knowledge that they had beaten the best pitcher in baseball on a day when the middle of their order—the Robinsons and Powell—had managed only 1 hit in 12 at bats. They had done it, too, with Frank Robinson seriously depleted, having lost six pounds in the previous 24 hours, courtesy of a nasty virus. Robinson didn't seem to have his customary quickness with the bat, but his powers of observation were unaffected. He told reporters after the game he thought the Mets looked "lifeless" in the dugout, even during the seventh-inning rally. "Their bench never made a sound. They just sat there showing no emotion," he said.

The Orioles, by contrast, were showing plenty. Buford, the hitting star with a homer and double, had planted the proverbial stake in the ground by knocking Tom Seaver's second pitch over the right-field wall. "When Buford hit that home run, I'm sure a lot of guys were thinking 'Shit, this is over,'" Powell said.

Like a boxer who gets knocked down in the opening round of a fight, the Mets' only option was to get back on their feet. They'd demonstrated deep resilience all season. Hodges wasn't discouraged. "We'll bounce back. If it's the fourth loss of the Series, then it would be a little discouraging," he said.

On his way off the field, Ed Charles had a chance encounter with Bamberger, his former minor-league teammate in 1961 with the Vancouver Mounties of the Pacific Coast League.

"George, you better enjoy this one, because this is the last game y'all are going to win," Charles said.

9

FARM FRESH

World Series Game Two
Baltimore, Maryland

JERRY KOOSMAN KNEW ONLY ONE WAY TO PITCH: YOU GET THE BALL, and you throw the ball. There was no reason to dawdle, go for long walks, or overthink things. He hadn't done it when he was pitching in the beer leagues in his native Minnesota. He hadn't done it during his spectacular rookie year in the big leagues in 1968, when he won a then Mets-record 19 games, pitched to a Mets-record 2.08 earned run average, and threw seven shutouts, the most by a rookie in 55 years.

He hadn't done it in the 1969 regular season or in the debacle of a start against the Atlanta Braves in the NLCS.

Nothing was going to change because it was World Series time.

"I just have never found nothing to do between pitches," he said. "I never threw a spitter, so I never had to figure out how to get my hand wet."

When the Mets sought comfort after the Orioles had beaten Seaver in game one, they knew exactly where to look: Koosman was pitching game two. This was no slight to Seaver, the staff's undeniable ace, nor to Dave McNally, the Orioles' game two starter, who won 20 games during the regular year, including his first 15 decisions. It was just that they knew all about Koosman's makeup and his competitiveness. He had proven it all season, never more than in the first game against the Cubs in September at Shea.

"To me Koosman was our toughest pitcher," Ed Kranepool said. "You wanted him out there when everything was on the line. He didn't get the credit he deserved because he was outshined by Tom Seaver, but he was a great pitcher. I wanted Koosman on the mound if it was a tough game or a knockdown situation. He would protect guys at all costs. Some pitchers would just throw over somebody's head. He would throw right at a guy."

• • •

GAME TWO FEATURED an unusual pairing of World Series starters, two young left-handers from the northern plains. Dave McNally was from Billings, Montana, Koosman from a speck of a farming community outside Appleton, Minnesota, just south of Artichoke Lake. Though he was only 26, McNally had already proven his postseason mettle, shutting out the Dodgers in the Series clincher in 1966, throwing a four-hitter to beat Don Drysdale, and pitching an 11-inning shutout against the Twins in the ALCS. A skillful, crafty left-hander, McNally threw a big, looping curveball and was as good as any pitcher in the game at hiding the ball from the hitter's view, keeping it tucked in his glove until the last moments of his no-windup delivery. He spun off one of those looping breaking pitches to begin against Agee, a tantalizing start to a 1-2-3 inning.

Koosman took the mound and immediately went to work on the dirt in front of the rubber, scuffing at it with his shoe over and over until he had just the ditch he wanted. He completed his warm-ups, and when the Mets finished throwing the ball around the infield, Ed Charles stood next to the mound and plunked it in Koosman's glove. Nervous energy and excitement coursed through Koosman's strong, farm-built body; that was normal before a start, but the stakes ratcheted it up to a level he'd never experienced.

"You try to control your emotions as best you can, so you can just go out there and do your best," he said. "That was always my goal. I feared losing. I never wanted to embarrass myself. It's hard to explain, but the fear of losing and not doing my best is always what bothered me the most, so I never wanted to let that happen. And of course the fear of losing a World Series game was that much worse, because there was so much more tension."

Nobody needed to remind Koosman how the Orioles' leadoff man, the switch-hitting Buford, had greeted Seaver a day earlier. Koosman had never faced Buford. He had never faced anyone in the lineup.

He busted Buford with a fastball on the hands on his first delivery. After missing with a couple of curveballs, he struck him out with another inside fastball. Koosman fooled Blair with a slow breaking ball, inducing a grounder to Charles. Up stepped Frank Robinson, and Koosman challenged him with a fastball away. Feeling more himself with the virus behind him, Robinson drove the ball deep to right-center. Off the bat, it looked as if the Orioles were going to grab a lead with a first-inning home run for the second game in a row.

Ron Swoboda raced back to the wall. He raised his glove directly in front of the 390 mark.

He caught the ball with his back pressed against the fence.

Koosman got more help from his fielders in the third, when Buford smoked a low liner between short and third that the diving Bud Harrelson snared just inches from the ground to close out the inning.

Koosman was working at a typically brisk pace and was in a much better rhythm than McNally, who threw six straight balls in the third inning and missed badly with an outside curveball to start off Donn Clendenon in the fourth. McNally came inside with a fastball to even the count and went with another fastball on the 1-1 pitch. Clendenon swung and launched a drive to right. The instant Clendenon made contact, McNally's head dropped. He knew. Pitchers always do. Frank Robinson raced back, but the retreat did nothing but give him a good view of the ball going over the wall.

The Mets had their first lead of the Series, and a surprising number of fans in Memorial Stadium were making noise about it; Mets fans clearly did not mind commuting for a World Series game. Koosman was the first to greet Clendenon in the dugout.

McNally recovered nicely, retiring the Mets in order, but Koosman was emerging as the story of game two. He set the Orioles down in order in the fourth and got the first two outs in the fifth, bringing up Andy Etchebarren, the Orioles' catcher. Though Etchebarren batted from the right side, the Mets' scouting report, prepared by Bob Scheffing and Warren "Sheriff" Robinson, called for defending him as if he were a left-handed pull hitter. So Agee shifted toward right-center and Swoboda edged over to the line. The report was right on: Etchebarren took an inside-out swing and drove a fastball to deep right. Swoboda, perfectly positioned, backed up near the fence and made the catch.

Through five innings, sixteen Orioles had come up. Fifteen of them had been retired. Koosman had thrown only 49 pitches. He had allowed no hits. After closing out the fifth, he walked off with his head down and paid no attention to the hijinks of 12-year-old Linda Warehime, baseball's first female ballperson and base cleaner. Warehime landed the gig with the help of her three brothers on the Orioles' grounds crew. After the bottom of the fifth, she made her way around the bases with her broom, cleaning them off, brushing off the shoes of the Orioles infielders for no extra charge, being careful as she went.

"It was the World Series. What if I went out there and tripped on a base or something?" she said. On her way back to her post along the third-base line, she stopped and gave the Mets' third-base coach, Eddie Yost, a peck on the cheek.

The bases had been freshened, and Koosman intended to keep them that way. The crowd grew restless, waiting for the Orioles to do something—anything—against Koosman. It was getting late early in Baltimore, as Yogi Berra once said.

Koosman started the sixth by retiring Mark Belanger on a fly to right. McNally hit a comebacker, and Buford bounced to short. The Orioles hadn't had a base runner since Dave Johnson's walk in the second inning. They had nine outs left.

• • •

A sight to warm the hearts of Met fans everywhere—Tom Seaver on the hill.
(Getty Images/Focus on Sport)

Casey Stengel and Gil Hodges—current and future Mets managers—talk shop on the first day of spring training in 1962.
(Getty Images/ Bettmann)

Al Weis, the Mets' Mighty Mite, hit the game-tying home run in game five and showed plenty of guts hanging in at second with the Orioles' Elrod Hendricks trying to take him out.

(Getty Images/Focus on Sport)

Donn Clendenon's opposite-field blast off Dave McNally in game two gave the Mets their first lead of the series.

(Getty Images/New York Daily News Archives)

(*Left to right*) Ken Boswell, Tommie Agee, Nolan Ryan, and Wayne Garrett show who's number one in the National League after the Mets finished off their three-game sweep of the Braves in the NLCS.
(*Getty Images/Bettmann*)

New York Mayor John Lindsay, a clubhouse regular late in the 1969 season, received a Champagne shampoo from Jerry Grote (*left*) and Rod Gaspar (*right*) after the NLCS. The Mets helped him get reelected.
(*Getty Images/New York* Daily News *Archives*)

Gary Gentry *(left)* shut out the Cardinals at Shea, 6–0, to clinch
the NL East on September 24, 1969, and manager Gil Hodges
(right) thinks it was a job well done.
*(Getty Images/*New York Post *Archives)*

Reliever Ron Taylor *(left)* loved throwing to catcher Jerry Grote *(right)* and
enjoying pregame laughs with him, too.
(Getty Images/Focus on Sport)

Ron Swoboda's sprawling grab of Brooks Robinson's liner in the ninth inning saved game four for the Mets. Mickey Mantle said it was the greatest catch he'd ever seen. *(Getty Images/New York* Daily News *Archives)*

Jerry Koosman *(right)* looked thirsty after shutting down the Reds at Shea in late July, so his pal Ed Charles *(left)* offered him a beverage. *(Getty Images/New York* Daily News *Archives)*

J. C. Martin *(left)*, had a huge pinch-hit in game one of the NLCS and had a chance to discuss it with Casey Stengel *(right)*, who was covering the playoffs for the New York *Daily News*. *(Getty Images/Bettmann)*

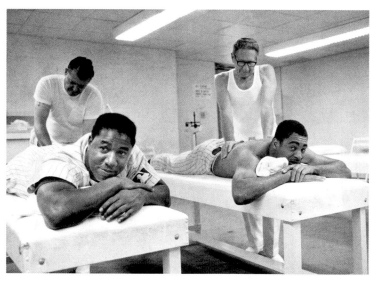

The Mets' men from Mobile, Cleon Jones *(left)* and Tommie Agee *(right)*, were never far apart, even in the training room. The rubdowns were administered by trainers Joe Deer *(left)* and Gus Mauch *(right)*.
(Getty Images/New York Daily News *Archives)*

This Spalding glove—a Johnny Callison model worn by Tommie Agee—cost the Orioles at least five runs in game three of the 1969 World Series.
(Photo courtesy of John Horne/Baseball Hall of Fame)

Karl Ehrhardt, the famed Sign Man of Shea, weighed in after Ed Kranepool homered in the eighth inning of game three of the World Series.
(AP Photo)

Orioles manager Earl Weaver (4) gave umpire Shag Crawford a mouthful in the third inning of game four and got ejected for his trouble. Frank Robinson and Jerry Grote listened in as Weaver became the first manager to get tossed from a World Series game in more than 30 years. *(Getty Images/New York* Daily News *Archives)*

After vanquishing the Orioles in five games, the Mets had a much wilder assignment: surviving their euphoric fans. *(Photo courtesy of John Horne/Baseball Hall of Fame)*

THAT JERRY KOOSMAN was in such a position, or in the big leagues at all, had as much to do with a serendipitous connection as his powerful left arm. He never played Little League or high school or college ball. He never even played in an organized game until he was a teenager. He was raised on a 320-acre farm with hogs and feed cattle and chickens, doing lots of chores and lots of throwing, just not baseballs. Instead he threw everything else. Corn cobs. Snowballs. Rocks on the lake, to see how many skips he could get, and not the flat ones, because anybody could skip those. Koosman would pick up stones and see if he could hit the sparrows on the roof of the barn, lined up as if for roll call.

"He got so that he would hit them almost every time," said his big brother, Orville.

Jerry would've played high school ball had it been an option, but there was no team at the school he attended, West Central School of Agriculture, a boarding school in Morris, Minnesota, primarily for farm kids. The school year went from early October to late March, allowing youngsters to work on family farms in the early fall and spring. Since there was no baseball season, Koosman gave football a try. He liked playing quarterback, but the coach said he didn't know the plays so he had to play tackle.

"We didn't have face masks. I was 180 pounds going against guys who were 220 pounds. I got a bloody nose every day," Koosman said.

His football career lasted one year. He wrestled and swam, and then Orville had a better idea.

Eight years Jerry's senior, Orville Koosman was a good baseball player and an equally good recruiter. Jerry was almost 14, a strong, athletic kid. Orville saw his potential and convinced Jerry to play on Orville's local semipro team in nearby Fairfield, Minnesota. Orville, also a left-handed pitcher, put Jerry in the outfield. One day when Orville didn't have it on the mound, he called for another pitcher and moved himself to center field. Jerry was in left. A batter hit a line drive into the left-center-field gap. Jerry raced to his left and called for it. Orville raced to his right and called for it.

Unfamiliar with baseball protocol, Jerry didn't know to defer to the center fielder. He just knew that Orville probably wasn't going to get there in time to make the play. He went down to one knee and made the catch, and the next instant Orville slammed into him, a collision that shattered Orville's leg, an injury so serious he would spend the next 28 days in the hospital.

"Now we had an open spot in the rotation," Jerry said. "That's how I got to be a pitcher. I broke my brother's leg."

For six months, Jerry went to Orville's farm morning and night to do Orville's chores. In the winter, when Orville's leg finally healed, the brothers would go up into the hayloft of the barn to throw. For a long time, Jerry had caught for Orville. Now the roles were reversed. Jerry became an American Legion star and the Sandy Koufax of the central Minnesota beer leagues, his compensation coming in the form of mileage reimbursement and occasional postgame beverages. He pitched in towns called Holloway, Fergus Falls, and Norcross, where he once struck out the first 21 batters he faced. A bird dog scout at the game was duly impressed, and after Koosman finished the seventh inning, the scout told him that as hard as he threw, he could throw even harder and be more effective if he altered his mechanics a bit.

"Thanks. I'll give it a try," Koosman said.

Returning to the mound for the eighth, he hit the first batter he faced, then walked a guy. An error followed, and two runs scored. Koosman abandoned the scout's advice and went back to his own approach for the last two batters, striking out both of them to finish with 23 for the game.

"I think I would've had twenty-seven if I hadn't listened to the guy," he said.

After studying engineering in college for a year, Koosman was about to be drafted and opted to enlist instead, thinking that he could fulfill his commitment and get his education paid for at the same time. He did his basic training at Fort Leonard Wood in Missouri, passed the test for Officer Candidate School, and was assigned to a missile base in Grafton, Illinois. By now he knew he really wanted to play baseball, and with the help of a National Guard connection in Minnesota, he was able to get transferred to Fort Bliss in El Paso, Texas, home of the 1st Armored Division as well as a strong baseball team. The day Koosman reported, his captain, the company commander, did not send out a Welcome Wagon.

"He chewed my ass for not going through the chain of command, and then he pointed to a big pile of paperwork," Koosman said.

"Do you know how much it costs the government to fill out all this?"

"No, sir, I don't," Koosman said.

"It costs forty dollars," the captain said, and then told him to report to the baseball field at 1300 hours. Koosman reported and met Pete Peters, the manager.

"What are you doing here?" Peters asked.

"I'm here to try out for the baseball team."

"What position do you play?"

"I'm a left-handed pitcher."

"Okay, let's see what you've got," Peters said.

The manager fetched a catcher's mitt. After a few very uncomfortable minutes he told Koosman to stop and found someone to put on a full set of equipment and catch him. When Koosman's audition was done, Peters said, "You're starting our next game."

Said Koosman, "I've been a pitcher ever since."

Koosman's batterymate on the Fort Bliss team was a New York kid named John Lucchese, a prospect himself who was being scouted by the Boston Red Sox. When Lucchese saw what Koosman had, he called his father, who was a Shea Stadium usher.

"We have a pitcher down here the Mets should check out," Lucchese told his father. The elder Lucchese relayed the tip to Joe McDonald, the Mets' scouting director. McDonald got tips all the time from mothers and fathers, aunts and uncles, coaches and neighbors.

"You check everyone out, because you never know," McDonald said.

McDonald mailed an assignment memo—long-distance calls cost too much—to Red Murff, the Mets' Texas-based scout. Murff scouted Koosman for a few games and liked what he saw. Murff offered Koosman $1,600 to sign with the Mets. Koosman talked to his father and decided to turn down the offer. The Twins were scouting Koosman as well and had offered $10,000. The Twins were his home-state team, and the money was enticing, but Koosman still passed; the Twins were a strong club, and he figured it would be much harder to get to the big leagues with them.

Murff circled back to Koosman. This time he offered $1,500.

Koosman declined.

Murff again told Koosman how much the Mets wanted him. Now the offer was $1,400.

So it went until Murff's offer dropped to $1,200.

"I figured I better sign before I owed them money," Koosman said.

. . .

THE ONLY NO-HITTER in postseason baseball history was the Yankee Don Larsen's perfect game against the Dodgers in the 1956 World Series. Koosman fantasized before the game about outdoing Larsen by pitching a perfect game and getting hits in every at bat. As he came out for his seventh inning of work, he didn't have any hits and had allowed one man to reach base on a walk, so he recalibrated his goals. He turned his attention to retiring the next hitter, Paul Blair.

Blair had had a breakout year in 1969, hitting .285 with a career-high 26 home runs and making his first All-Star team. Koosman had handled him easily in his two at bats. He started Blair off with a fastball on the inside corner. Blair swung and missed. Jerry Grote called for another fastball, but for one of the few times all game, Koosman shook Grote off. Koosman had twice popped up Blair with curveballs. He wanted to attack him the same way again—set him up for another fastball with a curve that wasn't in a spot he could hit.

Ray Miller, one of baseball's most respected pitching coaches, once described pitching as "the art of missing bats." You do it with deception, with delivering the unexpected. You change speeds.

Change locations. Change patterns from one at bat to the next. Koosman's instincts told him that this would be his best shot at retiring Blair for a third time. He curled his index and middle fingers around the seams of the ball, his curveball grip. He rocked back slightly, brought his hands up just over his head, and kicked his right leg up above his waist, an easy, fluid motion that belied his power. When he was younger, Koosman had had a Juan Marichal–type leg kick, almost over his head. During his Fort Bliss days, he had met Syd Cohen, a former big-league pitcher who managed the El Paso Sun Kings, a double-A team in the Texas League. Cohen had the distinction of giving up Babe Ruth's final home run (number 708) as a New York Yankee. His coach on the Sun Kings was his brother, Andy, another former big-leaguer. Both Cohens had urged Koosman to lose the big kick and make his motion more compact, convincing him that it would make him a better, more consistent pitcher. Koosman agreed to give it a try. He was easy to pick out in the Fort Bliss barracks.

"I'd stand in front of the mirror and do windups about a thousand times a day," he said.

Minus the Marichal-esque kick, Koosman spun the ball toward the plate. It came in higher than he wanted.

It had more of the plate than he wanted, too.

Blair jumped on it, smacking a clean single between third and short.

The Memorial Stadium crowd stood and cheered. Finally there was something to get excited about. Blair stood on first, representing the tying run.

Koosman got the ball back and showed no more emotion than a Buckingham Palace guard. Ed Charles came to the mound for a visit, a check-in to make sure Koosman was okay. Koosman and Charles were good buddies. When the Mets had a doubleheader, Koosman used to tease Charles, telling him he'd get to sit out two games today, not just one. The Mets called Charles "The Glider," and Koosman was fond of saying, "Never throw a slider to The Glider."

But Koosman didn't want to talk to The Glider or anybody else right now. He got back onto the rubber, in the stretch position. He was hugely disappointed, but in a one-run game you can't allow emotions to creep in and screw things up. This was only the most important game of the 167 games the Mets had played in 1969. And the heart of the Orioles' order was coming up. The next batter was Frank Robinson.

Koosman pawed at the dirt in front of the rubber and looked in for the sign. He started Robinson with a fastball that the two-time MVP fouled off. Robinson checked his swing on a curveball, and then Koosman missed outside with another curve, falling behind 2-1. Koosman came back with a low fastball. Robinson went down to get it but flied out to Agee in center.

Dropping down a bit against the left-handed Boog Powell, Koosman went with inside heat, but Powell was ready. He ripped a line drive down the right-field line that hooked foul. After fooling Powell with a couple of off-speed pitches, Koosman came back with a fastball and got him on a pop to short.

Powell hoisted his bat up and looked ready to slam it to the ground. He lumbered back to the dugout.

Koosman needed just one more out to get out of the seventh inning with his one-run lead intact. Brooks Robinson took a sweeping curveball on the outside corner for strike one. Blair edged off first, getting more aggressive with his lead. Koosman threw over to chase him back, then came back at Robinson with a high fastball. Blair took off for second, getting a good jump. Grote's throw was strong and right on the bag, but Blair slid in under Al Weis's tag.

Blair dusted himself off, the tying run now in scoring position. Koosman got Grote's sign and delivered a fastball, and Brooks Robinson grounded a ball up the middle. Harrelson raced to his left but had no chance. The ball rolled into center field, Blair wheeling around third and racing home, pounding his left foot onto the plate, as if the run would count twice if he hit home plate hard enough.

In a matter of minutes, Koosman had lost his no-hitter, his shutout, and his lead. And he wasn't out of it yet.

The next hitter was Dave Johnson. Koosman got him to chase a curveball outside for strike one. After missing with a curve, Koosman came inside with a fastball. Johnson roped a hard shot between third and short.

Ed Charles lunged to his left, getting his glove down, but the ball was right on him and seemed sure to be headed into left field. He stretched his left arm and somehow speared the ball a millisecond before it went by him. Charles quickly stood up and fired to Weis across his body, hoping to get the force at second.

With Brooks Robinson barreling toward him, Weis would've been forgiven for having flashbacks of another Robinson—Frank—charging toward him. Weis was one of the Mets' bantamweights, but his teammates will tell you he was a total gamer, 160 pounds of pure guts. He held the base, took Charles's throw, and got the force play.

It was the Mets' best defensive play of the first two games. Charles couldn't have channeled his inner Brooks Robinson at a better time.

10

SUNDAY SCOOP

World Series Game Two
Top of the eighth

	1	2	3	4	5	6	7	8	9	Runs
Mets	0	0	0	1	0	0	0	-	-	1
Orioles	0	0	0	0	0	0	1	-	-	1

LOST IN JERRY KOOSMAN'S NO-HIT QUEST WAS THE BRILLIANCE OF Dave McNally, who had limited the Mets to three hits as he faced the top of the order in the eighth. McNally fell behind Tommie Agee 2-0, before Agee rapped a hard grounder to Mark Belanger at short for the first out. Bud Harrelson hadn't had a good swing against McNally all day, and that wasn't entirely surprising; during the season, the switch-hitting Harrelson hit .268 against right-handed pitchers and only .186 against left-handers. After missing inside with a sweeping curveball, McNally stayed inside and got Harrelson to hit a bouncer to Brooks Robinson for the second out.

Cleon Jones came up, trying to get something going. A natural left-handed hitter, Jones learned to hit right-handed as a kid in Africatown. He and his friends played ball wherever they could, in vacant lots or on the street. Their main location for street games was Best Street, where left field went on and on but right field had little houses and a trash-filled lot not too far beyond first base. Almost every time the left-handed Cleon came up, his shots would break a window or disappear into the trash heap, never to be found again. Baseballs were a precious commodity for kids in Africatown, and you couldn't be wasting any by hitting them in places where you couldn't get them back. So Cleon taught himself to switch-hit. If

Mickey Mantle—Triple Crown winner in 1956 and Cleon's favorite ballplayer—could do it, why couldn't he? The transition went so well that by the time he got to junior high school, Jones decided to bat right-handed all the time.

Jones was the only Met who took two of his own bats into the on-deck circle. He liked swinging both of them. Most guys used a weighted bat, but Jones wanted his hands on the weapon he would be taking to the plate. He was much more of a line-drive hitter than a true power hitter, but if ever there were a time to think about knocking one out of the park, this was it. He grabbed a fistful of dirt at the plate, took a couple of practice swings, and got into the box. Jones had one of those batting stances that told you he was a hitter even before he swung. He was perfectly balanced, neither open nor closed. He had a slight crouch, but not too much. He held the bat high, but not too high. You looked at him, and you saw a hitter ready to do some damage, with the strength and hand-eye coordination to drive the ball wherever he wanted to.

McNally threw a sharp curve to get ahead 0-1, missed with his next two pitches, and then had Jones way out in front of a changeup for 2-2. Jones drove an inside fastball hard down the third-base line, just foul, then barely got a piece of a curve. McNally was showing him everything he had, in all locations, and came with a fastball away. Jones hit it squarely toward Frank Robinson in right. Robinson had slammed a foul ball off his instep in batting practice and was moving gingerly, but he ranged back and made the play.

Koosman came back out for the eighth. Andy Etchebarren, a two-time All-Star, led off. Known for his defensive prowess and his handling of pitchers, Etchebarren had one of the hardest-hit balls of the day off Koosman in his previous at bat. He jumped on another outside fastball but lined it right to Al Weis at second base. Koosman had worked over Belanger, the number eight hitter, with his big curveball all day. It was a weapon that was getting more and more effective for Koosman and one he could thank his manager for. During Koosman's rookie season, Hodges had called him into his office to meet two special guests. One of them was Chuck Connors, who had briefly been Hodges's Dodgers teammate before going on to much greater acclaim as the star of the hit television show *The Rifleman.*

The other guest was Sandy Koufax.

"Maybe you can show him how you throw your curveball," Hodges said to Koufax.

Koufax grabbed a baseball, and he and Koosman had an impromptu curveball clinic right in Hodges's Shea Stadium office. Koufax's long fingers enabled him to spin off one of the great curveballs the game has ever seen. Koosman was a willing pupil. Koufax showed him where to put his fingers on the seams and how to get maximum rotation upon release. Koosman's curveball wasn't Koufax's, but it was a reasonable facsimile.

Koosman dropped one big-breaking curve on the outside corner against Belanger and then another. Quickly, the count was 0-2. Belanger, choking up maybe five inches on the bat, more than any player on either team, took three quick practice swings and assumed his straight-up stance, a stick figure with eye black. Koosman fired again, a fastball on the outside corner. Belanger didn't budge. Umpire Frank Secory rang him up.

It may have been Koosman's best sequence of the game.

Orioles manager Earl Weaver had his 6-foot, 6-inch reliever Dick Hall, a former position player and economics major at Swarthmore College, warming in the pen but decided to let McNally hit for himself. McNally didn't hit for average, but he was no joke at the plate and would finish his career with nine home runs. He took an earnest cut at a Koosman fastball, driving it to the warning track before Jones made the catch.

The game went to the ninth, the starters still in, the score still tied at one. The first Mets batter was Clendenon. McNally attacked him with fastballs up and away and struck him out. Swoboda bounced out on a nice play by Powell, who ranged well to his right and threw to McNally covering.

The oldest Met, Ed Charles, stepped in. Charles had already made an immense contribution with his glove in the seventh. He

prided himself on never letting the moment, or his emotions, over-
whelm him. Though he hit only .207 as a part-time player in 1969,
Charles hit .375 with runners in scoring position that season. He
embraced pressure, wanted the pressure.

"That's what turned me on—coming through in the clutch," he
said. "Some people can deliver. Some people can't. It's part of what's
inside a person."

• • •

WHEN YOU WAIT as long as Charles did to get a chance to play in the
big leagues, you don't want to squander even a moment of it. Ed
Charles started writing his life story late in his career and worked
on it right through the 1969 season. He began the book with a verse
of his poetry:

> *What is it that makes a man*
> *What is that makes him stand?*
> *What is it that makes him rise?*
> *When he is persecuted, when he is despised?*

Charles grew up in an impoverished, violent world in a shabby
little house, one of nine kids on the wrong side of the tracks in Daytona Beach, Florida, a quarter century before the Daytona 500 made
the town a destination in the stock car world. He recited the Pledge of
Allegiance in school each day, read the Constitution, and wondered
how the high-minded principles of those documents—the more perfect union, the liberty and justice for all—allowed for WHITES ONLY
signs, lynching parties, and the shackles of segregation.

He never got the answer to that question—or many others.

"You read everything that is being taught, and you can't understand why you can't go here and you can't go there," he said. "Why
is that off-limits to me? You are not a human being. It eats at you. A
lot of people couldn't take it, and then they do something and wind
up dead."

One Sunday, Charles and his brothers and sisters came home

from church to find a toy missing from their front porch. Turned out it had been stolen by some white kids on the other side of the tracks. Charles and his brothers went to get it back, and a big fight broke out. One of the white youngsters said he was going to get a shotgun. It was the Agee family plantation story, recast on the Florida coast. The Charles kids took off for home with the white kids and their father in hot pursuit. Charles's grandfather had to beg the white kids' father for forgiveness. Then he gave Ed and his brothers a terrific beating with a stick.

"Don't you know they could've lynched you for that?" he hollered.

Abuse was a regular occurrence in the Charles home. His father beat his mother and wound up going to jail for trying to stab her. When Ed tried to intervene, his father beat him, too. One time his father pistol-whipped him in the head. Sick of living this way, Charles, then in seventh grade, reached out to a friend and asked if his family would take him in. The friend lived eight blocks away. He said yes, you can move in with us. Soon after Ed moved out, his father spotted him walking down the street, pulled over in his car, and hauled his son in. He took him to the local jailhouse.

"He told the desk sergeant I had run away from home and he wanted to send me to reform school," Charles said.

The sergeant took down all the information and put Ed into a cell. His father left. One cell over was a black woman who had arrived a short time before. Charles couldn't see anything, but he heard it all, the guards demanding sexual favors and the woman refusing. Then he heard the sounds of them beating her and her crying and begging them to stop, until she complied with their wishes.

After two nights, Charles was taken to the county jail in Deland. His mother came and got him released.

For Ed Charles, there was but one positive aspect about Daytona: across the street from his house was City Island Ball Park, the winter home of the Montreal Royals. In 1946, the Royals had a rookie named Jackie Robinson. The team had started spring training in Sanford, Florida, but when the local authorities padlocked the field and refused to allow a black man to play baseball with white men, it relocated to Daytona. Charles would watch Robinson and the Royals practice. He would sit on the left-field fence and watch them play spring training games.

Charles was a good young ballplayer, and Robinson instantly became his idol, but he never chased him for an autograph. It would've been like asking God for an autograph. His friends would swarm Robinson after games, and Charles would be with them but always on the periphery. He would just stare at Robinson in awe. "I couldn't even get a word out," Charles said. It was almost too much to comprehend. He was watching a man who had the same color skin as he did playing pro baseball before a crowd that included black and white baseball fans, not segregated by sections. He studied Robinson's every move. At night he prayed that Jackie Robinson would succeed, that he would show white people that black people were capable of excellence, too.

"You could see what you hoped for right before your eyes," Charles said.

Robinson and the Royals headed north to Montreal. Charles's mother and sisters fled to St. Petersburg to escape his father. Ed was left alone in the house across from the ballpark. His grandfather was a block away, but that was small comfort.

"It was miserable," he said.

He dropped out of school and moved to Miami to live with an older brother. His brother told him if he didn't go back to school he'd have to get a job, but before he could do that, they lost the apartment. Now Charles had a new problem: he was homeless. He broke into a car and slept in the backseat for a night. The next night he slept in a movie theater until he got chased out. The night after that, he collected a bunch of newspapers, laid them out by the railroad tracks, and slept there until it started to rain. He got cold, so he sought shelter in a building that was under construction.

"The next thing I know, there is a flashlight in my eyes and voices tell me to get up," Charles remembered.

It was the Miami police. They took him to the local precinct and then to the city jail. Eventually he was brought before a judge, who told him he better go find his mother or he would get into a whole lot more trouble. And so 14-year-old Ed Charles reconnected with his mother and made his way to St. Petersburg. He got a job as a dishwasher at a place called Orange Blossom Cafeteria. He met a girl with whom he was completely smitten, but she told him she didn't have any interest in dating a dropout.

Charles quit washing dishes and enrolled in Gibbs High School, where he became not only a baseball star but the quarterback of a state championship football team and got another glimpse of his hero, now a Brooklyn Dodger. Before heading north at the end of spring training, the Dodgers stopped in St. Petersburg to play a game against the Yankees. After the game Charles and his friends chased the Dodgers' bus to the train station. They ran along the platform until they found the car where Jackie Robinson was sitting, playing cards with his teammates. Charles and the other kids waved at Robinson, and he waved back. Then the train started to pull out. The kids ran alongside. The train started going faster. Charles kept waving and running, waving and running, wishing he could somehow express to Jackie Robinson how much he meant to him.

"We ran as long as we could, until the train was out of sight," Charles said.

Charles graduated from Gibbs High School and played semipro ball, drawing some attention from scouts. The Indianapolis Clowns of the Negro American League offered him $250 a month, but his mother wouldn't let him go. A chance meeting with an executive of the Boston Braves resulted in a tryout in Myrtle Beach, South Carolina. After an impressive showing, Charles was assigned to the Quebec City Braves, in the Class C Provincial League, which had a history of welcoming black athletes.

The year was 1952. Charles was 19 years old and went to Canada without even a sweater, never mind an overcoat. He lived with Canadian schoolteachers and finished the year hitting .317 with 11 triples, a star by any measure. He had another fine year in Class B in Fort Lauderdale, then did a hitch in the US Army in Germany and came back to hit .333 in Corpus Christi with 19 homers, 14 triples, and 35 doubles in 1955, by which time the Braves had relocated to Milwaukee. Charles was one of the Braves' top prospects, but still he did not get the call to the majors, victimized by the unstated quota system that was in place. Yes, baseball was integrated, but club owners were a long way from being color blind. Eight years after Jackie Robinson stepped onto Ebbets Field in a Dodgers uniform for the first time on April 15, 1947, only 5.2 percent of all Major Leaguers were African-American.

Charles's frustration grew in inverse proportion to the scarcity of opportunity.

"It almost destroyed my love of the game," he said.

Years came and went, and Charles continued to excel on the field and endure prejudice off of it. He would travel through the South with his teammates and not be able to eat in restaurants with them or stay in the team hotel. He wanted to love his country. But why was his country making it so hard? Why could he serve overseas in the military and come home and be treated as if he were a stray dog? How is a man supposed to feel when he has to relieve himself in the bushes because he's not welcome in a whites-only bathroom?

In 1957, when Charles was in the midst of a standout year in the South Atlantic League, his Jacksonville team visited Knoxville. The Knoxville club had a notorious fan with a foghorn voice, the kind you could pick out from a crowd of a hundred thousand. For nine innings, the foghorn spilled venom on Ed Charles. N-this. N-that. Go back to Africa. It was horrible, the worst racist taunting Charles had ever heard—even worse than what Agee would be subjected to in North Carolina some five years later.

Charles responded by having one of his best games of the year. He smashed hits and made superb plays at third base. As he headed off the field at the end of the game, the foghorn was right there.

"By golly, nigger, you are a hell of a ballplayer," the voice said.

Charles walked on by without a word. For most of his life, he had been victimized, but he refused to be a victim. At times he felt beaten down, but he refused to be beaten.

"Background is not the primary concern, but backbone is," he once wrote. "To quit is cowardice. To lose faith is to doubt the working of God through man, and to shirk responsibility is to live a life void of purposeful meaning, another liability on the backs of those who are the true heirs of life."

Charles's break finally came in 1961. After a tremendous year in triple-A ball, he was dealt to the Kansas City Athletics. The Athletics were a fixture in the depths of the American League standings, but they held one huge draw for Charles: they were a big-league team. In 1962, 29-year-old Ed Charles made it to the majors. He hit .288 with 17 home runs, 74 RBI, and 20 stolen bases, establishing himself as a bona fide big leaguer, an A's mainstay until they traded him to the Mets early in 1967 for a minor-league outfielder named Larry Elliot and $50,000.

The deal was not the stuff of major headlines, but Charles became a key contributor after the arrival of Hodges, who had seen Charles for five years in the American League. Charles hit .276 with 15 home runs for the 1968 Mets, and though his numbers weren't close to those a year later, Hodges still had deep faith in Charles's ability and his character.

• • •

MCNALLY DROPPED A sweeping curve on the inside corner to get ahead 0-1 on Charles and then came with another. Charles swung so hard he spun all the way around. McNally was a strike away from ending another tidy inning and sending a tie game into the bottom of the ninth.

Charles stepped out and rubbed dirt on his hands. Shadows covered home plate and the third-base line; the rest of the field, including the pitcher's mound, was still in bright sunshine.

McNally, looking to mix it up, came with a high fastball that he hoped Charles would chase. Charles spanked it into left field for a single, past Brooks Robinson. It was Charles's second hit of the game and right out of his personal playbook: he wanted to be at the plate when the game was on the line.

Jerry Grote worked the count to 2-2. Knowing the Orioles would never expect it, Hodges had Charles running on the next pitch. Charles wasn't slow, but at 36, he wasn't scaring anyone on the basepaths, either. He hadn't stolen a base since June. Charles took off, and Grote stroked a grounder in almost the identical spot that Charles had, past Robinson into left field, Charles wheeling around second and racing all the way to third.

George Bamberger, Charles's old Vancouver teammate and future manager of the Mets (1982–83), came out to the mound. He draped an arm around Etchebarren, and a few moments later second baseman Dave Johnson, manager of the 1986 world-champion Mets, joined the meeting. McNally pounded the ball into his glove. Dick Hall had stopped throwing in the bull pen. It was up to McNally to work out of trouble. Earl Weaver knew that bringing in a right-hander such as Hall would all but guarantee that Hodges would pinch-hit for Weis with Art Shamsky, Ken Boswell, or Wayne Garrett. Weis had hit just .215 for the year, and though he had singled and walked in game two, Weaver clearly preferred to pitch to Weis rather than one of the lefties.

McNally peered in for the sign, still in sunlight. Etchebarren called for a slider. Charles led off of third, Grote off first, both runners running on contact with two outs. Weis choked up on his bat and got set.

McNally's slider stayed up in the zone. Weis took a rip and lined a single to left, one hard hop in front of Don Buford. Charles trotted home from third. Three successive two-out singles had enabled the Mets to regain their one-run lead. If Koosman could put up one more scoreless inning, the 1969 World Series would be squared at one game apiece.

"A batter goes to the plate looking for a pitch he can hit, and I gave him one," McNally said. "It was a slider up in his eyes, and I wanted it down."

As he took the mound for the bottom of the ninth, Koosman had soaked through his uniform. He perspired so heavily that it wasn't unusual for him to lose 12 or more pounds in a complete-game start. He had limited the Orioles to a season-low two hits. The

Orioles had the top of their order coming up—Buford, Paul Blair, and Frank Robinson. The Mets had McGraw and Taylor, their best relievers, warming in the pen.

Koosman took a deep breath.

His first pitch to Buford was a fastball that sailed high and outside, his wildest pitch of the game. Buford swung through another fastball and then was late on Koosman's next offering, hitting a short pop fly to right.

One out.

Blair had broken up the no-hitter with a curve, and Koosman wasn't going to give him another breaking ball he could hit. He tried to get Blair to chase an outside curve and then came with a succession of fastballs. Koosman fell behind 3-1 but didn't give in, retiring Blair on a grounder to Harrelson.

Two outs.

Frank Robinson hobbled to the plate, and Weis ran out to left field from the infield, Hodges again opting to go with his four-outfielder alignment. Jones, Agee, and Swoboda all moved over a few steps to the right. Clendenon was all alone on the right side of the infield.

Koosman took a moment and surveyed his defense. He got ahead of Robinson 1-2 with two fastballs on the outside corner. He was one strike away. He came with a curve that dipped low. Robinson fouled off the 2-2 pitch and held up as a fastball ran a bit down and in.

On the payoff pitch, Koosman fired a fastball on the outside. Robinson started to swing but checked it. The pitch was close. Secory called it ball four. Robinson limped to first and was replaced by a pinch runner, Merv Rettenmund. A rookie and former running back at Ball State University who was drafted by the Dallas Cowboys, Rettenmund wasn't looking to score six points here—just one run.

Weis returned to his usual workplace at second. Memorial Stadium blared with the sound of "Charge!" and the fans belted out the word twice. Rube Walker came out for a word with Koosman. Clendenon also stopped by, pumping his fist as he departed. McGraw and Taylor were still throwing in the bull pen.

Koosman fell behind Boog Powell, 2-1, Grote doing a superb job of smothering a curveball in the dirt to keep Rettenmund at first. Koosman missed again to make it 3-1. Now Ed Charles trotted in to the mound for a positive word. Koosman's command, so stellar through eight and two-thirds innings, was beginning to falter.

He worked on the dirt in front of the rubber and wiped his face with the right shoulder of his gray flannel uniform. He came with a fastball, and Powell took a mighty rip but managed only a foul tip. The count was full. Again Koosman was one strike away. Rettenmund would be running. A long single could tie the game. Koosman looked toward the Mets' dugout and gave an almost imperceptible nod, then did the same with Grote. He took a deep breath.

He spun off a curveball. It missed low.

Powell headed to first. Gil Hodges emerged from the dugout.

Koosman stood on the mound with his hands on his hips. He knew that Hodges was coming to get him. The call went to Ron Taylor, Koosman's roommate. "Gil left me in to get Powell, and I screwed it up," Koosman said. "I should've gotten him out. I was mad at myself."

The lone Met with World Series experience, Taylor wasn't one of the bigger names on the staff or one of the hardest throwers. He was, however, as durable and reliable as almost anyone. Hitters talk about pitchers who throw what they call a "heavy" ball. Taylor's sinking fastball felt like an anvil when it was coming in right. Hodges knew Taylor had the seasoning to handle the moment. In game four of the 1964 World Series, Taylor, then playing for the Cardinals, came on in relief with a one-run lead and shut down the New York Yankees for four innings to help the Cardinals even the series at two games apiece. The Cards would end up winning in seven games.

Taylor was 9-4 with a 2.72 ERA and 13 saves during the season and had thrown 3½ scoreless innings against the Braves in the NLCS. Hodges trusted him implicitly.

All of the Mets did.

"He was a quiet man who contributed a great deal," said Joe Mc-Donald, the Mets' farm director at the time. "He was an inspiration to a lot of people, myself included. Unfortunately, they don't have stats for guts. Ron Taylor had guts. He wanted the ball no matter what the situation, and he was never scared."

Taylor's journey to the Memorial Stadium mound that Sunday had come by way of Toronto and would not have come at all but for a missed boat. Maude Evans, Taylor's mother, was a young woman from Cardiff, Wales, who was looking to emigrate to Australia after her parents had passed away.

"She had three siblings, and she organized them to get a fresh start," Taylor said. "She gathered their meager life savings to buy tickets for a boat, and when the day came they went down to the dock and she handed the tickets to the dockmaster and said, 'Where's the ship to Australia?'

"The dockmaster said, 'You're late,' pointing to a ship pulling out of the harbor." The young woman had spent all this money and here she stood on the dock, watching a ship heading out to sea without them. She had no clue when the next passage to Australia would be. Then she noticed another vessel in the harbor.

"Where's that ship going?" Maude Evans asked the dockmaster.

"To Canada," he said.

"Can we get on that one?" she asked.

Soon Maude Evans and her siblings were on their way to Montreal and eventually to Toronto, where the spoken language was English, not French. She met a young man, Wesley Taylor, who worked at the Dunlop Tire and Rubber Company. They married and had two kids, Carole and Ron.

Maude Taylor was "a brilliant woman who was frustrated because women couldn't really work in those days," according to her son. She raised smart kids. The Mets never had an IQ contest, but if they had, Ron Taylor would've been at the top of Gil Hodges's class. Taylor would read as many as a hundred books in a year. His standard off-field position was outside the team hotel, his head buried in whatever he was reading, waiting for the bus to arrive to go to the ballpark. Years before he became a Met, he took an engineering job in the off-season and moved to New York's Upper East Side. He went to Toots Shor's, the famous celebrity hangout, one night and wound up having a nice talk with Ernest Hemingway. Taylor's mind was always searching for new ideas and fresh intellectual challenges, and he found plenty after making a USO trip to Vietnam following the 1969 season. He saw all the wounded soldiers, the horrible human wreckage of war.

"It changed my life," Taylor said. "It made me want to be a physician. It made me want to pursue a career where I could help people get better."

Taylor started medical school at age 34. He became the team physician for the Toronto Blue Jays eight years later, sharing the same fascination with the human body as his mother, who had theories about human physiology, strong ones. When he was about 6 years old, Ron suffered from a blood-clotting disorder that required regular blood transfusions. The condition kept him away from hockey, the sport of choice among most young Canadians. Ron joined a local baseball league when he was eight. The youngster took to the game and had a strong left arm, at least until his mother intervened. She was concerned that Ron would develop cardiovascular issues doing all that throwing with his left arm, because of its proximity to his heart. So she insisted that her son throw right-handed.

"Insisted? She tied my left hand behind my back," Taylor said.

• • •

TAYLOR, A MOTHER-MADE right-hander, had struck out Brooks Robinson in game one, and now he was looking to get him again and get the Mets out of Baltimore with a split.

As Taylor reached the infield, Clendenon walked toward him. They were close friends, two men with the same wry sense of humor and a long history dating back to the Northern League in 1958, when Clendenon was a promising 22-year-old slugger with the Grand Forks (N.D.) Chiefs in the Pirates organization and Taylor was a promising 20-year-old pitcher for the Minot (N.D.) Mallards in the Indians organization. Starting against the Chiefs one day, Taylor gave up a home run to Clendenon. Clendenon came to bat three more times that night. Taylor hit him twice and knocked him down once. Afterward Clendenon charged into the Mallards' clubhouse, looking for Taylor, before multiple Mallards intervened. The men became good friends on the Mets. When Clendenon met Ron's young son, Drew, he clasped him on both shoulders and said, "I almost killed your dad one night in Minot, North Dakota. So you're lucky to be here."

Clendenon kept the conversation current as Taylor neared the mound.

"Keep it low, Ronnie," Clendenon said.

"Thanks for the tip," Taylor replied.

With his warm-ups complete, Taylor went to the back of the mound and took off his hat, wiping his brow with his sleeve. He picked up the rosin bag to dry his pitching hand, then looked in for the sign, leaning his glove on his left knee. Taylor had a pronounced swing of his arms before getting to the set position. He brought his hands together just above his waist.

His first pitch was a fastball way up and in. Brooks Robinson reeled backward. The Memorial Stadium crowd booed. Taylor came inside again, and Robinson held up his swing to make it 2-0.

At second base, Rettenmund checked the whereabouts of Harrelson and Weis and took a big lead. Taylor threw a curve that had Robinson leaning back for strike one. Grote went out to the mound. Taylor missed inside again for 3-1. The Orioles were a pitch away from loading the bases after having two out and nobody on.

Taylor went with a breaking ball and it looked off the plate, but Robinson swung and fouled it off. With the count full again for a third straight hitter, the runners would be in motion.

Taylor got the sign, glove on the knee, and swung his arms to get set. He came inside with the pitch.

Robinson hit a sharp grounder to third.

Charles, guarding the line, had already gone through his mental checklist. He knew that running fast was the one thing Brooks Robinson could not do. He also knew the runner at first, Powell, was equally slow afoot, in case Charles needed to go to second.

Rettenmund had good speed and would be running on the pitch. Charles was playing deep, a few steps behind the bag, giving him a better chance of keeping the ball in the infield. The ball got to him quickly, but his glove was down and his hands were soft and ready. He wanted to be the guy to make the play.

"If you don't want to be a star, you shouldn't be out there," Charles said.

The ball reached him on an in-between hop, probably the hardest play for an infielder, because the reduced reaction time makes it easy for the ball to skip by you. Charles fielded it cleanly. He took two quick steps to the bag to try for the game-ending force, but Rettenmund had gotten a huge jump and was almost at the bag already.

Charles alertly pulled up and decided to go with Plan B, immediately setting his feet and pegging the ball across the diamond to Clendenon. His throw came in low. Clendenon made his stretch with the improper leg. First basemen are taught to stretch with the same leg as their glove hand to maximize their reach. As a right-handed player, Clendenon should've had his right foot on the bag and stretched with his left. He did the opposite. Wherever his feet were, Clendenon had only one job in that moment: to catch Ed Charles's throw. He could see it wasn't going to make it on the fly. He got down low. Brooks Robinson was a stride from the bag, head down, digging hard. The ball skipped into the dirt. With the webbing of his glove in the dirt, Clendenon scooped it. Even a momentary bobble would've loaded the bases. Clendenon dug the ball out cleanly with one hand, then held his big first baseman's mitt overhead for all to see.

Brooks Robinson was out, and the World Series was tied.

The New York Mets swarmed Taylor on the mound. There were handshakes and backslaps all around. The Mets had won their first World Series game. The Orioles had lost their first World Series game. Retreating to their clubhouse in Memorial Stadium, the Mets packed up and headed home to the former horticultural hub of Flushing, New York, which would be the site of the next three games.

11

MOBILE MAN

World Series Game Three
Queens, New York

THE FIRST WORLD SERIES GAME EVER PLAYED IN SHEA STADIUM took place under a gray sky, with the lights on, and on the eve of the biggest antiwar protest in the nation's history. People poured into New York for the protest. Nobody really knew what to expect, about anything. In Macy's, the world's largest department store, police found a sixth bomb in four days, a small device tucked into a Marlboro cigarettes box and slipped into a coat pocket. None of the bombs did major damage, but they didn't do much to attract customers, either. New York senator Charles Goodell gave a stirring antiwar speech at Queens College. Even Tom Seaver, the Mets' poster child, was on record as being against the war. The government of North Vietnam saluted everyone who took a stand against the Nixon administration's policies, calling demonstrators heroic comrades whose stand would "save their children and brothers from a useless death in Vietnam."

Some 4,200 miles northwest of Hanoi, meanwhile, Soviet officials in Moscow announced the launching of their third manned Soyuz spacecraft, putting the number of cosmonauts orbiting Earth at seven. The Soviets had lost the race to the moon in July, watching with the rest of the world as Neil Armstrong and Buzz Aldrin took their lunar stroll and left behind a plaque that read:

HERE MEN FROM THE PLANET EARTH
FIRST SET FOOT UPON THE MOON
JULY 1969, A.D.
WE CAME IN PEACE FOR ALL MANKIND

The latest Soyuz launching was the Soviets' answer, showing the world they were still major space-race players, and raising concerns among Cold Warriors that the Soviets might establish a space station and achieve outer-space supremacy.

In Flushing the concerns were much more terrestrial. The Mets wanted to take the lead in the World Series. That was their sole mission, even as hysteria swirled around them. The press box was bursting with reporters from around the country. Fans, many of whom camped out Gary Cohen style, to get tickets, poured through the turnstiles, and another supporter, the adult film star Fanny Hill, took out a big newspaper ad to promote her film and her allegiance to the Mets:

I WAS WITH YOU IN ATLANTA.
I'M WITH YOU IN NEW YORK.
NOW GO GET THE BIRDS—
FOR YOU'RE MY KIND OF MEN

(AND I KNOW I'M YOUR KIND OF WOMAN SO COME ON OVER TO SEE ME AT THE
34TH STREET EAST AND AVCO EMBASSY EAST THEATERS.)

Gil Hodges gave the ball to Gentry, the boyish-looking 23-year-old from Phoenix who owned the Mets' biggest dog (a Saint Bernard) and a deceptively live fastball, and won more games that year than any rookie pitcher in baseball. The day before game three, when the teams had an off-day workout at Shea, Hodges said that if the game were postponed—a possibility with rain in the forecast—he would switch starters and come back with Tom Seaver on three days' rest, followed by Jerry Koosman in game four, with Gentry getting bumped back to game five. It was how he had handled the rotation all year: Seaver and Koosman pitched when their turns came up, and the other starters—Gentry, Jim McAndrew, and Don Cardwell primarily—were moved accordingly.

No change turned out to be necessary. The rain held off, and Shea Stadium was stuffed with frenzy, and celebrities, among them Jackie Onassis and her young children, Caroline and John Kennedy. Pearl Bailey, the Tony Award–winning star of *Hello, Dolly!* was there, as she always was for big Mets games, and Ed Sullivan and Jerry Lewis were on hand, too. Roy Campanella threw out the ceremonial first pitch from his wheelchair and got a bigger cheer than anyone else, even the Mets players and Hodges. The recording star Steve Lawrence sang the national anthem, but the microphone malfunctioned and his voice could hardly be heard. Nobody seemed to mind.

Like Seaver and Koosman, Gentry had not had a memorable outing in the NLCS. He said, improbably, that the problem was that he had been too relaxed, that he pitched better when keyed up. Gentry wanted to be keyed up against the Orioles. He had not appreciated being pulled so early from game three against the Braves after Rico Carty's long foul ball. As Gentry took the Shea mound for the third game of the Series, he knew the one foolproof way to keep Hodges in the dugout was to put up zeroes on the scoreboard.

Gentry's first pitch was a fastball wide to Don Buford, the lone Oriole with two hits in the Series. Buford fouled off another fastball, before Gentry made him look silly on a 1-1 changeup, then struck him out with a curveball. Gentry got Paul Blair on a harmless fly to Tommie Agee and then battled Frank Robinson to a full count, challenging him with high fastballs, the imposing Robinson leaning over the plate, as ever. Robinson was hit 13 times during the season, more than any other American League player. The wonder was that he wasn't hit more.

Robinson drew a walk, but Gentry busted Boog Powell's bat on a grounder to second, and the woes of the vaunted Orioles sluggers continued. A half inning into the third game, Baltimore's 2-5 hitters were a collective 2 for 30 in the World Series, with both of the hits singles. Earl Weaver was convinced that such an explosive lineup couldn't stay dormant for much longer. He was equally convinced that the all-Arizona pitching matchup for game three—Scottsdale High School's Jim Palmer versus Camelback High School's Gentry—strongly favored the Orioles.

Pitching a day before he would turn 24, Jim Palmer was only a year older than Gentry and one of the most promising young hurlers in baseball, already battle tested on the big stage; three years earlier, he had thrown a four-hit shutout against the Dodgers, beating Sandy Koufax in game two of the 1966 Series. After blowing out his rotator cuff in 1968—an injury so severe that the Orioles hadn't protected him in the expansion draft (the Kansas City Royals and Seattle Pilots passed on him)—Palmer started taking an anti-inflammatory pain reliever suggested by a friend who worked for a drug company. Almost miraculously, his arm healed, and he returned to dominance in the '69 season, putting up the best earned run average (2.34) among Orioles starters and the best winning percentage (16-4) in the league. Palmer's signature was a fluid, high-kicking motion and a high, riding fastball that he could get by just about everybody.

Agee stepped in against Palmer to start things off for the Mets and took a couple of his trademark half swings, tapping home plate after each one before assuming his stance. He was hitless in the first two games, hitting only one ball with any authority. The Orioles pitchers were keeping away from the low fastballs he preferred, working him instead with breaking stuff, mostly on the outer half, and fastballs up in the zone. Agee was looking for a fastball up.

With the count 2-1, Palmer kicked and delivered, and sure enough, it was a high fastball. Agee crushed it, driving the ball on a line to straightaway center, the ball clearing the center-field fence by 20 or 30 feet, heading straight toward the SERVAL ZIPPERS sign. Along the third-base line, the Mets' famous sign man, Karl Ehrhardt, held up the words MET POWER!

As Agee rounded third, he clapped his hands and then smacked the hand of Eddie Yost, the third-base coach. Buford had led off the first game with a home run. Now Agee had done likewise in the third game.

Palmer, a future Hall of Famer, got a new baseball and did a superb job of acting as if nothing had happened. The thunderous cheers of 57,000 people in Shea Stadium suggested otherwise.

With a right-handed pitcher on the mound for the Orioles, Hodges did what he had done all season, sticking with his platoon system. That may have been his greatest managerial strength—his unfaltering consistency, his rock-ribbed belief that to win in baseball you need all 25 men to buy in, to feel valuable. He was not a man easily seduced by emotion or outside clamor. He believed in his people. He had given everyone a role in the 165 games that had preceded the World Series. He was not going to abandon doing so now. His left-hander hitters—Art Shamsky, Ken Boswell, Wayne Garrett, and Ed Kranepool—had been a huge part of the sweep of the Braves in the NLCS, but hadn't gotten off the bench in the first two games of the Series, as the Orioles had gone with left-handers Mike Cuellar and Dave McNally. Now their chance was here.

Palmer struck out Garrett swinging with a smoking fastball on the outside corner, and while he got Cleon Jones and Shamsky to fly out, both Mets took the ball to the warning track. Palmer allowed only one run, but three of the four Mets hitters had hit the ball hard. He was struggling to throw his curveball for strikes and knew he had to find the answer if this start was going to go well.

Gentry, by contrast, looked more comfortable than he had at any point in his brief NLCS outing. He wore his cap so high on his head, you wondered if he'd attached it with bobby pins, and with the brim pulled so low hitters could barely see his eyes. In his baggy pin-striped flannels, looking as if he needed a meal, Gentry had most of the Orioles swinging late on his fastball from the outset, as if they were unprepared for the fact that someone so skinny could throw so hard. He spotted his fastball in different locations and deftly mixed in breaking balls and off-speed pitches, cruising through an easy second inning.

Palmer got two quick outs in the home second, but missed badly with two sweeping curves to Grote before walking him on a high fastball. Palmer kept looking down at the mound, as if he didn't like his landing spot. Harrelson lined a fastball right over Palmer's head into center for a single, Grote holding at second.

That brought Gentry and his .081 average to the plate. Palmer checked the runners and delivered a fastball. The pitch was up, in the middle of the plate. Gentry took a slashing swing, driving the ball on a line to right-center. Blair, a brilliant outfielder, played the shallowest center field in the game and was even shallower with Gentry up. He sprinted back and to his left but couldn't catch up to it. The ball rolled to the wall, by the 396 mark. Grote scored easily, and Harrelson tore around the bases from first to double Gentry's RBI output for the season. Gentry pulled into second as the crowd let loose with an earsplitting roar. It was Gentry's first hit since August 3, ending an 0-for-28 spell.

"The ball sort of hit my bat," Gentry told reporters later.

Karl Ehrhardt held up a sign that read INCREDIBLE. An inning that seemed to be heading nowhere had yielded two of the most improbable runs of the Mets' season. For a second straight game, the bottom of the order had come through in a big way.

The Mets had a 3–0 lead.

Palmer stood on the mound, hands on hips, the picture of disgust. Elrod Hendricks and George Bamberger visited him. Two relievers started warming up in the left-field bull pen.

Gentry blew through the top of the third on eight pitches, making it look easy. The Orioles' hitters may have been surprised by Gentry's stuff, but the club's scouting department knew all about him: the Orioles had drafted Gentry in the first round of the secondary phase of the 1966 draft, 12 spots ahead of another well-known college pitcher, Tom Seaver of Southern California. But Gentry opted not to sign. He hadn't signed the year before, either, when he'd been drafted by the Houston Astros, and he wouldn't sign the next year when drafted by the Detroit Tigers. Instead, he had spent 1967 with Arizona State University, going 17-1 with 229 strikeouts in 174 innings and an earned run average of 1.14, winning a national championship along the way, highlighted by two epic performances. In a conference playoff game against the University of Arizona, Gentry threw 208 pitches over 15 innings, striking out 18 players in a 4-hour, 17-minute marathon that concluded with a 4–3 ASU victory.

"Considering the pressure, that was the greatest pitching performance I have ever seen," said Bobby Winkles, the ASU coach. In the national semifinal against Stanford, Gentry again worked overtime, going 14 innings and striking out 15. The Mets drafted him after the Arizona State season ended, and this time the 20-year-old Gentry was ready to pursue pro baseball, a transition that proved to be no problem; he reached the big club after just eighteen months in the minors.

Palmer started the third by throwing four straight balls to Garrett, the last of them a fastball that missed by a foot and a half. Palmer struck out Jones with a well-placed breaking ball before getting Shamsky on a hard grounder to first. Garrett was running, so the Mets stayed out of the double play.

That brought up Boswell, who was the Mets' leading hitter in the second half of the season, hitting .345, and got even hotter in September and October, hitting .378. That Boswell could be relied on in big spots was no revelation; he wore out the Mets' biggest rival, the Cubs, all season long, hitting .365 against them in 17 games. It was Boswell, in the first game of a doubleheader against the Expos on September 10, who delivered the twelfth-inning single to put the Mets in first place for the first time in their history.

A prep baseball and basketball star from Austin, Texas, Boswell would've signed out of high school, but his parents wanted him to go to college. He accepted a baseball scholarship to Sam Houston State, where the baseball end of things went extremely well and the academic side did not. He flunked out of school, which turned out to be an impeccably timed turn of events. Baseball rules stipulated that a college player could not be signed until his class graduated.

By flunking out, Boswell was no longer a college player. Red Murff, the busy scout who signed Koosman and Ryan, among others, recognized that because Boswell was not a college player, he would be draft eligible before the rest of his classmates.

Murff signed Boswell to an $8,000 bonus before the 1965 season. After winning Rookie of the Year honors with Auburn in the New York–Penn League and hitting .299 the next year in double-A Williamsport, Boswell almost certainly would've made the Mets in 1967, but he spent most of the year fulfilling his military duties. He hit .261 in part-time duty with the 1968 Mets, convincing Hodges and the front office the big leagues was where he belonged. On the day his hit put the Mets in first place in September, Boswell reflected on his 4-for-10 day with a champagne bottle in hand.

"What am I doing with this?" he asked. "My father drives a beer truck."

Stepping in against Palmer, Boswell settled into the box and took a single practice swing, pointing his bat menacingly at Palmer. Boswell held his bat farther away from his body than any other Met, prizing the freedom of movement the extra space gave him.

Palmer started Boswell off with a curveball that curled low. His next pitch was a fastball. Boswell jumped on it.

The minute the ball left his bat, the crowd at Shea stood and let out an anticipatory roar. Joe Pignatano, the Mets' bull pen coach, followed the ball's flight as it headed his way, getting ready to make the catch. Frank Robinson ran back to the warning track. He raised his glove. A shifting wind held the ball up. It was Robinson, not Pignatano, who made the play, comfortably in front of the wall. The score remained 3–0.

With one away in the fourth, Frank Robinson lined Gentry's 0-1 pitch straight at Jones in left. Jones charged hard, got low, and made a scooping play on the ball, snagging it on a short hop and then holding up his glove to try to sell the umpire on a catch. It didn't fly. Robinson's hit was the Orioles' first of the game, and the next batter, Powell, got their second, a single to right that sent Robinson around to third. Under pressure, Gentry smoked a high fastball by Brooks Robinson for the second out.

Now Hendricks, from the unlikely outpost of the Virgin Islands, stepped in. Gentry quickly went ahead 0-2 with off-speed stuff, and Hendricks fouled off another off-speed pitch to stay alive. Gentry looked to waste a fastball away, but he missed his spot and Hendricks tagged it, driving it hard and far to left-center.

Off the bat, it looked to be a two-run double, at least.

Agee, playing Hendricks to pull, was well over in right-center. He got a good jump on the ball, but he had much ground to cover and the ball was slicing away from him. Agee raced toward left-center. Robinson was already home, and Powell was heading there. Coming from left, Jones knew he had no chance and backed off so his friend could go after the ball with complete abandon.

Agee kept running, a diagonal blur in the Shea outfield. At the ball field Agee and Jones had played on back at Mobile County Training School, there had been no outfield fences and no dugouts; Agee could run as far as he wanted to track down a fly ball in Mobile. But not in Flushing. Shea Stadium had a fence, and Agee was fast approaching it.

"Lots of room, lots of room!" Jones shouted to Agee.

Agee changed his angle and veered sharply backward, toward the wall. He was nearing the warning track now. Hendricks would say later it was the hardest ball he'd hit to the opposite field in two years. Right in front of the 396 sign, Agee extended his glove—a Johnny Callison model—as far as it would go. It looked as if the ball would be beyond his reach. He kept closing on it. He extended his glove a little more. The ball was dropping quickly. Agee made one last strain to get there and the ball tumbled into the end of his webbing. His momentum carried him into the wall, Agee cushioning the impact with his right arm. The white of the ball made his glove look like a snow cone. His glove bumped the wall, but Agee held on.

Shea Stadium erupted, even louder than when Agee had led off the game with his home run. As he ran toward the infield, Agee kept his glove out in front of him, the ball still in the exact same spot at the tip of it, the snow cone there for all to see, as if to assure all of the Mets fans in the house that everything was okay.

The crowd gave him a standing ovation. Hendricks's drive had resulted in nothing but a 390-foot out. Gentry's shutout, and his three-run lead, were intact.

Agee finally took the ball out of his webbing when he arrived in the dugout, where he received a hero's welcome. Seaver grabbed Agee's glove and immediately went to work on his webbing, stitching it up tight. Seaver, the Mets' ace, a 20-game winner and that year's Cy Young Award recipient, was Agee's go-to guy when it came to webbing repairs.

"He was good at that," Agee said.

12

POSITIVE SIGNS

World Series Game Three
Bottom of the fourth

	1	2	3	4	5	6	7	8	9	Runs
Orioles	0	0	0	0	-	-	-	-	-	0
Mets	1	2	0	-	-	-	-	-	-	3

THE CROWD WAS STILL BUZZING OVER TOMMIE AGEE'S CATCH WHEN Ed Kranepool crushed a Jim Palmer fastball on a line to right, as hard a hit ball as there had been in the game. If he'd gotten it a little bit higher, it would've been a home run, but the topspin tugged the ball downward and Frank Robinson caught it on the edge of the track for the first out. Kranepool made a right turn just past first base and headed forlornly back to the dugout. He didn't need a reminder that baseball is a sport that, as much as any other, teems with caprice. You can hit a little flare and get a double in one at bat and the next time scald a ball on a 350-foot line and get nothing but an F-9. Supposedly it all evens out.

Palmer had secured a loud out, but still looked unhappy. He asked the umpire for a new baseball. Maybe that would help.

After getting Jerry Grote on a grounder to second, Palmer missed with three more breaking pitches and fell behind Bud Harrelson, 3-1. The wind had picked up, and suddenly the umpires' trousers were flapping like the flag in center field. Harrelson almost disappeared in a mini–dust storm that swirled in the batter's box before the 3-2 pitch. He stepped out of the box and wiped his eyes.

A wrapper blew by Palmer on the mound. He ignored it and then missed the strike zone, his slider cutting down and well inside. As Harrelson trotted to first, Palmer's shoulders sagged in annoyance that his wildness had wasted a chance to have Gentry lead off the next inning.

Palmer made a throw to first to keep Harrelson close before he even threw a pitch to Gentry. Harrelson had good speed, but it was highly unlikely he would be going anywhere; he had stolen just one base in the regular year and had been caught three times. Gil Hodges had clearly decided that he wasn't going to turn Harrelson loose on the bases in his first season after knee surgery. Still, Palmer watched him closely.

After throwing a 1-2 curveball in the dirt to Gentry, Palmer wheeled and made a snap throw to first. Harrelson darted back. Palmer's throw was well wide of the bag, and as Boog Powell moved to the right to get it, he and Harrelson bumped. The ball got by Powell and rolled toward the seats. Harrelson broke for second at the same time Powell broke for the ball, and an instant later they were all tangled up, the 250-pound Powell clipping the left leg of the 146-pound Harrelson, whose Mets teammates called him Twiggy, after the world's wispiest and most famous fashion model. Harrelson, way out of his weight class, went sprawling.

Home plate umpire Larry Napp called Powell for obstruction and awarded Harrelson second base. Elrod Hendricks, the catcher, screamed at Napp and pointed at first, telling him he'd blown the call. Powell charged in and made the same case, and Earl Weaver barreled out of the dugout as if he'd been launched. A man with a beer-keg body and a legendary temper—he had once been tossed out of all four games of a minor-league series by his longtime sparring partner Ron Luciano—Weaver started going nose to nose with Napp, his face reddening and his veins bulging. Napp wouldn't hear any of it, and the call stood. The tempest passed quickly after Gary Gentry whiffed on a high fastball to end the inning.

Any concerns the Mets had that the pas de deux with Powell might've hurt Harrelson were summarily dismissed one batter into the fifth inning when Orioles second baseman Dave Johnson rapped a grounder into the hole between short and third. Harrelson scooted to his right, deep into the hole. Scooting was exactly how Harrelson moved around the ball field, a little man who took little steps, a bunch of them, always in a hurry. He wasn't shading Johnson to pull, which added to the ground he had to cover. He backhanded the ball inches from the outfield grass. Without stopping to plant his back foot, Harrelson cut the ball loose, straight overhand. Johnson dug hard down the line. Harrelson's throw was straight and remarkably strong considering he had no body weight behind it; the ball hummed right by Gentry, flat as a clothesline. The 6-foot, 3-inch Kranepool met the throw with a huge stretch. Harrelson's throw was a first baseman's dream. Head high, right on target.

Johnson was out by two strides.

The next batter was Mark Belanger, Harrelson's Baltimore counterpart. It would be hard for a World Series to provide a better shortstop showcase than 1969 did. It was staged by two men born two days apart in 1944, Harrelson on the day of the Normandy invasion, June 6, in Niles, California, an old railroad town on the east side of San Francisco Bay, and Belanger on June 8 in Pittsfield, Massachusetts, an old manufacturing town on the state's western border. If Harrelson scooted on the field, Belanger danced, a baseball Baryshnikov who didn't cover ground so much as flow over it. Belanger, who was nicknamed "The Blade," seemed much taller than the 6 feet, 1 inch he was listed at. He never hit much—his lifetime average was .228—but he was so graceful and gifted in the field that it hardly mattered. He played with a little glove that he broke in with saliva and coffee and was vehemently against diving for balls, believing that with keen anticipation, knowledge of the hitter, and economical movement, a shortstop could make more plays and cover more ground on his feet than on his belly. Belanger would win eight Gold Gloves in the American League, becoming the league's gold standard both literally and figuratively. Playing alongside Brooks Robinson, he was one-half of as stellar a left side of the infield as the game had seen. Mayo Smith, the manager of the Detroit Tigers, once said that trying to get a hit through the left side of the Orioles' infield was like "trying to throw a hamburger through a brick wall."

Harrelson may have lacked Belanger's fluidity, but his own athletic gifts were unmistakable, which was how he had become a three-sport star at Sunset High School in Hayward, California, a standout running back and a good enough guard to earn a basketball scholarship to San Francisco State University. Then the big-league baseball scouts descended on him, and his point guard days were done. The Mets offered less money ($10,000) than some other teams, but, like Koosman, Harrelson weighed the money against the opportunity for rapid advancement. He made his Mets debut at age 21, pinch-running for veteran Roy McMillan and then taking over for McMillan at short against the Astros on September 2, 1965. By the beginning of the 1967 season, the starting job was his.

"With the kind of ball club we have," Hodges told *Sports Illustrated* in 1969, "if we don't have a great shortstop we're in a lot of trouble. I don't believe the club could have had the kind of year we had without Harrelson."

Harrelson and his roommate, Tom Seaver, had come up through the Mets system together. To Seaver, Harrelson and Agee were the most important defensive players on the team. Seaver loved how completely Harrelson got into the game, how his suggestions were invariably spot-on. Harrelson could often detect when Seaver was dropping his shoulder or not getting down enough on his right leg, sometimes even before Seaver knew it. Harrelson was always one to come to the mound to offer an encouraging word or tell him to slow down. "I wouldn't trade him for any other shortstop in baseball," Seaver wrote in *The Sporting News*. Giving was hard-wired into Harrelson. The Mets' television director, Jack Simon, had a son who was celebrating his Bar Mitzvah that year. Harrelson asked Simon if he could wait until the end of the year to give him a gift. Simon said of course. After the Series, Harrelson delivered the present: the glove he'd used to snag Don Buford's line drive in game two.

Belanger had tested Harrelson on his first trip to the plate, and now he pulled a 2-1 fastball in the same direction. Harrelson was on the balls of his feet, leaning forward slightly, the way his mentor, McMillan, had taught him. A former All-Star and Gold Glove winner, McMillan was winding down a stellar career, spent mostly with the Cincinnati Reds, when Harrelson arrived. The son of a Texas barber, McMillan never said much, and neither did Harrelson. The teacher and pupil were a perfect fit. Harrelson was a relentless worker. In his first full season as the starter, in 1967, he went through a brutal early-season fielding slump, making nine errors in his first 15 games, but soldiered through it by taking hundreds of extra ground balls before games. Harrelson had been hindered by a balky knee ever since he'd jackknifed out of the way of a takeout slide in Jacksonville in 1965, finally having surgery to repair it after the 1968 season. By 1969 he was tied for second in fielding among the league's starting shortstops.

Belanger's second grounder to short was Harrelson's easiest chance of the day, a chest-high three-hopper. Weaver had right-hander Jim Hardin warming but chose not to pinch-hit for Palmer. Palmer swung at a 1-2 fastball and hit a ground ball up the middle. Harrelson quick-stepped to his left, charged the ball hard, and got down low to scoop up the ball, making a strong sidearm throw to Kranepool for his third assist of the inning. Then he scooted off to a nice ovation, his arms bent and tight against his wiry physique, pumping like little pistons.

• • •

IN THE BOX SEATS behind third base, 44-year-old Karl Ehrhardt watched as Gentry headed back out for the top of the sixth inning. The scoreboard offered him a satisfying sight: Gentry had put up a neat line of zeros in the runs column of the Orioles' box score, in his longest outing since his division-clinching shutout on September 24.

Ehrhardt could see the number 9 on the back of the Orioles' Don Buford as Buford headed for the plate from the visitors' dugout. On Gentry's first pitch, Buford squared as if to bunt and took a fastball outside. He squared a second time and took a strike. He didn't swing the bat until he took a big hack at a curveball and struck out. Grote fired the ball to Garrett at third.

As Gentry tugged his cap, Ehrhardt stood up. He was wearing a mustard-colored sweatshirt and a black derby with a blue-and-orange band and a Mets logo on it. He unfolded a sign with white block letters, a black background, and a lime-green exclamation point.

It read BACK TO YOUR NEST, BIRD!

Ehrhardt had plenty of other signs—as many as twelve hundred of them—if you didn't like that one. He was as much a Shea Stadium staple as the air traffic overhead. Known as "The Sign Man of Shea," he was a commercial artist from Glen Oaks, Queens, who had been born in Unterweissbach, Germany, the son of Willie and Elsie Vight Ehrhardt. The family emigrated to the United States when Karl was six years old and opened a beauty parlor in Queens. He served in the army during World War II, working as a translator in POW camps holding German soldiers, before returning home and enrolling in Pratt Institute, from which he graduated with a degree in design art. Commercial art was his field, but his passion was the Mets. During the early, bleak years at Shea, Ehrhardt and a friend had hung a banner over an upper-deck railing that addressed not just the Mets' performance but the stuffiness of M. Donald Grant, the team's chairman.

The banner read WELCOME TO GRANT'S TOMB.

The Mets didn't care for the message and had security confiscate it. Ehrhardt was perturbed at the infringement on his freedom of expression.

"Just because it was a negative thing, it's no reason not to have it," said Bonnie Troester, Ehrhardt's daughter and frequent companion at Mets games. "What the banner said was true. The Mets were doing really bad."

Ehrhardt found his way into the press box and let the writers know what happened. Stories came out the next day. Long before anybody had ever heard of the Internet, the blowback was immediate and the Shea editorial police backed off. Ehrhardt became a fixture behind third base with his clever and carefully catalogued signs, sitting in box seats provided by a typographical house he worked with. He always had a message for the moment, standing up in his derby, chewing his gum, a Shea sideshow for no extra charge.

Ehrhardt made his signs on the floor of his daughter's room. They were foldable 20-by-26-inch rectangles of black cardboard, with white block letters he cut out by hand and spray-glued onto the cardboard. Some of his signs were straightforward—MET POWER! was a staple—and others were cute and sometimes cutting. During journeyman outfielder Jose Cardenal's brief stay in Flushing in 1979 and 1980, his strikeouts would be greeted with a sign that read JOSE, CAN YOU SEE? A Mets error would often prompt another favorite: LOOK MA, NO HANDS. A fine outing by the Mets' ace would result in the unveiling of LEAVE IT TO SEAVER.

Ehrhardt used color-coded tabs to help him quickly find the right sign. He would typically take about 60 signs to any given game. On weekdays, he'd drive his car to a gas station near Shea Stadium and leave the signs in the trunk. He'd take the number 7 subway line into Manhattan for work and, at the end of the day, take the number 7 back to Shea. He'd change clothes in the car, get his signs out of the trunk, and report to the seats behind third.

"Before I went to the ballpark, I would try to crystal-ball what might happen that particular day," he told the *New York Times*. "I would read all the newspapers to learn who was hot and who was in a slump, stuff like that, and create my signs accordingly."

Ehrhardt loaded up on bird puns to welcome the Orioles and was delighted to send Buford back to his nest. Paul Blair followed him there, getting underneath a high fastball and popping it up to Harrelson. Quickly Gentry had two outs, but he lost the strike zone and walked Frank Robinson on four pitches. Gentry's pitches had started riding higher than intended, and he wasn't finishing them the way he'd done earlier, a telltale sign of a pitcher tiring. He fell behind Powell and then left a curveball up that Powell belted into right field to put runners on first and third. The tying run was coming to the plate.

Nolan Ryan, who had pitched so brilliantly in relief of Gentry in the third game of the NLCS, started to warm up in the bull pen.

Now it was Brooks Robinson's turn, and again Gentry fell behind, throwing a couple of fastballs to run the count to 3-1. Gentry rubbed up the ball with both hands. He came to the set position and paused to exhale deeply. It was the most critical juncture of the game for Gentry. Grote called for another fastball. Gentry stayed on top of this one and fired it about thigh high, on the outside. Robinson may have been expecting something in, because he was pulling off the ball. He swung late and without conviction, lifting a fly into shallow right. Shamsky ran over to the line and made the play easily.

Despite fighting himself from the outset, Palmer had kept the Orioles in the game. His first challenge in the sixth was Ken Boswell, who rapped a grounder between first and second that just eluded the lunging efforts of Powell to reach it. Dave Johnson circled behind him, stabbing the ball in the webbing of his glove, a superb play. Six feet deep on the outfield grass, Johnson spun and threw to Palmer, who was just getting to the first-base bag. The throw sailed a bit, and the 6-foot, 3-inch Palmer stretched high to catch it. The ball beat Boswell by a stride, but Palmer's reach pulled his foot off the base.

Crouched right next to the bag was Henry Charles "Shag" Crawford, the first-base umpire. Crawford was a former milkman and cabdriver who started umpiring high school games to make a few extra bucks in his native Philadelphia, going on to umpire more than three thousand big-league games and raise two sons, Jerry and Joey, both of whom went on to officiating careers, Jerry in baseball and Joey in the NBA. Shag Crawford's trademark was the same crouch he assumed on Boswell's bouncer. When he umpired behind home plate, in fact, he would get so close and low to the catcher that he would steady himself with a hand on the catcher's back. Hustling to the bag and getting down low, Crawford fixed his eyes on first base. Boswell arrived at the bag. Palmer's foot lifted off it by the width of a shoelace. It all happened so quickly. Crawford started to raise his hand to call Boswell out, then paused for an instant with his arms wide to signal Boswell safe, lifting up his left leg to show all parties the reason why.

Palmer looked down at first base once, then again, but he never argued, nor did any other Oriole. Boswell, credited with a base hit, stayed at first.

Up came Kranepool, who fell behind 0-2 but worked the count even. On the 2-2 pitch, Hodges had Boswell running, another aggressive, run-and-hit play. Boswell hadn't stolen a base in almost two months, but Hodges had faith that Kranepool would make contact and get Boswell into scoring position. Kranepool did precisely that, grounding to Johnson as Boswell advanced to second. Grote came up next and swatted a slow, arching curveball down the left-field line for a double, scoring Boswell to make it 4–0.

Gentry struck out, leaving Grote stranded at second, but he had to like the larger landscape. He was a rookie pitcher who had a four-run lead and a three-hitter going, with nine outs remaining in a World Series game. He would take that anytime. Now it was back to work.

13

FIELD DAY

World Series Game Three
Top of the seventh

	1	2	3	4	5	6	7	8	9	Runs
Orioles	0	0	0	0	0	0	-	-	-	0
Mets	1	2	0	0	0	1	-	-	-	4

GARY GENTRY CAME OUT FOR HIS SEVENTH INNING WITH THE SKY the color of cement. The afternoon edged toward three o'clock as a wicked wind gust blew past him, wrappers blowing behind him as he stepped on the rubber to face Elrod Hendricks. Hendricks, who had driven Tommie Agee to the wall in left-center in his previous at bat, took a robust cut at a 2-1 slider and just missed it, fouling it back. He flipped his bat in frustration, knowing he'd had a good pitch to hit. Gentry came back with a fastball, a little above the belt, and Hendricks was right on that one, too, driving it high and deep to right-center. Agee ran to his left and caught the ball just a few steps in front of the wall. The wind almost certainly kept the ball in the park.

Gentry was starting to live dangerously. He fell behind Dave Johnson 2-0, the third consecutive hitter to get ahead in the count. The Orioles were too strong a hitting team for Gentry to get away with that for long. He came back with a knee-high fastball on the outside corner before Johnson fouled off another fastball. After four straight fastballs, Jerry Grote called for a breaking ball. It was over the plate, and Johnson hit it well, sending it to deep center. Agee retreated but suddenly slipped and nearly fell, kicking up a hunk of grass and steadying himself by planting his glove on the ground.

Back upright, he made the catch and then dutifully replaced the divot, tamping it down with his spikes.

It fell to Mark Belanger to try to get something started for Baltimore. He saw six pitches and looked at every one of them for a leadoff walk. Dave May, a left-handed pinch hitter, came up to bat for Palmer, and Gentry walked him, too, missing with a fastball on the payoff pitch. Gentry looked away in disgust. He snapped his glove after receiving Grote's throw. In the dugout, Gil Hodges made no move. Gentry had just missed striking out May, and he'd had success against the next hitter, Don Buford, all day.

Hodges was giving Gentry one more batter.

With runners leading off first and second, Gentry started Buford off with a curveball that missed high and wide. It was the eleventh time in the last 12 batters that Gentry had thrown a first-pitch ball. In the corner of the Mets' dugout, Hodges sat with his hands folded on his lap, fingers interlocked, looking as serene as a man on a park bench.

After a checked-swing foul ball, Buford took a fastball high and another inside. Neither pitch was close. The count was 3-1, the bases one ball away from being full. Hodges folded his arms. A restless murmur, growing louder, rippled through the sold-out stadium. Gentry rubbed up the ball again, touched his hat, and bent down to get some rosin. He came set and fired one more fastball.

It missed outside.

Buford hadn't taken more than three steps toward first before Hodges started out of the dugout. He tapped his right arm to signal that he wanted Ryan. Still, Gentry's performance rated as an unqualified triumph. He had faced 28 batters over 6⅔ innings, yielding three hits and no runs against one of the best lineups in baseball. He had outpitched Jim Palmer. It was all the Mets could've asked for.

It was hard for Gentry to let go of the three walks that ended his afternoon. On the mound with Kranepool, Grote, and Hodges, he tossed the ball into the air and snatched it with angry vigor. He pounded the ball into his glove. He looked vacantly toward the out-field as he waited for his replacement, handed the ball to Hodges, and walked off to one last ovation.

Now it was Nolan Ryan's game, a 22-year-old Met taking over from a 23-year-old Met. Hodges had used Ryan in high-pressure moments before, most recently in game three of the NLCS, when he had relieved Gentry with two on and nobody out in the third inning. But this was altogether different. It was the World Series, the Orioles were a far more dangerous team, and although Ryan may well have had the best young arm in the game, he was also capable of being wilder than spring break in Miami. With an average of 5.3 walks per nine innings, he was the most strike-challenged pitcher in the Series. He was in a spot with no margin for error.

Hodges had a gift for understanding both pitchers' repertoires and their psyches. His knack for putting players into situations in which they could succeed was almost unparalleled. But handing the ball to your wildest pitcher with the bases loaded in a World Series game? Even some of the Mets were surprised, including Jerry Koosman, who rode to the park with Ryan before almost every home game.

"We all knew Nolie could throw hard, but we also knew he was capable of walking the ballpark," Koosman said.

The Orioles' hitter was Paul Blair, who relished every opportunity to show his former team what they let go. In left field, Cleon Jones knew Blair would never let him forget it if he delivered a big hit here. In fact, the two men had a friendly bet about who would get more hits in the Series. Jones always enjoyed Blair's animated, chatty personality—Blair's nickname was "Motormouth" because he rarely stopped talking—and had fond memories of the spring of 1962, when Jones, Blair, and Choo Choo Coleman had rattled around Homestead, Florida, in a 1957 Dodge they had bought for $100. Blair constantly teased Jones that he—not Jones—would've been the Mets' big hitting star now if the Orioles hadn't signed him away.

Wanting to make Ryan throw a strike, Blair took the first pitch all the way. Ryan came right at him with a fastball on the outer half of the plate.

Strike one.

Ryan wound and fired again, another fastball. Blair swung and missed.

Strike two.

In his young career, Ryan had struck out more than one batter an inning. He was looking for another one.

He pitched from a full windup and launched another fastball, this one belt high and over the plate. Blair had already seen two of Ryan's fastballs and was starting to get acclimated. He swung and drove a ball deep to right-center.

With two outs, the runners took off on contact. Buford, the fastest of the Orioles, was all but certain to score from first if the ball fell in, which would make it a 4–3 game.

Agee, shading Blair to left-center, was on the move immediately. The ball tailed away from him. Agee kept running and pounded his glove a couple of times as he went. He'd learned to pound his glove years before, at Grambling. It was his way of deepening the pocket, getting it ready to receive a baseball.

"Whenever I saw him pounding his glove, I knew he had it," Jones said. "The only times Tommie did that was when he was sure he would catch it."

At first Agee thought Blair's drive would not be that hard to catch up to, but the ball kept slicing away from him. For an immensely gifted athlete, Agee had a wobbly running style, his weight seeming to shift from leg to leg; he looked as if he might fall down at any moment. He kept running, kept wobbling. The ball continued to curl away from him. Now he wasn't so sure if he could catch up to it. At the edge of the grass, he dived. The ball was dropping fast. He leaned down low, extending his glove until it was maybe six inches off the ground. He reached just far enough to snag the ball in his webbing an instant before he sprawled and skidded onto the warning-track dirt. Just as he'd done earlier, Agee held his glove up to make sure the umpires knew what was tucked inside.

The Shea crowd erupted once more. The side was out, the Orioles threat extinguished.

Agee had single-handedly saved five runs—and possibly more—with his two catches. Hodges thought the second catch was the better of the two and later rated it even better than the grab by Dodgers left fielder Sandy Amoros on Yogi Berra in the sixth inning of game seven of the 1955 Series. Agee, for his part, believed that the first catch was harder because he had to reach across his body and backhand it.

"I thought I had the second one all the way, but the wind caught it and it dipped suddenly, so I had to dive for it," he said.

Agee was bathed in cheers on his long run to the first-base dugout, and it didn't stop there; he was the first Met up in the bottom of the seventh. The crowd stood for the seventh-inning stretch and remained standing as he walked to the plate. Behind third base, Karl Ehrhardt held up two big red letters—an A and a G—and pumped them up and down.

The new Baltimore pitcher was Dave Leonhard, the first reliever Weaver had used in the three games. Leonhard hardly fit the profile of a typical big-league pitcher; he was a former high school history teacher who had a degree from Johns Hopkins. He was greeted by 56,000-plus fans still throbbing with excitement over Agee's latest catch. A hearty "Let's go, Mets!" chant started up.

The 28-year-old Leonhard had had the best season of his six-year big-league career in 1969, pitching to a 2.49 earned run average and winning seven games out of Earl Weaver's bull pen. He put up a scoreless inning against the middle of the Mets' order. Nolan Ryan now faced the same challenge in the eighth, and had two new defensive players to help him do it: Al Weis at second for Ken Boswell, and Rod Gaspar for Art Shamsky in right. Hodges always wanted his best defenders on the field when the Mets had a late lead; both players had finished all three games of the NLCS with good results.

Ryan threw seven pitches to Frank Robinson to lead off the eighth, every one of them a fastball. Robinson battled his way to a full count, fouled a ball off, and then drove a long fly to left-center. Jones raced back and to his left, onto the warning track. Agee raced back and to his right. Jones seemed to have it lined up, but at the last moment Agee called him off and Jones stopped running, knowing to defer to the center fielder. A step in front of the wall, Agee made the catch. The man was ubiquitous. It was his sixth putout of the game. For once he didn't need to use his webbing. In the box seats behind third, Ehrhardt held up a sign that read, A BIGGY.

The Orioles had five outs left and needed four runs to tie. Boog Powell, who had two of the Orioles' three hits, stepped in for his first look at Ryan. Ryan started him off with a curveball, a wicked overhand breaker that dropped right at the knees on the inside corner, all but unhittable, and followed with gas. Powell took a massive cut and missed. The crowd *ooh*ed. The fans were alive on every pitch. The end was in sight, and they wanted to help the Mets get there.

After Ryan came in high and hard on an 0-2 pitch, Powell hitting the dirt to get out of the way, Grote wanted to go away. He was a masterful pitch caller with a sharp sense of how to exploit a hitter's weaknesses. Shamsky, who had played with Johnny Bench in the Cincinnati Reds organization, believed that as tremendous as Bench was as a catcher, Grote had a stronger arm and a better glove. No less an authority than Lou Brock said that Grote was as tough a catcher to steal on as any he'd ever seen. A native Texan, Grote had become such an indispensable Met that he had caught every inning of every game in the 1969 postseason. It continued a remarkable turnabout for a player who, two years before, would've been a leading candidate for Most Volatile Met but surely not the most valuable one. If not for a freakish turn of events, he wouldn't even have been the Mets' starting catcher.

After coming over from the Houston Astros after the 1965 season, Grote was superb behind the plate but hit just .237, then endured a nightmarish 1967, when he hit .195 and incurred the wrath of his manager, Wes Westrum, and some of his pitchers, too, for constantly yapping at umpires, virtually assuring that no Mets pitcher would ever get a borderline strike call. The low point came in Los Angeles. Westrum, a former catcher himself, had already used two catchers when Grote came on as a pinch-hitter in the seventh inning. He stayed in the game to catch and immediately started in on home plate umpire Bill Jackowski, complaining about his calls as the Dodgers loaded the bases on two walks and a single.

The Mets got out of the jam, but back in the dugout Grote stayed on Jackowski. Grote tossed a towel on the field and then Jackowski tossed Grote, which presented a problem: the Mets were out of catchers. Now the enraged Westrum had to go find a volunteer to catch. Rookie outfielder Tommie Reynolds took over and did a creditable job until the eleventh inning, when the inevitable happened, a swinging strike getting by Reynolds with a man on third, handing the Dodgers a 7–6 victory. The tantrum cost Grote a $100 fine and a telephone scolding from team president Bing Devine.

Grote's hotheaded ways and inconsistent hitting compelled the Mets to explore some new catching options. When Hodges came aboard in the fall of 1967, he told the front office that J. C. Martin of the Chicago White Sox would be a good man to have. Not even six weeks later, the Mets acquired Martin as the player to be named later in a deal that sent Ken Boyer to the White Sox.

Hodges was delighted. Martin, who found out about the trade while he was on a hunting trip with White Sox pitcher Gary Peters, was not. Indeed, he was crushed. The son of a small-town deputy sheriff in Virginia, he'd been with the White Sox since they had drafted him as a teenager. The White Sox were a contending team, right up there with the Yankees every year, and the Mets were awful. Martin hadn't seen the trade coming, and when it did it had the sting of dismissal. Only when he arrived at spring training and got to know Hodges and got to see all the young talent on the Mets' pitching staff did his thinking change.

Martin was expected to be the Mets' number one catcher in 1968, relegating Grote to backup, but in the first game of the season, in San Francisco, a Willie Mays foul tip smashed into Martin's finger.

The X-ray showed that it was broken. Martin was going to be out for nearly a month. Hodges, his new manager, said, "Why don't you get on a plane in the morning and go home and be with your family for a week and then meet us back at Shea Stadium."

Martin deeply appreciated the offer.

"That's just how he was," Martin said. "He was such a fatherly figure. He had those big hands and arms, but he was so kind and had a sense of humor you wouldn't believe. He was just so important."

In Martin's absence, Grote played his usual stout defense and hit over .300. Hodges had worked with Grote to lower his hands at the plate, shorten his swing, and be more selective. Grote more than tripled his walk total, wound up hitting .282, and was named the starting catcher for the National League in the All-Star Game, getting more votes than Hank Aaron or Willie Mays. Martin, as selfless a man as there was on the team, couldn't argue with Hodges's decision to keep Grote as the number one catcher after Martin's finger had mended.

"He was doing a tremendous job. You had to leave him in there," Martin said.

Martin's bad break turned out to be a career-altering event for Grote, who suddenly was an anchor of the club and a pitch-calling drill sergeant behind the plate. When he wanted to deliver a wake-up call to a pitcher, Grote would sometimes throw the ball back to the mound faster than the ball had come in. It would get the pitcher's attention, though one guy Grote learned not to do it to was Jerry Koosman. The last time Grote tried it, firing a ball back to him, Koosman caught it on his hip, glared at him, and called Grote out to the mound.

"If you ever do that again, I will kick your ass," Koosman said.

• • •

GROTE DIDN'T THROW his fastball back to Ryan after Ryan had sent Powell reeling backward. There was no wake-up call necessary. With the count at 1-2, Grote called for another fastball; it was away.

Ryan hit the glove on the outside corner. Powell, leaning backward, took a halfhearted swing.

Two outs.

Ryan got ahead of Brooks Robinson 1-2 with another big curveball, but Robinson battled hard, fouling off a fastball and working the count full after Ryan barely missed with a 2-2 curveball. Ryan wanted the call but didn't get it. He went into his motion, rocking backward, swinging his arms overhead, and bringing up his left leg almost to the letters, an effortless motion that delivered a pitch that would become known, a bit later in his career, as the "Ryan Express." The Express was what Grote called for, and Ryan brought it on his next pitch. Robinson swung and couldn't catch up to it.

A trio of hitters who had accounted for 92 home runs and 305 runs batted in that season had gone down in order. The Orioles, who had had 16 runs and 36 hits in their sweep of the Twins in the ALCS, had 1 run and 5 hits in their last 17 innings against the Mets.

Paul Richards, the Braves' general manager, the man who had mocked the Mets for refusing to trade all their untouchables (Ryan among them), was at Shea Stadium and was astounded by what he was watching.

"It is absolutely impossible for a human being to throw the ball harder than he does," he said. "If he threw it any harder, it would have to be a cinder when it got up there."

With one out in the bottom of the eighth, Kranepool launched a curveball from Leonhard far over the right-center-field fence, growing the lead to five and bringing the fans out of their seats yet again.

• • •

UP IN THE Shea press box, a former bedspread salesman named Arthur Friedman recorded Kranepool's clout in his scorebook and made the necessary updates to his numbers. Friedman was the Mets' statistician, a man who was so good with digits he would also become the New York Rangers' statistician and the stat man on *Monday Night Football*. He met Hodges on the first day of spring training in 1968, and Hodges told him, "I want to see you every day. You are going to be a very important part of what we do."

Long before computers made their way into the sports world or anyone ever heard of advanced metrics, Friedman, who grew up in Brooklyn with sportscaster Marv Albert, kept all his stats by hand, providing Hodges with precise daily breakdowns of statistical trends on the Mets and their opponents. Hodges wanted splits on how players fared against right-handed and left-handed pitchers, on baserunning tendencies, starting pitchers' track records, everything.

"Gil wanted to know every piece of information you could give him," Friedman said.

Friedman saw every regular-season Mets game, home and away, for 16 years. He had been there when they stunk, and now, as he hunched over his stat sheet in the press level behind home plate, he was three outs away from seeing the Mets take a 2-1 lead in the World Series. A consummate pro who tracked everything that happened on the field, he had no time or inclination to get swept up with the burgeoning excitement in the park.

He had numbers to keep, after all. But still . . .

"It was hard to fathom what they were on the brink of doing," Friedman said.

· · ·

RYAN CAME OUT for the ninth. Elrod Hendricks had hit long shots to left-center and right-center in his previous two trips, both of them run down by Agee. This time Hendricks tried Gaspar, a short fly to right for the first out. Johnson followed with a line drive, also to Gaspar, and the Orioles were down to their final out and then their final strike after Ryan went ahead of Belanger. Belanger fouled off a couple of pitches and made Ryan work and wound up drawing a walk. The crowd, all set to let loose, had to wind back down for the moment. It was difficult to do.

Weaver went with veteran catcher Clay Dalrymple to pinch-hit for Leonhard. On a 2-2 pitch, Dalrymple hit a grounder up the middle. Weis dived and smothered it and fired to Bud Harrelson at second, but Belanger just beat the throw. The crowd, again ready to explode in delight over a game-ending force play, collectively groaned about having to defer gratification once more.

Weaver brought in Chico Salmon, a reserve infielder, to run for Dalrymple. The Orioles had two on with two out and, curiously, nobody warming up in the bull pen, even though Leonhard was out of the game.

Buford drove Ryan's first-pitch fastball deep to the opposite field, toward the left-field foul pole. Jones broke for it hard but quickly saw that the ball wasn't going to be playable; it was going to be either a home run or a long foul ball. It all hinged on where it landed. Jones tracked its flight, and so did Ryan and every other human being in the park. The ball rocketed onto the concourse, into the standing-room crowd, about six feet left of the foul pole and the 341 feet sign.

That's how close Buford came to making it a 5–3 game.

Ryan got a new ball from Larry Napp, the home-plate umpire. He got back onto the rubber, and Grote called for a fastball down in the zone. Ryan missed low, then missed with a couple more. Finally a Baltimore reliever—Eddie Watt—started warming up. Ryan missed with a 3-1 pitch, and now the bases were loaded.

Hodges went to the mound. Grote joined him. Hodges patted Ryan on the leg and said a few things. The meeting lasted 13 seconds, and Hodges went on his way, back to the dugout.

Paul Blair stood in. He was the first batter Ryan had faced in the game, two innings before, with the bases loaded then, too. Blair had been taking great cuts; he would've had the Orioles' biggest hit of the day had it not been for Tommie Agee.

Ryan started him off with a fastball on the outside corner. Blair barely moved as the ball left Ryan's hand; he appeared to be taking all the way, hoping that Ryan was lapsing into one of his wild patches. The pitch came in about knee high, and Napp came up with his right arm. Ryan was ahead 0-1. Wasting no time, Ryan fired again, another fastball, more in the middle of the plate. Blair took a strong cut and fouled it back.

The count was 0-2. Ryan needed just one more strike. The question was how he would try to get it. Blair had seen five pitches from him over two at bats, every one of them a fastball. Blair may have been in a hole, but he'd already shown he could catch up to, and drive, Ryan's fastball.

Grote put down the sign. Ryan tugged at his cap. He checked Belanger at third and went into a full windup. Blair gripped the bat with a small gap between his top and bottom hands, his face taut with concentration. Expecting another fastball, he strode toward the ball the instant Ryan let it go. He was out in front, committed, and then the ball started to break, a roundhouse curve that buckled Blair's knees and dropped into Grote's glove over the inner part of the plate. Napp jerked up his right arm, immediately took off his mask, and did an about-face, marching toward the umpire's exit behind home plate, his day's work done.

Blair dropped the bat onto his shoulder and stood for a moment at home plate as Shea Stadium throbbed with joy all around him. Grote bounced out of his crouch and ran toward the mound, tucked the ball into Ryan's glove, and slapped him on the chest. The Mets poured out of the dugout. They were 5–0 victors in the first World Series home game they had ever played and led the Series two games to one.

One of the last Mets off the field was Tommie Agee, the man who had done more than anyone to make the outcome of game three possible. It was Agee who knocked the long home run off Jim Palmer to start the game. It was Agee who might have had the greatest game afield of any outfielder in World Series history. Grote waited by the dugout steps to welcome him, which he did with a huge smile and an arm around his waist. Right behind Grote was Donn Clendenon, who gave Agee a big slap on the backside.

Back in Mobile County Training School, the kids were out of class and watching every play on NBC, celebrating over the fact that one of their own had changed everything.

There was an almost palpable giddiness around the Mets' clubhouse after game three, not because the players were cocky about taking the series lead, but because of the breathtaking manner in which they had won. Most ball games, even 5–0 games, are decided by the most slender of margins—a big hit in a big moment, a big catch in a big moment. On a windswept October Tuesday in Flushing, every big moment belonged to the New York Mets. And it certainly didn't dampen the mood any knowing that for game four, Hodges would be handing the ball back to the man who had won more games than any other pitcher in baseball.

Game one of the Series had not gone the way Tom Seaver had hoped. Neither had game one of the NLCS. Seaver was the Mets' best pitcher, the man who had altered the course of the franchise upon his arrival two years earlier. Now he had before him a clean easel on which to paint. Game four would be played on October 15, as millions of protesters around the country participated in the Vietnam War moratorium. Seaver, an ex-Marine, shared their convictions, but the only place he would be marching on Wednesday afternoon would be to the Shea Stadium mound.

14

PITCHING IN PROTEST

World Series Game Four
Queens, New York

THE AFTERNOON OF OCTOBER 15, 1969, BROUGHT AN AUTUMN CHILL and charged emotions to Flushing, Queens, along with 225 special guests of the New York Mets. They were directed to an area beyond the center-field fence, near the Shea Stadium flagpole. The guests were veterans from nearby St. Albans Naval Hospital, most of them arriving in wheelchairs, the more fortunate ones on crutches, all of them wounded in combat in the Vietnam War. As they made their way through the parking lot, the veterans were surrounded by antiwar protesters who were circulating leaflets with the heading "Mets Fans for Peace," featuring a photo of game four's starting pitcher, Tom Seaver. Prominently displayed was a story in which Seaver discussed his plan to place an advertisement in the *New York Times* that said, "If the Mets can win the World Series, then we can get out of Vietnam." Seaver was, in fact, an ardent opponent of the war, but he hadn't authorized the use of his likeness and didn't appreciate seeing the leaflets when he showed up for his workday.

The war was at the forefront of American consciousness everywhere that day, as hundreds of thousands of people, demonstrators and counterdemonstrators alike, voiced their opinions about the war with rallies, church services, and candlelit processions, organized mostly by the Vietnam Moratorium Committee, a group headed by supporters of former antiwar presidential candidate Senator Eugene McCarthy. In Boston, an estimated 100,000 protesters gathered on Boston Common. In Washington, tens of thousands held a silent vigil on the steps of the US Capitol, gathered by the Washington Monument, and marched on the White House.

Students at Monmouth College in New Jersey put the names of all of the state's Vietnam War fatalities in a casket and buried it on an athletic field, and at the trial of the so-called Chicago Eight—the activists charged with conspiracy to incite violence at the 1968 Democratic National Convention—defendant Abbie Hoffman entered the courtroom with a black armband and a large Vietcong flag that he attempted to drape over the defense table, along with a small American flag. Hoffman's decorative plans were interrupted by a federal marshal, the two men engaging in a tug-of-war before both flags were confiscated. On the *CBS Evening News*, Walter Cronkite called the nationwide outcry against the war "historic in its scope."

In New York alone, there were an estimated 175 different moratorium events, one of them in Washington Square Park, where Steve Zelkowitz joined thousands of other NYU students. In Bryant Park on 42nd Street, some 50,000 people gathered to listen to music by Peter, Paul and Mary, and hear Mayor Lindsay call it "one of the most peaceful and greatest days we've had in our city." The mayor ordered all US flags in city buildings—including the one at Shea Stadium—to fly at half-staff to honor those who had died in the war, an edict that did not go over well in the city's police precincts and firehouses. Most police and firefighting union officials refused to go along, and the mayor was also rebuffed by Baseball Commissioner Bowie Kuhn, who ruled that the Shea flag would fly high and was backed by the 225 wounded veterans seated by the flagpole.

"They would have had to fight us first," said Sergeant Maurice Kaplan, a soldier who had been wounded twice in Vietnam, when asked what would have happened if anyone had touched the Shea flag. That lowering the flag, a time-honored means of mourning the loss of life, would trigger such controversy underscored how deeply divided the nation was.

After Casey Stengel theatrically wheeled his left arm a few times and threw out the ceremonial first pitch to Jerry Grote, eight Mets took the field. The missing Met was Tom Seaver. Donn Clendenon whipped underhanded grounders to the other three infielders. The outfielders got loose. Grote kept looking into the Met dugout, wondering where the ace was. Finally, almost a minute and a half after his teammates, Seaver, apparently needing a last-minute stop at the dugout latrine, emerged from the dugout and ran out to the mound. He picked a few pebbles off the front of the rubber and started scuffing up the dirt to get it right. He warmed up quickly.

Game four was an exact rematch of game one: Seaver versus Mike Cuellar. Both managers went with the same lineups they used in the first game. Only the venue had changed. Seaver hoped the outcome would change, too. He took the mound knowing full well that if the Mets could manage to take a third straight game, they would be in a commanding position. In a best-of-seven series, the difference between being up three games to one and being tied at 2-2 is massive. It made every pitch and every at bat in game four vitally important. One hit, one pitch, one fielding gem could be the difference maker, and you never knew when that might be. The Orioles didn't need to look farther than Tommie Agee's glove to be reminded of that.

• • •

AS SEAVER READIED to make his first pitch, scores of writers from around the country were poised over their portable typewriters in the Shea press box, the air thick with cigarette smoke and the clacking sound of typewriter keys. The writers would pound out their stories on paper, edit them by hand, then hand them to a press box aide who would retype a clean copy and send it via telex machine to the various newspaper offices. There was no women's room in the Shea pressroom, because no women worked there. George Vecsey of the *New York Times* was one of the reporting horde. It was the work he'd envisioned himself doing since the day he had accompanied his father, the original George Vecsey, a sportswriter himself, to Ebbets Field. It was 1946, and young George was 7.

"From the time Louie the bartender slid me a Coke at the end of the Ebbets Field pressroom bar, I knew I wanted to be a baseball writer," he said.

Vecsey covered the Mets from the beginning. He was fascinated by the funny stories and fractured syntax of Casey Stengel and forged a strong connection with the so-called New Breed—young players such as Ron Swoboda, Tug McGraw, and Cleon Jones—whom Stengel invariably referred to as the "Youth of America." When Ed Charles joined the club in 1967, it didn't take long for Vecsey to regard him as one of the most thoughtful and gentle souls he'd ever met, in baseball or out. Vecsey had seen Gil Hodges as a player and now as a manager and appreciated his low-key earnestness and his underappreciated drollness, as well as the way he never bullied anyone, something that his powerful physical presence would've made easy to do. After a bad stretch early in the season, Hodges closed the clubhouse door and reamed his team out without raising his voice, and when the press pushed him for details, he declined to give them any. When they kept prodding, he said calmly, "We had a meeting. It's a clubhouse thing. It pertained to the game."

Vecsey had a genuine fondness for the Mets as people, but even with the wholesale changes in the club's ability and attitude under Hodges, he watched the start of game four and couldn't imagine that the Series would continue on this path.

"As a writer who had been around the Mets all those years, I was conditioned to expect them to lose," he said. "I never saw that a team that was changing kaleidoscopically would turn into this. I never saw the Mets coming. It was just very easy to think that Frank and Brooks Robinson and everybody else would start to hit and the Orioles would win in seven."

* * *

SEAVER'S FIRST GOAL in game four was not to let Don Buford lead off the game with a home run. He started him off with a high fastball on the inside corner. He fired another well-located fastball that

Buford fouled off on a 2-2 count and then struck him out with a curveball away.

This was a much better beginning, Seaver decided.

Paul Blair laced a single to center, and that brought up Frank Robinson. He had been unusually quiet through the first three games, managing but one single in nine trips and no runs batted in, but Seaver knew that could change with one swing of the bat. Robinson was as dangerous as any hitter in baseball. Seaver got ahead with a fastball on the outer half that Robinson missed and challenged Robinson with heat again, but this time Robinson swung and put serious wood on it, launching it deep to left-center.

Tommie Agee—him again—was in full retreat, sprinting to the warning track and settling under the ball, catching Robinson's drive just in front of the green eight-foot wall.

Seaver worked the inner half of the plate against Powell, then painted a fastball on the outside corner to catch him looking. Powell gave home-plate umpire Shag Crawford a you've-got-to-be-kidding look, then tossed his helmet and bat toward the dugout, where Weaver, his pepper-pot manager, was fuming about the call.

Cuellar finished his warm-ups and then Brooks Robinson handed him the game ball. Cuellar was all set to go to work when he realized he was missing a left fielder. It was a day for late arrivals. Buford had started up the dugout stops and felt something catch in his lower left leg. He had floating cartilage from an old knee injury during his days as a USC running back. It flared up periodically, and he had aggravated it the previous day. He returned to the dugout and called for the trainer, who worked on his calf and the inside of his knee. Weaver came over to see what the problem was. The massage seemed to help, and Buford gingerly ran out toward left field, noticeably favoring his right leg.

With a full complement of fielders, Cuellar got Agee on a bouncer to third before Harrelson, batting from his weaker (right-handed) side, pounded a hard single to left between Brooks Robinson and Mark Belanger. Cuellar made sure to keep Harrelson close to first, throwing over once and then again. Down a game and not hitting at all, the Orioles couldn't afford to fall behind early, and when Cuellar got Jones to bounce into a crisp 6-4-3 double play, they had put up the desired zero.

In the second, Seaver had two outs and Dave Johnson on first when Belanger stepped up to the plate. Seaver missed with his first pitch before he got a call on the corner to even the count at 1-1. The moment Crawford made the call, Weaver started chirping at him.

"Outside corner, my ass."

"That's not even close."

"You better give us that call, too."

Crawford glared into the dugout but didn't say anything. It was only the second inning, and the umpire's patience was already getting tested. Belanger swung at a fastball away and hit a foul ball down the right-field line, Swoboda galloping in hot pursuit. Swoboda's nickname was "Rocky" because of his muscular physique and his full-throttle style of play, with little regard for his physical well-being. Swoboda hit the sidewall but couldn't get to the ball. Belanger was still alive.

One pitch later, Johnson took off for second. Seaver's pitch was up and in. Grote bounced up and fired a strike to Harrelson, who put the tag on Johnson for the third out.

Sending Johnson was a curious decision by Weaver. Johnson had had an All-Star year, but he was not a base stealer, having been caught more times (four) than he had been successful (three). Grote was one of the best-throwing catchers in the game. Weaver was trying to get something going and catch the Mets unaware, but the result was that his number eight hitter and his pitcher would be the first two hitters in the top of the third.

• • •

DONN CLENDENON led off the second inning. At 6 feet, 4 inches and 215 pounds, Clendenon had a long, chiseled face that was a perfect complement to his body. He set up deep in the box, well off the plate, wheeling his bat a couple of times before settling into his stance, feet wide apart and knees bent, leaning in at the waist, a man with the unmistakable, long-limbed aura of a power hitter.

Clendenon hadn't become a Met until the June 15 trading deadline, when Johnny Murphy, after his fortuitous accidental phone call to Clendenon's hotel room, had sent four players to the Montreal Expos to get him. By then Clendenon may have had the most bizarre season of any player in baseball. In a span of months, he'd been taken in the expansion draft by the Expos, traded to the Houston Astros, announced his retirement, and then found himself at the center of a squabble involving two clubs and the commissioner's office. Clendenon was tired of being bounced around, and wasn't one to be pushed around. He had no interest in playing again for Astros manager Harry "the Hat" Walker, a self-styled hitting guru and lifelong Alabaman who had managed him in Pittsburgh. Walker had a profound influence on Matty Alou, among others, but he also had an acerbic style and a history of prickly relationships with some of his players of color. The trade prompted Clendenon to say goodbye to baseball and accept a VP position with Scripto, an Atlanta-based pen company, a stunning career move that never came about because Bowie Kuhn convinced him to unretire, arranged for him to remain in Montreal, and got the Expos to send the Astros other players in his stead.

Murphy's belief was that the 33-year-old Clendenon wasn't a fading malcontent but a right-handed slugger who would beef up the Mets' power-challenged attack, and he was right. Clendenon's impact with the Mets was far greater than his half-season stat line of 12 home runs and 37 runs batted in might suggest. He was a bright man with diverse interests and a college degree, and a noted needler with a gift for keeping the clubhouse loose amid the daily grind and competitive stresses of a baseball season.

Hodges's son, Gil Jr., quickly became one of Clendenon's favorite targets. Clendenon used to tell the younger Hodges that you weren't really a man until you tested your father. Two or three times every road trip, Clendenon would see Gil Jr. and holler, "Hey, Junior, have you done it yet?"

Gil Jr. idolized his father. He also knew he was one of the strongest human beings anywhere. One year, Gil Jr. got a set of weights for Christmas, loaded up about 80 pounds on a barbell, and watched his father hoist it overhead with one hand.

"It was like he was lifting a Tootsie Roll," Gil Jr. said.

The son wasn't going to test his father, ever, but Clendenon kept it up. As Gil Jr. walked by Rube Walker one day, Clendenon started in again. "Junior, have you done it? Are you a man yet?"

"Leave me alone. Are you crazy?" Gil Jr. said.

Walker asked what all this was about. Clendenon explained the backstory.

"Why don't *you* test Hodges?" Walker said to Clendenon. "Why don't we see what kind of man *you* are?"

Clendenon laughed. "I'm not testing him. Are you crazy?"

Gus Mauch, the Mets' trainer, had spent nearly two decades as the Yankees' trainer before joining the Mets in 1962, taking care of Joe DiMaggio, Yogi Berra, Mickey Mantle, Whitey Ford, and Elston Howard. When Clendenon walked into the training room one day and saw Mauch giving a rubdown to Joe Pignatano, he said, "Why in the hell are you wasting those marvelous hands on a horseshit player like Joe Pignatano, who couldn't even hit his weight?"

Pignatano—"Piggy" to everyone on the Mets—got off the table and chased Clendenon out of the room.

Like his new teammates Ed Charles, Tommie Agee, and Cleon Jones, Clendenon, of Atlanta, Georgia, was raised in the South in a time when segregation still held sway in daily life. There were no well-organized Little Leagues for African-American kids; there were makeshift fields on vacant lots or dirt roads. Each season began not with a new uniform and a fresh stockpile of bats and balls but with your regular clothes and whatever equipment you could get your hands on. You knew your place and you stayed there, far from the whites-only bathrooms, water fountains, and restaurants.

The difference for Clendenon, though, was that he came from an educated, academically minded family. His father, Claude, had a doctorate and was the chairman of the mathematics department at

Langston University in Oklahoma. His mother, Helen, was a college graduate who went on to work as a librarian. Clendenon was just six months old when he lost his father to leukemia, but the academic road map had been laid out before him.

Clendenon was a superb student and equally gifted as an athlete. When his mother married a man named Nish Williams, a graduate of Morehouse College, a historically black university that had educated generations of Atlanta's most prominent African-Americans and had become the hub of the civil rights movement, Clendenon gained a loving, devoted second father and baseball mentor. Williams had been a standout player in the Negro Leagues, a man who would've had a shot at the major leagues had he been born twenty years later. He was friends with Jackie Robinson, Satchel Paige, Roy Campanella, and Joe Black, among others, all of whom would stop by the house periodically. When Donn was 10 years old and already showing athletic promise, his stepfather arranged for him to have a batting-practice session against Paige. The kid grabbed a bat, stood in, and took his hacks. Clendenon said later he would never forget it because his parents got into a fight about it; his mother wanted him to go to his violin lesson.

Clendenon became a three-sport star in high school and was set to accept a scholarship offer from UCLA before his parents—and a prominent Morehouse alumnus—convinced him to stay home and attend Morehouse. Enrolling at age 16, Clendenon was assigned a "big brother" in the school's mentoring program. His big brother was the same man who helped change his mind about UCLA: Martin Luther King, Jr. Clendenon sought his big brother's counsel often and was a regular visitor at the King home. If Martin Jr. was on the road, Martin Luther King, Sr. (Morehouse Class of 1926), was always around to help. Clendenon did well academically, earned 12 varsity letters in football, basketball, and baseball, and ran a 9.6 100-yard dash on the side. The Cleveland Browns made him an offer right out of school, but Clendenon's first love was baseball, so he passed and took a job teaching fourth grade. In the spring of 1957, he was invited to a 10-day Pittsburgh Pirates tryout camp in Jacksonville,

Florida. He stood out enough among the five hundred players trying out that the Pirates offered him a professional contract for $300
a month.

It didn't take long for Clendenon to experience the harshness of
minor-league life as an African-American in a sport, and a country,
that was embracing the idea of integration hesitantly. In his first season in the minors, he played for Jamestown in the New York–Penn
League. While the white players lived in homes in the community,
Clendenon and the other black and Hispanic players were herded
into the Jamestown YMCA. In rookie ball in Salem, Virginia, Clendenon and other players of color did get to stay in homes, but the
homes were invariably in poor neighborhoods, in conditions that
were often rodent-infested or otherwise substandard. In 1959, in the
newly integrated Carolina League, Clendenon played for the Wilson Tobs, getting off to a torrid start with a .370 average. Early in the
season, Wilson—a club with nine players of color—traveled to Raleigh. A local newspaper referred to the visitors as the Wilson Black
Tobs. Carolina League and Tobs officials decided that nine was too
many black players for one team, so in hopes of heading off any
racial unrest, the Tobs demoted Clendenon to Idaho Falls, Idaho,
and the Pioneer League. The move so incensed Clendenon that he
told the Pirates he was done. He went home to Atlanta and called
the Cleveland Browns, who still wanted to sign him. The Pirates
contract, however, barred Clendenon from playing other sports.
And baseball's reserve clause barred him from finding work with
another baseball organization.

Branch Rickey, Jr., son of the Pirates' GM and the organization's
farm director, traveled to Atlanta and showed up at Clendenon's
home, imploring him to change his mind. Rickey told Clendenon
he had a bright future and said if he went to Idaho he would give
him $100 for every point he hit over .300. As the son of the Dodgers
executive who had opened the door for Jackie Robinson, Branch Jr.
deserved more benefit of the doubt than most baseball officials, in
Clendenon's mind. Clendenon agreed and wound up hitting .356
with 15 home runs, 15 triples, 26 doubles, and 96 RBI in 105 games.

The extra $5,600 was a handsome salary bump. Clendenon continued to put up big numbers in the minors and got his first call-up to the big leagues in 1961. He became a Pirates fixture through the 1960s, highlighted by a 1966 season in which he hit .299, with 28 homers, 22 doubles, 10 triples, and 98 RBI.

Throughout his years with the Pirates, Clendenon showed again and again he wasn't afraid to go his own way or speak his mind. During his early years with the Pirates, Clendenon worked in the off-season as a Mellon Bank management trainee and in the Allegheny County District Attorney's Office. Later he got his law degree. When he heard the shattering news that his big brother, Martin Luther King, Jr., was assassinated on April 4, 1968, and baseball took no immediate action to postpone the start of the season, Clendenon mobilized his Pirates teammates, arguing that playing baseball on the day of the slain civil rights leader's burial was unthinkable.

"We feel we cannot play these games out of respect to Dr. King," he told *The Sporting News*, "since we have the largest representation of Negroes in baseball on the Pirates."

Major League Baseball ultimately decided to delay the start of the season by two days.

Gil Hodges had a good idea of the kind of man, and hitter, he was getting in Donn Clendenon. In their first meeting after he arrived in New York, Hodges told Clendenon how glad he was to have him on board, how he believed that Clendenon's big bat and veteran leadership would be vital ingredients for the young Mets in their first pennant race. Clendenon had never played in a World Series. He had joined a club on a rapid rise, and now that club was two games away from becoming world champions.

• • •

CUELLAR KNEW he had to be careful with Clendenon, the only Met with two hits off of him in game one. Cuellar would often get right-handed batters to chase his screwball, and though Clendenon was extremely prone to striking out (he had led the National League with 163 strikeouts the year before in Pittsburgh), he rarely seemed to bite on Cuellar's best pitch. So Cuellar didn't throw it, firing seven pitches that weren't screwballs, the last of them a slider that Clendenon rocketed to the back of the Orioles' bull pen, the ball flying right over the cart where a couple of Orioles relievers were sitting.

For a third straight game, the Mets had jumped out to an early lead, doing it with their fourth home run of the Series. It was only a single run, but you got the sense it was only going to ratchet up the pressure the Orioles felt to get themselves going.

Cuellar thought he had Clendenon struck out on a slider on the corner right before the home run, a call that caused Weaver to throw a fit in the dugout. Weaver kept up the barking to umpire Shag Crawford when Grote came up with two outs and checked his swing on a 1-1 pitch that looked to have the inside corner. Again Crawford didn't give Cuellar the call. When Grote took a high fastball up in the zone for strike three, Hendricks spiked the ball into the dirt on his way off the field.

Belanger returned to the batter's box to begin the third, having been left there when Johnson was gunned down by Grote. Seaver dropped a curveball on the outside corner to even the count 1-1 and was on the rubber, about to throw his third pitch of the inning, when Crawford took off his mask and walked toward the Orioles' dugout. Weaver and Hendricks were both hollering about the last strike call.

Although managers are typically given more leeway in postseason games, Weaver was treading a perilous path by arguing balls and strikes, which is grounds for automatic ejection. That did not stop him. His team was getting outplayed. He wanted to stir things up. If that meant baiting the home-plate ump, so be it. Weaver had started beefing on the second pitch of the game.

When Seaver's curveball to Belanger was called a strike, Weaver screamed that it was low and wanted to know why the Orioles weren't getting the same call. Crawford pointed at Weaver once, then again. "Shut your damn mouth," he said, and then turned back for home plate. Weaver followed him out, still yapping.

Later Weaver claimed he hadn't heard what Crawford said, and that was the only reason he followed him out onto the field.

"If he didn't hear me, then his ears are as bad as he thinks my eyes are," Crawford said.

Weaver kept it up and finally Crawford had heard enough, turning around and jerking up his hand, throwing Weaver out of the game. The Shea crowd went berserk. Weaver made sure he got his money's worth before departing, getting right into Crawford's mask to air a few more gripes, then trotting back to the dugout and heading for the clubhouse. Weaver was the first manager to get tossed from a World Series game since Charlie Grimm of the Cubs in game three of the 1935 Series. Billy Hunter, the third-base coach, took over the managerial reins.

Perhaps Weaver's dust-up had some effect, because the Orioles came to life. Belanger took a Seaver fastball to right for a single, and Cuellar, after squaring around to bunt three times, served a soft liner just over Harrelson's head. The Orioles had two on and nobody out.

Buford came up, and the Mets were looking for another bunt. Clendenon moved way in on the grass as Buford squared around on an 0-1 curveball. He stayed there on the next pitch, but Buford took a full swing, pounding a high chopper right at him. Clendenon leaped, stretching his glove as high as it would go, snaring the ball in his webbing, and throwing to Harrelson for the force-out.

Had Clendenon been 6 foot 3, the ball would've been in right field, and the game would've been tied.

Paul Blair was in a position to do some damage, with runners on the corners and one out. As the 1-1 pitch came in, the Mets' infield at double-play depth, he laid a bunt down the third-base line, thinking he'd catch the Mets off guard and keep the rally going for Frank Robinson and Powell. Blair didn't execute the bunt the way he'd hoped, though, popping it up to the left of the mound. Seaver threw Blair out at first, Belanger holding third.

With runners at second and third, Frank Robinson came to the plate. He'd backed Agee onto the warning track in his previous at bat. A single would give the Orioles the lead.

Seaver fell behind 2-0 but refused to give in, throwing a breaking pitch off the plate that Robinson chased. Robinson looked ticked off that he'd swung at ball three. Seaver came in with a rising fastball, and Robinson took a big rip at it, getting underneath it and lifting it into foul territory near first base. Clendenon made the catch. A half inning after crushing a long home run—his fourth hit and second homer in eight Series at bats—Clendenon had two assists and a putout. He was getting a lot done. He underhanded the ball toward the mound like a slow-pitch softball pitcher.

The Orioles' scoreless streak had reached 14 innings, their last run coming in the seventh inning of game two. In the quiet of the clubhouse beneath the third-base stands, the banished Weaver wondered when Baltimore's booming bats would come out of hibernation and tried not to think about Shag Crawford.

15

GLOVE STORY

World Series Game Four
Bottom of the third

	1	2	3	4	5	6	7	8	9	Runs
Orioles	0	0	0	-	-	-	-	-	-	0
Mets	0	1	-	-	-	-	-	-	-	1

MIKE CUELLAR FOUND HIMSELF IN A TIGHT SPOT IN THE BOTTOM OF the third. Al Weis singled off of Brooks Robinson's glove, and Tommie Agee roped a long single to left-center. With one out, Dave Johnson, the Orioles' second baseman, made a superb play to run down a Bud Harrelson grounder, leaving the Mets with men on second and third and their best hitter, Cleon Jones, stepping to the plate.

Jones, who had the third best batting average in the majors in 1969, had hit .429 in the sweep of the Braves and singled against Cuellar in his first at bat of the Series. Since then, though, he'd gone 0-13. He had not been held hitless in three consecutive games the entire season.

At age 27, Jones had grown into an elite hitter with no holes in his offensive game. He could hit any pitch to any field. He hit .340 against right-handed pitchers and .338 against lefties in 1969. He hit .341 the first half of the season and .337 the second. He was as consistent as the tides. Jones wasn't a man who was going to beat himself up over a few at bats, having learned a long while ago that the best way to hit is to step up to the plate with a calm mind and a sound plan. He bent down to get some dirt on his left fist, then rubbed his hands together and took a pair of practice swings. He rearranged the dirt in the box, got set, and after hitting a nubber foul down the first-base line, he looked for a pitch he could drive.

The sound of "Let's go, Mets!" filled the ballpark.

Cuellar's screwball came over the middle, then cut away and down, and Jones swung and knocked a grounder between third and short. Brooks Robinson reacted quickly, pouncing to his left. He gloved it cleanly and fired across to Powell to end the Mets' rally.

Cuellar hadn't put up 23 victories without being able to throw his best pitches in the biggest moments. Seaver hadn't won his 25 games without the same skill. In the top and bottom of the same inning, both pitchers had navigated some choppy seas nicely, and you had the feeling that the starters were beginning to seize control of the game.

Seaver kept it going in the fourth, with his tidiest inning of the game, needing only nine pitches to secure three outs, the last of them against Elrod Hendricks. Seaver started him with a curve so slow it almost qualified as an eephus, then busted him with a fastball, Hendricks hitting it wide of first. Donn Clendenon made a nice backhand play but threw low to Seaver covering, the pitcher having to reach down to his shoe tops. Seaver caught the ball just ahead of Hendricks, who clipped the back of his left foot. Clendenon ran over to offer his apologies for almost getting Seaver mowed down. Hendricks made sure that Seaver knew he hadn't meant to hit him.

Seaver waved them off, but when he got to the dugout, he sat down next to Gil Hodges and took off his left shoe and sock. He had a gash on his heel that Gus Mauch cleaned up and bandaged, Hodges carefully watching the whole process.

After Clendenon was caught looking and Swoboda threaded a single up the middle, Charles stood in. Cuellar came in with a high, tight fastball that bore in on Charles, who jumped and twisted to get out of the way. The ball caromed off his hand and the bottom of the bat.

Foul ball, Crawford said. Charles couldn't believe it. He showed the umpire his left pinky. Crawford wouldn't budge. The ball wouldn't have bounced so far away if it hadn't hit the bat first. The crowd booed lustily. Hodges walked slowly out of the dugout. Mauch was right behind him. As Mauch tended to Charles's pinky, Hodges calmly discussed the play with Crawford, who told him the ball had hit Charles's bat and then his pinky, and that made it a foul ball. Having gotten an explanation, Hodges headed back to the dugout.

The contrast between Hodges's measured calm and Weaver's blustering fury was striking. Hodges didn't bully or berate Crawford to help him get the next call. He listened and departed. His expression never changed. Not that Hodges would never argue—sometimes even vehemently—with umpires. It was just that he saw no need, or gain, to belittle them or attack their character. He would always remind people that umpires are human beings and that the human behind the plate had to make about 250 decisions every single game. Some mistakes were inevitable. You cannot demand perfection. To Hodges, it showed respect for both the umpires and the game to understand how difficult their job was.

The next inning, Seaver went back to work, pounding Dave Johnson with fastballs inside before the Orioles' second baseman hit a looping liner to short left field. Jones, oddly, hadn't had a fly ball hit his way since the eighth inning of game two.

The first step for an outfielder often determines whether he will catch the ball. If he takes a step back on a short fly, it's nearly impossible to recover. If he takes a step in on a ball over his head, it's even harder to catch up to it. The best outfielders go after a fly ball with the same urgency as a base stealer going for a bag, bursting low and hard like a sprinter coming out of the blocks.

Jones broke fast for Johnson's ball and thought he had a good chance to get it. With nobody out, it was worth the risk. As the ball descended, he sprinted a few more strides and went into a slide, extending his glove in front of him, so low it was touching the grass. An inch or two before it hit the ground, the ball dropped into his glove. He squeezed it tightly to make sure it stayed put and Frank Secory, the umpire on the left-field line, emphatically confirmed it was a catch, not a trap. Stealing a hit from an opponent can give a team almost as much of an emotional lift as scoring a run. The Mets were doing all kinds of hit stealing in this Series.

By the end of the fifth inning, Seaver had retired nine straight Orioles, closing it out by blowing Cuellar away with a fastball. Seaver was in the best groove he'd had in weeks. Cuellar was nearly as good, but his offense had scored one run in the previous 23 innings and were 12 outs away from falling behind in the Series, 3-1. Hitting is contagious, and so is not hitting. When a team goes into a prolonged slump, it's natural for every hitter to try a little harder, and when a hitter tries harder, his results are almost always poorer. "I *have* to get a hit," is the worst tape a hitter can have winding through his head.

That the Orioles' lineup was being overmatched by the Mets' young pitchers had become the dominant narrative of the Series. During the Orioles' stay in New York, Joe Cronin, the American League president, ran into O's coach Billy Hunter, a longtime friend whose playing career as a backup infielder had resulted in a .219 career average.

"Your guys are hitting like you used to," Cronin said.

After Buford bounced to Clendenon to start the sixth and Paul Blair worked out a walk, Seaver fired fastballs up and away to Frank Robinson, getting him on a pop-up to Harrelson. With Clendenon holding Blair at first, Seaver started Powell off working the outside edge but missed with a fastball and a slider. Ever the perfectionist, he snapped his glove when he got the throw back from Grote on the slider, frustrated that his command had fallen off. He fell behind 3-0, but battled back to get a full count. Clendenon looked into the dugout to see if Hodges wanted him to continue to hold Blair on. All three of Powell's hits in the Series had been slotted into the hole between first and second. Hodges wanted Clendenon to keep holding Blair on anyway. In a one-run game, Hodges reasoned, you had to keep the speedy Blair as close to first base as possible. The battle continued, Seaver coming at Powell with two fastballs up in the zone, Powell fouling them both off.

Oddly, Seaver chose that moment to walk off the mound, toward the second-base umpire, Lee Weyer. Seaver handed him the ball.

"This is an American League ball. Do I have to use it?" he asked.

Weyer looked at it, and indeed, the ball had Joe Cronin's signature on it.

"No, you don't," Weyer said, calling for Crawford to throw Seaver another ball, one that bore the signature of Warren Giles, the National League president. Crawford complied. There wasn't supposed to be any difference between the leagues' balls, but Seaver had become the top winner in baseball pitching with Warren Giles baseballs and saw no reason to switch brands now.

Behind the mound, Seaver vigorously rubbed up the new ball with both hands. He had been working Powell almost exclusively on the outside corner, and he stayed out there, bringing more high heat. Powell swung and hit a high fly to left-center. Agee held his hand up as he fought the bright sun. Jones, hustling over from left, circled right behind him in case he lost it. Agee pounded his glove.

The Orioles had nine outs left.

• • •

CUELLAR SET DOWN the top of the Mets' order on nine pitches, and Seaver was back on the hill so fast he probably wondered why he had ever left. For reasons known only to Jane Jarvis, the Shea Stadium organist, she played "O Tannenbaum" between innings. A supremely gifted musician, Jarvis was well versed in jazz and classical piano and had been the house organist since Shea opened, forging a successful performing career after enduring an unspeakable loss at age 13, losing both of her parents when their car had been struck by a train in her native Indiana. Jarvis was a petite woman—she was 5 feet tall but played bigger—who had been recognized as a major talent long before any Mets players were. She played the Thomas organ with bold, jazzy riffs and a sharp sense of humor. At the end of the second game (it took 7 hours, 23 minutes for the Mets to lose) of the longest doubleheader in big-league history, on May 31, 1964, Jarvis played "Gee, I Hate to Get Up in the Morning." She liked to play "Mr. Wonderful" for Tom Seaver and "When Irish Eyes Are Smiling" for Tug McGraw.

In her previous ballpark work, with the Milwaukee Braves, Jarvis would knock out Charlie Parker's "Scrapple from the Apple" when managers and umpires argued. Once, in the fourth inning of a Mets game, she played "Four," a tune recorded by Miles Davis, and later composed "Let's Go, Mets!"—the song she would play when the Mets took the field.

Seaver and Grote were in perfect harmony in the seventh, Seaver punctuating a 1-2-3 inning by blowing Johnson away with a high fastball. The shadows had overtaken home plate by the bottom of the inning, making it even tougher on the hitters. Pitches that started in bright sunshine got much harder to see 55 feet into their journey.

In the last of the seventh, Swoboda lined a one-out single to left, and when Charles smashed a line drive to left—the hardest-hit ball of the day outside of Clendenon's home run—the Mets seemed to have something going, but Buford flipped down his glasses and snagged Charles's shot a few feet short of the track.

As strong a game as Cuellar had pitched, Hunter, the interim Orioles manager, had no choice but to pinch-hit for him with one out in the top of the eighth. His team was running out of time—and outs. Dave May came up to hit for Cuellar. Seaver went after him with gas from the first pitch. Pinch-hitting is one of the hardest jobs in baseball, and when you are coming into a game in the eighth inning to face a Tom Seaver fastball, it's that much harder. May tried to catch up with a 2-2 offering but went down swinging, and when Buford popped up another Seaver fastball to Charles, the Mets were three outs away.

Up in the press box, even the doubting George Vecsey was starting to think that Gil Hodges's Mets might prove him wrong and change the franchise narrative.

The Orioles' top relief pitcher, Eddie Watt, a pudgy man who threw sidearm and wore his hat to the side, too, made his first appearance of the Series in the bottom of the eighth and tied a record that will never be surpassed. He did not throw a single pitch out of the strike zone. Seven pitches were all he needed to record three outs, and now Seaver came out to try to finish the job against the middle of the Orioles' order.

The Shea crowd was ready to explode, more taut with tension than during any game since the night of July 9, when Seaver had taken his perfect game into the ninth against the Cubs. As everyone knew, stuff can happen in the ninth inning.

Seaver started Blair off with a knee-high fastball on the outside corner for a strike. It would have been hard for a pitch to be more perfectly placed. Blair kicked his head back, stepped out of the box, and cursed. Shag Crawford was clearly in the Orioles' heads now. Blair got back in, only to see Seaver spin off a sharp curveball to make the count 0-2. Two pitches later, Seaver delivered another fastball on the outer half, and Blair skied it to Swoboda in right.

Seaver had retired 19 of the last 20 Orioles and hadn't given up a hit since the third inning. He had only two more outs to get. Frank Robinson strode to the plate, and Charles camped on the third-base line to guard against an extra-base hit. Clendenon did the same at first.

Seaver threw seven straight fastballs to Robinson, almost every one up in the zone. Robinson put some good swings on them, fouling off three in a row at 2-2, then drilling a single to left on a ball Seaver didn't get high enough.

Powell muscled an 0-1 fastball into the hole between first and second, not a hard-hit ball but a most timely one for his team. Robinson raced to third.

Hodges came out of the dugout and walked to the mound. Ron Taylor and Tug McGraw were getting loose. It was a difficult decision for Hodges to make. His team was up by just one run, and the O's had put runners on the corners. He had baseball's best pitcher on the mound, but he also had evidence that Seaver was tiring and two topflight relievers ready to go. Hodges's stay on the mound was brief.

This was Tom Seaver's game to win or lose.

Now it was Brooks Robinson's turn. Robinson had gone 1 for 15 for the World Series and 0-3 for the day, and he hadn't made good contact against Seaver all game, not getting the ball out of the infield.

Frank Robinson took a lead off third, Powell off first. Grote set up inside. Seaver started Robinson off with a fastball. It drifted out over the plate.

Robinson took a slashing swing and hit it solidly toward right-center, heading toward the gap. It looked to be serious trouble for Tom Seaver and the New York Mets.

"I thought it was going to bust the game open," Powell said.

16

CATCH ME IF YOU CAN

World Series Game Four
Top of the ninth

	1	2	3	4	5	6	7	8	9	Runs
Orioles	0	0	0	0	0	0	0	0	-	0
Mets	0	1	0	0	0	0	0	0	-	1

WHEN THE BALL LEFT BROOKS ROBINSON'S BAT, ROCKY SWOBODA had a microsecond to make perhaps the most important decision of his baseball life: Should I go for the catch or play the ball on the bounce? Nobody who knew Swoboda or had ever watched him play would have expected him to choose the latter. Swoboda's name is the Polish word for "freedom." He played the game with something approaching reckless abandon, slugging soaring home runs and running circles around fly balls, sometimes in the same game.

Strength and effort were never in question when it came to Swoboda. Grace and elegance were another matter. More than any other Met, he brought an element of unpredictability to the ballpark. You didn't know what he would do or what he would say. Smart and funny and a keen observer of his own foibles, he would weigh in on almost any subject, as he did on June 22, 1969, when the surging Mets were in the midst of a hot stretch, winning seven of eight games. Playing a Father's Day doubleheader at Shea against the Cardinals before almost 56,000 fans, the Mets swept behind superb pitching by Gary Gentry and Jerry Koosman, but somehow a Swoboda sideshow in game one elicited the biggest roar of the day.

Swoboda ended the bottom of the first by striking out against Steve Carlton. Carlton struck him out again in the third. When Swoboda came up an inning later, Carlton was gone and the Mets had a 5–1 lead, but Swoboda met with the same result, striking out against reliever Chuck Taylor. Each strikeout was greeted with progressively louder boos. When Swoboda led off the bottom of the seventh with strikeout number four against another reliever, Ron Willis, the boos amounted to some of the loudest noise of the year.

That figured to be the end of it, except that the Mets got a couple of guys on with two outs in the eighth, bringing Clendenon to the plate and Swoboda to the on-deck circle. When the Cardinals walked Clendenon intentionally, the Shea crowd cheered. Swoboda would be coming up a fifth time, with a chance to tie a major-league record of five strikeouts in one game.

Willis threw a strike to get ahead. The fans roared. When Willis threw a ball, the fans booed. They had brutalized Swoboda all day long for striking out, but now there was a complete emotional turnabout; now they wanted to see history.

Now they were rooting for him to strike out.

When Swoboda fouled off the next pitch, the fans exulted again. Rocky Swoboda was one strike away. Willis threw the 1-2 pitch off the outside corner. It was a good distance from the strike zone. Swoboda swung weakly and missed. He had the record and the crowd went wild.

"When I struck out the first time, I figured I'd get him the next time," Swoboda told reporters after the game. "When I struck out the second time, I wondered what was going on. The third time it seemed funny that I couldn't connect. The fourth time it was just a big, bad joke. Now, the fifth time, it was history.

"I guess if we had lost the game, I would've been eating my heart out. As it is, I'm only eating out one ventricle."

Swoboda majored in extremes, and it had always been thus. In his first game in the minor leagues, with the Mets' triple-A affiliate in Buffalo, he homered and went 3 for 5. The next day, against the Yankees' Richmond farm team and a promising pitcher named Mel Stottlemyre, he struck out four times.

Swoboda came from a working-class family in Baltimore. His

father, a waist gunner over Japan during World War II, worked as a mechanic, his mother in a variety of social service jobs. He signed for $35,000 out of the University of Maryland after an impressive showing at a big tournament in Johnstown, Pennsylvania, where the Mets' scouting contingent included Wid Matthews, the same scout who signed Stan Musial. Swoboda put on an equally good performance in his first big-league camp in the spring of 1964. Among those impressed was Casey Stengel, who couldn't pronounce Swoboda's name—he called him Suh-boda—but thought his potential made him the Mets' version of a young Mickey Mantle.

"Amazing strength, amazing power—he can grind the dust out of the bat," Stengel said. "He will be great, super, even wonderful. Now, if he can only learn to catch a fly ball."

The 20-year-old Swoboda came up to the Mets in 1965, a muscular frontman for Stengel's "Youth of America." Cleon Jones, Tug McGraw, and Bud Harrelson—all of them joined the big club that year. The next year brought Nolan Ryan, followed by Seaver, Koosman, and Ken Boswell in 1967. Jim McAndrew and Duffy Dyer arrived in 1968, a year before Gary Gentry, and Wayne Garrett, maybe the biggest surprise of them all, became Mets in 1969.

Swoboda would say later he had no business being in the big leagues so quickly, but his power was too enticing for the organization to ignore. In his second at bat in the major leagues, Swoboda socked a ball off the Astros' Turk Farrell that he said was the hardest ball he had ever hit, before or since. The ball hit the back wall of the left-field bull pen on the fly. About six weeks later in St. Louis, the Mets had a 7–0 lead in the middle of the seventh against the Cardinals and a 7–2 lead going into the bottom of the ninth. The Cardinals scored twice with the help of an error, then loaded the bases with two outs when Cardinals shortstop Dal Maxvill lofted a fly to right field. Swoboda had left his sunglasses in the dugout, not thinking the sun would be an issue. It was. He lost the ball in midflight, and all three runs scored to tie the game. The play was scored as a triple because Swoboda had never touched the ball. After

Swoboda lined out to start the tenth, he stomped on a helmet in anger. His foot got stuck in it, and he furiously began to try to shake it off, creating a major scene.

"You're done for today," Stengel said.

The Cardinals won in 12 innings.

Swoboda finished his first year with 19 home runs, a record for a Mets rookie that stood until Darryl Strawberry hit 26 in 1983. He also had 11 errors and a batting average of .228. He worked hard on his fielding. His average improved to .281 in 1967, and when he hit seven home runs in April 1968 and Koosman provided Seaver with a dominant southpaw sidekick, the Mets had something going. Swoboda was their quirky, charismatic power source and, quite unexpectedly, a *Sports Illustrated* cover boy. The issue was dated May 6, 1968. THE MOVIN' METS, it read above a closeup image of "Slugger Ron Swoboda" at the plate, gaze fixed squarely on the incoming pitch. Swoboda wound up hitting only four more homers the rest of the year, and though the Mets had patches of respectability, the team still finished in ninth place.

When Swoboda reported to camp in the spring of 1969, his stated goals were to be more professional and consistent and to prove to Hodges that he could be trusted. It was a necessary goal. Hodges was an old-school baseball man to the core. The game had enough maddening variables without creating more of your own. But Swoboda at times appeared to be moving in the opposite direction. In his first start in spring training, he misjudged a wind-blown fly ball and let it land a foot or two behind him. Later in the game a line drive caromed off his midsection for an error. After leaving the game in the sixth inning, he went to the bull pen area with his bat to work on his swing. When he returned to the dugout, he stumbled and nearly tumbled down the steps.

Swoboda played fewer games in 1969—109—than in any previous year in his career. He platooned with Art Shamsky in right and also shared time with rookie Rod Gaspar. A smooth and reliable outfielder, Gaspar came on for defensive purposes late in games for much of the year. Swoboda could've moped about it, but instead he redoubled his commitment to get better in the field. Coach Eddie Yost hit him fly balls and grounders before almost every game. Nobody on the club took more extra fielding practice than Swoboda. Gradually all of the reps paid off. Swoboda was never going to have the athleticism or outfielding instincts of Agee, but by dint of unstinting effort, he made himself a serviceable big-league outfielder. After September 1, Hodges did not remove Swoboda in the late innings even once.

If he never developed into the big-time slugger Stengel had envisioned, Swoboda nonetheless was a dangerous hitter, especially in big moments, an all-in Met fully committed to the cause. On September 13 in Pittsburgh, the Mets took Forbes Field with a nine-game winning streak and a two-and-a-half-game lead on the Cubs. Seaver and the Pirates' Luke Walker were locked in a taut battle, the score 1–1 in the eighth. Walker walked two batters and was replaced by Chuck Hartenstein. The Pirates didn't want to tangle with their former teammate Donn Clendenon, so they walked him intentionally. That brought up Swoboda, who knocked a 1-0 pitch over the left-field wall for his first grand slam.

The winning streak stretched to 10, the lead over the Cubs to three and a half games.

Two days later, the Mets were in St. Louis, facing the Cardinals' All-Star left-hander, Steve Carlton. In the early years of a Hall of Fame career, Carlton wasn't just overpowering that night in Busch Stadium; he was historically overpowering, striking out a record 19 hitters. Carlton said it was the best stuff he'd ever had in his life. His strikeout victims included Swoboda twice, once swinging and once looking. In his other two at bats, Swoboda drilled a pair of two-run home runs, accounting for every run in a 4–3 victory that was arguably the most improbable outcome in club history.

"He got me twice. I got him twice," Swoboda said.

. . .

SWOBODA WAS PLAYING Brooks Robinson a bit more shallow than usual in the top of the ninth of game four. Robinson had yet to have a good swing against Seaver, so Swoboda readied himself mentally to aggressively charge anything that came his way. With Frank Robinson on third, ninety feet away from tying the game, Swoboda wanted to give himself a shot at throwing him out at the plate if he tried to tag up. Next door in center, Agee got into his customary crouch, pounding his glove, weight on the balls of his feet. Grote smoothed out the dirt in the catcher's box and set up on the inside. Seaver's fastball came in over the plate. Brooks Robinson went after it.

You knew instantly from the sound that Robinson had hit the ball well, his line drive zooming over Al Weis's head at second and heading toward right-center. Swoboda got an excellent jump, but the ball was sinking fast. When he was a few feet away, Swoboda launched himself toward the descending ball, a full-out, headlong dive. He extended his left arm as far as it would go and made a backhand reach for the ball. It smacked into his webbing not even an inch or two from the ground. He rolled over, and his hat flew off. The ball stayed put. Swoboda held his glove aloft to show Lee Weyer, the nearest umpire, that it was a clean catch and came up throwing to the plate.

Frank Robinson, displaying keen baserunning instincts, had held at third to see if the ball would be caught. When it was, he tagged up and easily beat Swoboda's throw home. The Mets ran an appeal play at third to see if Robinson had left early, but it was denied. The Orioles had tied the game 1–1, but the Mets would happily take that; off the bat it looked as if the ball might be in the gap and would score two runs. At the very least it would've put runners on first and third. Probably thinking that Swoboda would play the ball safely on a bounce, Agee had been slow to back up his teammate. Had the ball gotten by Swoboda, even the slow-footed Powell would've scored and Brooks Robinson likely would've had a double or a triple.

For the third time in two games, a Mets outfielder had made a spectacular, potentially game-saving catch, one that none other than Mickey Mantle called "the best play I've ever seen in my life."

Clay Dalrymple, the Orioles' backup catcher and a former Philadelphia Phillie, had seen Swoboda many times in the National League.

"If he had tried that last year, he would have landed on his head and the ball would have rolled to the wall," Dalrymple said. "Then he would have had trouble picking it up and would have missed the cutoff man with his throw. He's hopped up like all the other [Mets]. I've never seen him make a catch like that."

Swoboda said the play unfolded too fast for him to do anything but rely on instinct.

"This is a game of chance, and if I have one chance in a million, I'll try to make it," he said.

. . .

ELROD HENDRICKS stepped up. He wasn't a high-average hitter (he hit .244 for the season), but he had a live, left-handed bat and hit 12 home runs in just over 100 games. Seaver started Hendricks off with a breaking pitch and fastball, both of which missed outside. He kicked his head back, ticked off that he couldn't hit his spots. Seaver caught Grote's toss back to the mound with two hands, as if he wanted to press pause and take stock of himself for a moment.

Hodges still had his two relievers ready to go but elected to stay with his ace. Seaver had thrown 18 complete games during the regular year, and all indications were that he would be completing game four.

Powell led off first. Seaver came set and delivered a fastball over the plate. Hendricks turned on it, hitting a bolt toward the right-field foul pole, 341 feet from home plate. Hendricks's shot had plenty of distance. It crashed into the stands just to the right of the foul pole. By a matter of inches, the game was still tied.

Seaver got a new ball and walked to the back of the mound. He took off his hat and wiped his brow. In the dugout, Hodges sat as impassively as ever, his hands in his jacket pockets.

Two pitches later, Hendricks made good contact again and drove a ball to right. This time Swoboda caught it on the run, no dive required. Having been robbed by Agee a day earlier, Hendricks probably wondered what he needed to do to get a hit against the Mets.

The score was 1–1 heading to the bottom of the ninth. With one out, Jones bounced a single to left, bringing up Clendenon, whose home run had accounted for their only run. Don Buford played him deep, almost on the warning track in left. Watt got ahead 0-2 and then struck Clendenon out with a high fastball. With two outs, Swoboda came up and got a huge hand for his catch. He got more cheers when he hit a single to right for his third hit of the game. Jones raced to third. Art Shamsky pinch-hit for Ed Charles but on the first pitch tapped a grounder to Dave Johnson at second.

Game four was going to extra innings—the first time there had been an extra-inning Series game in five years. Home plate was completely in the late-afternoon shadows, but Seaver stood in bright autumn sunshine as he squinted in to get Grote's sign.

Leading off the inning, Johnson reached on an error, his bouncer glancing off the glove of Garrett, who had come on for Charles at third. The ball caromed against the tarpaulin, but the hustling Harrelson backed the play up and kept Johnson at first. With one out, Dalrymple batted for Watt and hit a single to center. Seaver had given up three hits in the last inning and a third, and multiple hard-hit balls. Still Hodges stayed with him. Seaver was a man who wanted to finish what he started. His manager trusted him to do that.

Buford drove a 1-0 pitch deep to right that Swoboda caught at the edge of the warning track. Johnson tagged and moved to third.

Up stepped Paul Blair, a man who could handle anyone's fastball. Seaver and Grote went after him with breaking pitches on the outside. Before almost every pitch, Grote pounded his glove and swiped his right hand in the dirt. Ahead 1-2, Seaver threw a slider low and away. Blair took it for a ball. Seaver came right back with a breaking pitch that was well out of the strike zone. Blair swung wildly and missed. It was Seaver's sixth strikeout of the day, and the most important.

Blair fired his bat and helmet away in anger. The Mets ran off
the field for their first crack at extra innings. On the Thomas organ,
Jane Jarvis played "I'm Looking Over a Four-Leaf Clover."

It was the bottom of the tenth.

The Orioles' new pitcher was Dick Hall, who, at 39, was the oldest player in the World Series. At 6 feet, 6 inches, he was also the
tallest. A sidearming right-hander, he had an ungainly, no-windup
delivery, hiding the ball behind his back and then taking an exag-
gerated bend at the waist, looking like a praying mantis in a hat as
he short-armed his delivery to the plate. It was a motion unlike any
other pitcher in baseball, and it worked; Hall had a 1.92 earned run
average for the season, allowing only 49 hits in 65⅔ innings.

His first batter was Jerry Grote, who worked the count full and
swung at a letter-high fastball, lifting a high pop to medium left
field. It was a routine play, but Buford misread the ball off of Grote's
bat, taking a couple of steps back and then momentarily losing the
ball in the late-afternoon glare. Brooks Robinson and Mark Belanger both hollered "In!" to Buford, who reversed gears and franti-
cally tried to make up ground.

Belanger, who had broken back for the ball on contact, kept running into the outfield, back to the plate. Belanger knew he was the
only one who had a shot at making the catch. As the ball descended,
Belanger ran a final step or two and picked up the flight of the ball
over his head. He reached out with his left hand. The ball missed
the tip of his glove by a fraction of an inch. The late-arriving Buford
picked the ball up and fired to second, but Grote, running hard, slid
safely into the bag.

Shea rocked with energy over the gift double as Hodges replaced
Grote with pinch runner Rod Gaspar, who would have a much better chance of scoring on a single, or on a sacrifice fly if the Mets
could get him to third. Al Weis came up but never got to swing;
Billy Hunter had Hall intentionally walk him to set up a force at
second or third. Hendricks, the catcher, tried to catch Gaspar nap-
ping after Hall threw his third intentional ball, lobbing a throw to
Belanger at second, but Gaspar had returned to the bag.

As soon as Weis got to first, Hodges called Seaver back from the on-deck circle and sent up J. C. Martin to pinch-hit. Martin had delivered a huge pinch hit against Phil Niekro in game one of the NLCS. Hodges trusted Martin so much that even when the Orioles brought in left-hander Pete Richert to pitch to him, Hodges stuck with Martin.

Hodges had instructed Martin to swing away against Hall, but now he called Martin over to the corner of the dugout.

"J, let's change our strategy," Hodges said. "Let's bunt the ball down the first-base line and get the runner over to third, and then we'll have two chances to win the game. Just make sure you keep it away from Brooks and make the pitcher or the catcher field the ball."

Martin had become an adept bunter during his years with the White Sox, a team that counted on good pitching and sound execution to win, along with some creative Comiskey Park groundskeeping. The White Sox grounds crew would bore holes into the dirt in front of home plate, fill them with sand, and soak the field overnight. It was almost like quicksand, slowing down any ball that got pounded into it. The grass was kept thick and long.

"The field was manicured to hurt hitters," Martin said. "Trying to hit the ball through the infield there was impossible." Once, a few minutes before game time, he looked up to see about half the Minnesota Twins' roster stomping around in front of home plate to try to pack the ground a little harder. The White Sox gave the baseballs some special attention, too. Whether they were soaked or frozen, Martin wasn't entirely sure, but sometimes he'd pick up a ball that felt as if it could be used as a shot put. Twins slugger Harmon Killebrew once mashed a ball to right-center in Comiskey that he thought would be far over the fence, and it wound up hitting the wall. The next time up, Killebrew tapped Martin on the shin guard.

"Hey, I know when I hit a ball good, and I had that last ball good. What is going on with these baseballs?" he said.

"Harmon, you must be losing your power," Martin said.

Martin was going to get no special help from the Shea infield to get his bunt down. It was going to be a challenge against Pete Richert, a hard-throwing left-hander. Richert had pitched for Hodges with the Washington Senators, and he wasn't surprised at the impact Hodges had made on the Mets.

"He was a tough taskmaster in a lot of ways," Richert said. "He let everyone know where we stood. He said, 'This is how we're going to play.' We can be better, but we can only be better if we do the basic things right and make as few mental mistakes as possible. He was a great fundamental teacher. It showed when he went to the Mets. He made them good because he made them play good, fundamental baseball."

Richert knew Martin would be bunting. Martin knew Richert would probably come in high and hard, the most difficult pitch to get down. It was the first World Series appearance in the careers of both men.

Martin squared around early, kept the bat level, and followed the pitch all the way in. He laid down a little roller about 10 or 12 feet up the first-base line, with backspin, so the ball would come to a stop. He could not have dropped it in a better location.

Richert charged toward the line. Hendricks sprung from behind the plate and knew that it was an easier play for him to make than Richert. For one thing, Hendricks was going forward, toward the ball. For another, the left-handed Richert would have to spin around to throw. Hendricks called Richert off, but with 57,000 Mets fans screaming, Richert never heard him. He got to the ball first, whirled, and threw. With Powell also charging, Johnson, the second baseman, covered first.

Martin, not a fast man, ran the 90 feet with all he had, slightly inside the foul line. He was maybe 15 feet from the bag when Richert let loose with his throw as Gaspar raced for third, Weis for second. Johnson waited for the throw on the bag, his glove up and open. It was hard to track the ball with Martin running toward him.

An instant before Johnson expected the ball to arrive, it hit the back of Martin's left wrist and bounced toward second base. Johnson took off after it. In the first-base coaching box, Yogi Berra started wheeling his right arm. Gaspar rounded third and couldn't hear anything the coach, Eddie Yost, was saying. But Yost was wheeling his arm, too, so Gaspar kept running, Yost following not far behind. By the time Johnson ran the ball down, Gaspar was gleefully running toward the plate, looking like a kid at recess. He planted his left foot on the plate and was immediately greeted by Seaver, who had run out of the dugout to welcome him home. The rest of the dugout emptied, and the Mets hugged and danced. The Mets mobbed Martin, who had put down a perfect bunt on the only World Series pitch he would see in his 14-year big-league career.

Before Richert left the field, he said to Shag Crawford, "I think he was inside the baseline."

Replied Crawford, "No, don't even think about it."

Photographs in the papers the next day clearly showed that Martin was running slightly inside the foul line.

Rule 5.09 in MLB's *Official Baseball Rules* book states, "A batter is out when . . . In running the last half of the distance from home base to first base, while the ball is being fielded to first base, he runs outside (to the right of) the three-foot line or inside (to the left of) the foul line, and in the umpire's judgment in so doing interferes with the fielder taking the throw at first base."

Weaver, who was long gone, obviously couldn't protest the game. Hunter, who could have, did not.

After scoring one run in 19 innings at Shea Stadium, after watching Mets outfielders turn game-changing extra-base hits into highlight-reel putouts while one of their own outfielders was turning a certain out into a game-changing double, the Baltimore Orioles were one game away from elimination.

That night, one of the Mets' biggest and most vocal fans, Pearl Bailey, performed at her usual venue, the St. James Theatre, in the title role of the hit musical *Hello, Dolly!* The show's audience included two out-of-towners, Don Buford and Frank Robinson. Bailey invited the Baltimore outfielders backstage after the show.

"What are you fellows doing here?" she asked. "The way you're going, you should be home—rehearsing."

17

THERE ARE NO WORDS

World Series Game Five
Queens, New York

THE THIRD THURSDAY OF OCTOBER 1969 WAS A REGULAR SCHOOL day at Jamaica High School, but not for Bobby Sacca. He had to be at work, and so did his friend and schoolmate Bill Curtin. There was no chance Sacca was going to miss work that day. He met up with Curtin and caught the Q65 bus near his home on 84th Avenue, taking it to the number 7 subway line, riding it one stop to Willets Point. They arrived at work three and a half hours early. They were a little excited. Their office was in Flushing, just off Roosevelt Avenue, on the first-base side of Shea Stadium, in the New York Mets' dugout. It was the day of game five of the World Series. Sacca and Curtin were the Mets' batboys and had been the whole season. They made $6.95 per game, and while their friends were pumping gas or sweeping out movie theaters on Jamaica Avenue, Sacca and Curtin were handing bats to Cleon Jones, long-tossing with Rod Gaspar, and playing pepper with Donn Clendenon.

"The coaches would yell at Clendenon because he was taking full swings at us," Sacca recalled.

A standout catcher on the Jamaica High baseball team, Sacca learned the game under the tutelage of coach Joe Austin, a local legend who would be inducted into the New York State Baseball Hall of Fame and have a city playground named in his honor. Austin ran a team called the Emeralds in the Queens-Nassau Baseball League.

One of his former ballplayers had been a center fielder in the Pirates organization named Mario Cuomo. Austin was friends with Mike Becker, a bird-dog scout for the Mets who knew that Austin had a pipeline of talented kids who loved the game. When the Mets needed a batboy, they turned to Becker, who turned to Austin. A youngster named Joey Fitzgerald, a promising pitcher for Jamaica High, had the batboy job for several years, but then the Mets signed him to a contract in 1968 and he left to play pro ball.

Austin had a question for Fitzgerald's favorite catcher, Bobby Sacca.

"Do you want to be a Mets batboy?"

A blocky 5 feet, 5 inches, Sacca looked the part of a catcher. Yogi Berra nicknamed him "Shorty." Sacca even got to warm up Tom Seaver one time. There were occupational hazards, as in any line of work; you had to look out for wicked foul balls and errant throws—and, as Curtin found out, swinging bats. Ron Swoboda was in the on-deck circle and backed up just as Curtin was running to retrieve a ball. Swoboda's leaded bat slammed into the underside of Curtin's chin.

Swoboda felt terrible and apologized.

Curtin went into the clubhouse, got seven stitches, and was right back out there.

Sacca's baseball season was great at the start and then got even better. The excitement kept building. National media outlets descended on Shea, and so did celebrities. The dugout got to be very crowded before games. Nick Torman, the equipment manager, told the batboys to keep a close eye on the equipment. Before one game Sacca saw a guy in a fancy suit holding two baseballs.

"Hey, you can't take those balls," Sacca told him.

A security man tugged on Sacca's arm.

"Hey, Bobby, do you know who that is?"

"No," Sacca said.

"That's the governor, Nelson Rockefeller."

"I'm just doing my job," Sacca replied. "He owns half the world. What does he need two baseballs for?"

From the moment Bobby Sacca and Bill Curtin walked into Shea Stadium on the morning of October 16 for game five of the World Series, they were sure that the baseball season would end that day, with no return trip to Baltimore necessary. The Mets hadn't lost at home since the Pirates' Bob Moose had no-hit them on September 20. "One thing led to the next," Sacca said. "They kept coming back and kept finding ways to win." The ballpark was empty when the batboys arrived. Soon Shea Stadium would have enough emotional current to power the eastern seaboard.

"At that point in the season, the Mets couldn't do anything wrong," Curtin said. "They made all the plays. They got all the big hits. They made all the pitches when they had to."

• • •

THE PITCHING MATCHUP for game five was a reprise of game two, Dave McNally versus Jerry Koosman, and it favored Koosman if only because the Orioles' offense had gone anemic. After Don Buford's leadoff home run in game one, they hadn't hit another homer. Through four games, their team batting average was .143. Brooks Robinson acknowledged what was becoming obvious: the Mets' pitchers were handling the Orioles' lineup better than that of any other club they had faced all year.

The visitors knew how important it was to get ahead early so that the sellout crowd of more than 57,000 didn't turn into a cauldron of full-throated Mets mania. Back from exile after getting tossed out of game four, Earl Weaver insisted that his team wouldn't panic in the face of the 3-1 deficit, and so did Frank Robinson.

"I think we'll win three straight. I'm not just saying that to hear myself talk," Robinson said.

The Orioles had had winning streaks of three or more games 17 times during the regular season. Just one year earlier, in the 1968 World Series, the Detroit Tigers had been in the same hole before coming back to win games five, six, and seven over the St. Louis Cardinals.

In the runway next to the Mets' bull pen in right field, Koosman was pacing anxiously, waiting for his time to warm up, when he looked up to see Pearl Bailey, who was also waiting—to sing the national anthem. She wore a brown suit and matching fedora.

"Hey, Kooz, just relax," she said. "Everything is going to be good. You are going to win this game."

"Thank you, Pearl," replied Koosman. "It's nice of you to say that."

"No, really. You are going to win it. I see this number eight, and you are going to win."

Koosman got on the bull pen mound and started getting loose. Soon he would take the real mound for the 1,146th game in the history of the New York Mets. It was hard to imagine that a farm boy from Appleton, Minnesota, who owed his baseball career to a tip from an usher was in such a position, but no less imaginable than his club being in such a position. Bailey belted out "The Star-Spangled Banner," and Joe DiMaggio, a 54-year-old icon from another New York team and borough, threw out the ceremonial first pitch as fans continued to pour out of the number 7 subway station beyond the right-field fence.

Eight Mets took the field and Buford, the Orioles' leadoff man, came to the plate. After toweling off in the dugout, Koosman ran to the mound, dug his desired ditch in front of the rubber, and commenced his warm-up tosses. Donn Clendenon came over from first and stood on the edge of the mound, monitoring Koosman as if he were Rube Walker's assistant. Ed Charles, the other corner infielder, pinched in from third to stand near Koosman, too. Koosman had almost 70 years of human wisdom on his flanks, his veteran corner infielders offering a word of encouragement before returning to their stations.

Koosman started Buford off with a fastball, then came back with a slow curve. Buford bounced to Bud Harrelson at short for an easy out. Koosman fooled Paul Blair—the man who had broken up his no-hitter in the seventh inning of game two—with a changeup that he popped to center, and then Frank Robinson put an inside-out swing on a fastball, hitting a ball to short right that a charging Ron Swoboda caught at his waist.

Koosman needed just six pitches to get three outs. It was one of his quickest innings of the season. When Tommie Agee came up in the bottom of the first, Karl Ehrhardt held up his old standby letters—A G, A G. Agee kept with his routine, too, taking four half swings and tapping his bat on home plate after each one, then settling into his stance with a slightly backward movement that looked almost like a twitch. McNally, who had pitched superbly in defeat in game two, got ahead 1-2 but struggled to locate his curveball and walked Agee on a 3-2 pitch. It's never good to walk the best base stealer on the opposing team, and Agee made him pay, stealing second as McNally struck out Harrelson. Cleon Jones flied to the edge of the warning track in right, moving Agee to third. The crowd surged with energy at the prospect of another early lead.

Up came Clendenon, who had homered off McNally in game two. On the 1-0 pitch, Agee bluffed toward home. The crowd roared, and McNally, deeply distracted, missed badly with a curveball. This was just what McNally did not want—a stressful first inning. He spent almost as much time looking at Agee at third as he did at Andy Etchebarren's target.

On the 2-1 pitch, Agee danced off third again. Clendenon swung through a fastball, and Etchebarren faked a throw to third. Agee dived back in safely. Agee loved every bit of it, siphoning off attention, making the Orioles worried, getting into McNally's head. The count to Clendenon went to 3-2, the third full count of the inning. McNally missed with a fastball.

With two on in the first, Weaver got Dave Leonhard up in the bull pen. McNally, at his best, was a pitcher who relied on command. He did not have much of it in the first inning.

Swoboda was next, and McNally started with a fastball that ran inside for ball one. He missed again with another fastball. McNally came back to even the count at 2-2. Agee led off third, Clendenon off first. McNally picked up the rosin bag and then called for time to tie his left shoe. He knew how big a pitch this was. He got Etchebarren's sign. McNally had had trouble with his curveball the entire inning, and Etchebarren wisely called for a fastball. McNally delivered it, up and away, and Swoboda swung and missed. It took 29 pitches, but McNally had kept the Mets off the board.

Koosman had another easy go of it in the second, working around Dave Johnson's first hit of the Series, and McNally answered with a 1-2-3 inning that he badly needed. In the top of the third, Mark Belanger led off with a bloop single to right. As Belanger took his turn, Jerry Grote sprinted from behind the plate to cover first base. Swoboda fired a strike to Grote, who slapped a tag on Belanger and then tried to push him off the base. Belanger wasn't happy. Umpire Lee Weyer rightly called him safe, but Grote's hustle showed how ready the Mets were to contest everything, how committed they were to being unrelentingly aggressive.

Now it was McNally's turn to bat, an obvious bunting situation. Gil Hodges instructed his pitchers to throw high fastballs when hitters were bunting to set up a trap play, a strategy designed to get a double play off of a poor bunt that is popped up. High fastballs make it harder for the hitter to get the ball on the ground. If the hitter squares around early, the pitcher can throw the fastball at his chest, making it almost a self-defense bunt, another method to get the ball into the air. If the strategy results in the desired pop-up, the closest fielder—usually the pitcher because he is charging the plate after he throws—hollers, "I got it! I got it!" loud enough for the runner on first to hear. Thinking the pitcher is going to catch the ball, the runner freezes. Then the pitcher lets the ball drop and plays it on a bounce, throws to first to get the bunter, and then the first baseman throws to second to put a tag on the runner for the double play.

Koosman took something off his fastball on his first pitch to McNally to make sure he put it the right spot. But McNally never squared to bunt. Instead he took a full swing and belted the ball into the Orioles' bull pen. McNally had given himself a 2–0 lead.

Koosman was furious that he'd allowed the opposing pitcher to go deep on him and that he'd thrown something other than his best fastball. He got the next two outs, bringing up Frank Robinson. Koosman started him off with a fastball, but the ball drifted over the middle of the plate. Robinson mashed it over the left-center-field fence—so far that neither Agee nor Jones made more than a token move for it. It was the Orioles' hardest hit in four games and gave them a 3–0 lead.

Shea Stadium was quieter than it had been in a month.

Koosman closed the inning by striking out Boog Powell with a fastball. He walked off the mound in a quiet rage and was still angry when he got back to the dugout. He had a message for his teammates, and delivered it so everyone could hear.

"They're not getting anything more," he said. "Let's go, boys."

18

RIDING THIGH

World Series Game Five
Bottom of the third

	1	2	3	4	5	6	7	8	9	Runs
Orioles	0	0	3	-	-	-	-	-	-	3
Mets	0	0	-	-	-	-	-	-	-	0

JERRY KOOSMAN'S GUARANTEE WAS ATHLETIC BRAVADO, FOR SURE. But it was also absolutely how he felt.

"It was the confidence I had in myself," he said. "I knew how to pitch them, and I had confidence in my stuff. It's probably like when you hear of someone lifting a car to save the life of someone who was pinned under it. Before the game, I told myself to pitch the best I could so we wouldn't have to go back to Baltimore. It wasn't just me; the whole team didn't want to go back to Baltimore."

Koosman had another agenda, too. He wanted to make sure Gil Hodges and Walker heard and saw his resolve and had full faith that he hadn't lost his stuff.

"I knew I could pitch better than those three innings, and I didn't want to be taken out of that game," Koosman said.

It was a new experience for Dave McNally as he took the mound in the third inning: for the first time in the Series, he was pitching with a lead. Koosman came to the plate with his .048 average and his four hits for the season, and payback on his mind.

"I wanted to hit a home run off him," he said.

McNally's first pitch was a breaking ball that hung up. Koosman smacked it down the left-field line. It wasn't quite the home run he had been hoping for, but it was good enough for a double, his first extra-base hit of the year. Yogi Berra ran a jacket out to Koosman, the wind kicking up gusts of dust and a plane flying overhead, something that happened just about every 10 minutes. Suddenly Shea was loud and blustery and bursting with hope. If Koosman could rip a double, anything was possible.

Koosman took a lead off second, hands on his knees. Agee got ahead 3-1 but skied to Paul Blair in shallow center, before McNally, showing much sharper command, threw two hellacious curveballs to strike out Harrelson, then induced Jones to pop up to Powell.

Intent on making good on his promise to his mates, Koosman got Brooks Robinson on a fly ball to Agee and took care of Johnson with a series of sharp-breaking curveballs, just the way Sandy Koufax taught him. When he pounded two inside fastballs and dropped a curve on the outer half that Etchebarren rolled to Weis at second, Koosman clearly was in command again.

The Mets had managed only one hit over the first three innings against McNally, who started the bottom of the fourth with two roundhouse curves against Donn Clendenon, then struck him out looking with a fastball on the outside corner. Clendenon dropped the bat, put his hands on his hips, and glared at Lou DiMuro, the home-plate umpire, his face no more than a few inches from the umpire's mask. He told DiMuro in so many words that the pitch had not been a strike. DiMuro told him: yes, it was. Swoboda knocked an 0-2 single up the middle, but Charles popped up and Grote grounded into a force play and the Mets were done in the fourth.

The clouds over Shea had started to darken and thicken, and the lights came on for the start of the fifth. The Mets' offense was as dormant as the broken Serval Zippers clock. Koosman was not nearly the dominant pitcher who had taken a no-hitter into the seventh inning of game two, and McNally seemed to get sharper every inning. Objectively, you had to give the Orioles the edge in the pitching department.

Koosman's average time between pitches was a little over 10 seconds. He seemed to be working at an even faster pace in game five. He didn't want to be out there any longer than he had to be, and was a big believer in getting three outs any way he could. Fans love strikeouts, and Koosman had 180 of them during the season, but he thought they were overrated. "I'd rather get an out with one pitch than three. The fewer pitches I have to throw, the better," he said.

Koosman's work was typically brisk against Belanger to begin the fifth inning, going with his fastball and retiring the shortstop on a routine fly to right. That brought up the surprise slugger, McNally. Ehrhardt stood up in his third-base box with a sign that read MERCY. McNally struck out on three pitches. Buford hit a 1-2 curveball hard to right-center, but Ron Swoboda was at full gallop almost immediately, losing his hat but catching the ball with a nice backhand grab amid the hot dog wrappers that dotted the wind-blown outfield.

Koosman had now set down seven men in a row since Frank Robinson's home run. He had stopped the bleeding, just as he had told his teammates he would.

• • •

BOBBY SACCA WAS busy getting things ready for the bottom of the fifth, taking a weighted bat, doughnut, pine-tar rag, and knee cushion to the on-deck circle. All year long he'd seen the Mets get big contributions from small-name role players and come back when things looked bleak. Like his buddy Bill Curtin, Sacca never had a doubt that the Mets would rally. They had outplayed the Orioles three games in a row. They were gamers, playing with the same resolve they had shown all year. Sacca looked around the ballpark and thought how cool it would be to hear the place jumping again.

"Who's going to be the hero who gets them going today?" Sacca remembered thinking. "Who's going to come through? That's the way they thought—the game isn't over just because we are behind."

• • •

WITH ONLY 15 outs remaining, the Mets had but two hits and a restless throng of fans, who broke into a "Let's go, Mets" chant as Al Weis came up to lead off the fifth. Weis chewed gum with gusto and took a deep breath as McNally peered in for Etchebarren's sign, his orange-and-black hat tilted slightly to the right, his hands together at his chest, right index finger poking out of the back of his glove. McNally got Weis on a two-hopper to Brooks Robinson, and struck out Koosman on a big-breaking curve, and though the Mets had a flicker of hope when Agee dropped down a bunt single, McNally came back to get Harrelson on a fly to center.

For the Mets, the only thought was to keep the game close and hope they could break through against McNally. Agee did his part, yet again, in the sixth, when Blair belted a 2-0 Koosman fastball to deep center, Agee running back to the track, turning one way, then the other, then making a nice one-handed catch 400 feet from home plate. For four and a half games now, Mets outfielders had been diving and lunging, spinning and sliding, catching every fly ball in sight. Only baseballs that went over the wall were safe from their gloves.

Frank Robinson, who had hit one of those balls over the wall his previous at bat, knew the Orioles needed to keep the pressure on and get more runs to put the game out of reach. Down 0-2 in the count, he took a Koosman slider that broke sharply inside, the ball thudding into the upper part of his left thigh. Robinson dropped his bat and started to first when DiMuro stopped him, brushing his left hand with his right hand, indicating it was a foul ball.

"What?" Robinson hollered. "The ball hit me in the leg."

DiMuro said the ball hit Robinson's bat first, then his thigh. Here came Earl Weaver again, running out of the dugout. Robinson furiously pointed to his leg and then to Lee Weyer, the first-base umpire.

"Ask him! Ask him! You've got to ask him! You can't see the play from behind the plate!" Robinson shouted.

Weaver was no less furious, but he didn't want to get heaved for a second straight game, so he held up both hands as DiMuro took off his mask, as if to declare a truce. Weaver—restrained for him—still managed to tell DiMuro that he'd blown the call and lambasted him for refusing to check with Weyer.

Koosman, meanwhile, watched with amusement as Robinson stood at the top of the dugout tunnel, his pants unbuckled, getting ice applied to his upper thigh. Koosman knew the pitch had hit Robinson, but this was not information he was going to share.

Weaver departed, still barking as he paced in front of the bench. DiMuro walked over to the dugout. He wanted to get the game going again, but there was no batter.

"Where's Robinson?" DiMuro asked Weaver. "He's supposed to be at bat."

Weaver told DiMuro he was getting ice on the welt from the ball that did not hit him. Robinson, finished with the ice, buckled his pants and returned to home plate, to a hearty chorus of boos.

Koosman threw him a curveball. He fouled it off. Koosman missed with another curveball and, on a 1-2 pitch, came with another curveball, the ball breaking hard and down, right on the outside corner. DiMuro came up with his right hand. The Shea crowd went berserk. The unhappiest at bat of Frank Robinson's World Series was over.

Powell, the only left-handed hitter in either lineup, had trouble with Koosman's deliveries, especially when he dropped down and came sidearm, but Powell managed to poke a checked-swing grounder past Harrelson for the Orioles' first hit since the third inning. Brooks Robinson tried to pull an outside curveball and hit a short fly to left. Jones handled it easily and trotted toward the dugout. He would be the leadoff hitter in the bottom of the sixth. The middle of the Mets' lineup would get their third turn against McNally.

Shea swelled with noise as Jones walked to the plate and Clendenon followed to the on-deck circle. At a ballpark that sat hard by Grand Central Parkway, the crowd rooted for some traffic on the bases, for the Mets to get something going.

19

IN CLEON'S GLOVE

World Series Game Five
Bottom of the sixth

	1	2	3	4	5	6	7	8	9	Runs
Orioles	0	0	3	0	0	0	-	-	-	3
Mets	0	0	0	0	0	-	-	-	-	0

BORN IN BAY RIDGE, BROOKLYN, LOU DIMURO WAS AN AIR FORCE VET-eran who became interested in umpiring after his playing career was ended by a broken finger. He went to umpire school and spent eight years learning his trade in the minors before joining the American League in 1963. He was selected to work his first World Series in 1969. Game five was his first time behind the plate in a postseason game.

Not even 10 minutes after Frank Robinson took a slider in the thigh and had nothing but a bruise to show for it, Cleon Jones stepped in for his third at bat. Dave McNally had had a long stretch on the bench during the argument, and whether he was cold or out of his rhythm, his first pitch of the bottom of the sixth was his wildest offering of the game, a curveball that dived down and in toward Jones's front foot. Jones tried to skip out of the way and landed on his left knee. The ball bounced all the way into the Mets' dugout. Jones rose shakily to his feet and started toward first base, until DiMuro called him back.

The ball didn't hit you, DiMuro told him.

Jones stopped, turned around, and put his left hand on his hip. He was incredulous. Of course the ball hit him. Everybody saw it.

Did Lou DiMuro, a highly respected umpire, have some policy for game five that no batters would be hit by a pitch?

Yogi Berra came halfway down from the first-base coaching box to plead the case. Jones said nothing, just stayed in the baseline, leaning on his bat. Donn Clendenon, the next hitter, backed Berra up and told DiMuro to look in the dugout.

A few seconds later, Gil Hodges walked up the steps, a World Series baseball in his big, meaty hand. It seemed as if he were walking even more slowly than usual.

Hodges knew DiMuro well from his time in the American League. He handed DiMuro the ball, showing him a black smudge where the ball had made contact with a shoe. The manager spoke softly, in his deep, restrained voice.

"Lou, the ball hit him," Hodges said.

On the press level, George Vecsey, a sharp student of human behavior, had been around Hodges enough in the tight quarters of the manager's office to know how powerful Hodges's presence was, and how his wide, guileless face and pale blue eyes radiated with sincerity. One look from those eyes could convince you of the unquestioned veracity of whatever he was saying and, in the case of a prying press, convince his interrogators to stop a wrongheaded line of inquiry.

It felt almost as if time had stopped as Hodges walked out and talked to DiMuro—extra moments that might've given DiMuro an opportunity to be reminded of Hodges's essential dignity and decency. DiMuro had a reputation for being a patient umpire who didn't lord his authority over managers and believed in allowing them to state their case. Hodges had his own reputation; he was a man who had never been ejected from so much as one game in a playing career that had spanned 18 years and 2,071 games. He was almost universally regarded as a complete gentleman who respected umpires and the game and would not argue if he did not believe he was in the right.

DiMuro studied the smudged ball again. He looked at Hodges. And then he pointed Cleon Jones to first base.

Jones had, in fact, been hit in the shoe with the ball, DiMuro decided. The crowd roared in approval. Hodges walked slowly back to the dugout.

"Gil mesmerized DiMuro," Vecsey said. "I saw that."

Earl Weaver, of course, was apoplectic. He barged out of the dugout and arrived at home plate to a cascade of boos, demanding to know how DiMuro could reverse this call and never even consult first-base umpire Lee Weyer on the pitch that had hit Frank Robinson. McNally came off the mound and jabbed a finger at the umpire. Andy Etchebarren, behind his mask, let DiMuro know how unfair his double standard was. Weaver said that Hodges and the Mets had time to do whatever they wanted to the ball once it rolled into the dugout and that was a flimsy basis on which to award Jones first base. Weaver asked to see the smudged ball, but DiMuro had already tossed it away.

Mindful again that he could not afford to go ballistic, Weaver kicked no dirt and screamed no magic words that would result in banishment. He gestured toward the Mets' dugout, his arm out and his palm up. Weaver went back to the dugout in a huff, tipping his cap up as he reached the steps. (It was one of Weaver's oddest idiosyncrasies; every time he'd get back to the dugout after an argument, he would reflexively tip his cap upward.) The sight of Cleon Jones standing on first made him sick.

• • •

DIMURO'S REVERSED CALL harkened back to a similar incident in game four of the 1957 World Series between the Yankees and Braves. The Yankees were up two games to one and had a 5–4 lead in the bottom of the tenth when a pinch hitter named Nippy Jones came up for pitcher Warren Spahn. Tommy Byrne, a left-hander, was pitching for the Yankees. Byrne's first pitch of the inning was a breaking pitch that hit the dirt and skipped past catcher Yogi Berra. Augie Donatelli, the home-plate umpire, called it a ball, but Jones said the pitch had hit his foot. The ball rolled to the backstop and bounced back toward the plate. Jones promptly picked the ball up and showed Donatelli the shoe-polish mark on it. Donatelli awarded Jones first base. Casey Stengel, then the Yankees' manager, and Berra argued with Donatelli but got nowhere. The Braves went on to score three runs that inning to win it, then took the Series in seven games.

It was Nippy Jones's last at bat in the big leagues.

Stengel admitted later that after the Nippy Jones play, he always kept a couple of smudged baseballs nearby, in case he needed them. There was no evidence that Hodges followed the same procedure, and later virtually everyone, Weaver included, agreed that the ball had in fact hit Jones's foot and that he deserved first base.

Nobody who was in the Mets' dugout saw anything untoward happen. Nobody except Jerry Koosman, that is, who said his manager wanted to take every precaution, just in case.

"I was sitting in the dugout not far from Gil, and the ball rolled to me," he said. "Gil said, 'Swipe it against your foot.' So I did. Then he asked me to give him the ball, boom, boom, that quick. He took the ball out there and showed the umpires the shoe polish on the ball. Now, maybe there was shoe polish on there from Cleon, too. Maybe there wasn't any shoe polish from me. I don't know. Gil was a quick thinker. A lot of people thought he was a straight arrow, and he was, but there were little tricks he had. You do everything you can to win. It wasn't legal, but it was lawful—put it that way."

It wasn't the only time Koosman had seen Hodges engage in clever advocacy for his club. Once Koosman was pitching in a Mets exhibition game in New Orleans against the Twins. He described the field as a "stupid racetrack diamond" with a mound that was full of ruts and holes and not packed properly.

"I was digging in front of the mound, trying to get it the way I wanted it," he said. "I also had a ball that felt oversized, with stitches that were really small. I didn't like it, and I threw it back to the umpire. He threw it right back. I threw it in again, and he threw it back again. I said to the ump, 'I don't want to pitch with this ball.'

"He said, 'Play with the ball I give you.'"

Out came Hodges. He didn't get into any discussion with the

umpire. He went to the mound and spoke quietly to Koosman. "If you don't want to use that ball, put it on the ground and stomp on it with your spikes, and the ump will change it."

Koosman did as he was told, mashing his spikes into the ball.

The umpire gave him a new ball.

• • •

WHEN THE TEMPEST subsided, it was Donn Clendenon's turn. He'd homered off McNally in game two, and McNally needed no reminder of his power. This exact situation was the reason Johnny Murphy acquired Clendenon—a player who could change a game with one swing.

Clendenon fouled off McNally's first pitch, a fastball away. McNally missed high and outside with another fastball, prompting a visit from Etchebarren. The count went to 2-2. Jones took his lead off first, juking as if he might be going. McNally delivered a curveball, up and over the plate, and Clendenon jumped on it.

In the batboy circle, Sacca heard the sound and saw the contact. *That's got to be gone,* he thought.

The ball took off as if it had been launched, deep to left. Don Buford hustled back as far and as fast as he could go. He got to the warning track. He looked up and watched the ball sail over the auxiliary scoreboard, directly above where it displayed the number 22 to indicate who was at bat.

The fans in the left-field stands where the ball hit jumped up and down and let out a roar as loud as a blast furnace. Clendenon was one of the quicker home run trotters in baseball, and this trip was no different. When he reached third base, he gave coach Eddie Yost a big hand slap and kept going, crossing the plate and pounding the hand of Bobby Sacca.

"He'd slap you so hard that it hurt," Sacca said.

Behind third base, Karl Ehrhardt's sign read OUTTA SIGHT. The entire stadium was standing and cheering. A lineup of Mets queued up to greet Clendenon. Even the cops in the dugout congratulated him.

"Let's go, Mets!" the crowd chanted.

Two runs were in, nobody was out, and it was a one-run ball game. A hit by pitch and a home run had changed everything.

Ron Swoboda came to the plate. He had had the only three-hit game in the Series in game four, an achievement overshadowed by his epic, game-saving catch. McNally retired Swoboda on a soft liner to second and set down the next two hitters, Ed Charles and Jerry Grote, without incident. McNally had recovered nicely, but Shea still surged with fresh energy.

The Orioles' lead was down to 3–2.

Out for the start of the seventh inning, Koosman had allowed only one hit since the third, and that was Powell's checked-swing job. He was showing the world what Ed Charles had seen in him from the start. You could count on Koosman when it mattered most.

Koosman had worked Dave Johnson over with curveballs the last time, and Grote, always wary of falling into a predictable pattern, called for a fastball. Koosman hummed it in to get ahead 0-1 and then fired another, Johnson lofting it harmlessly to right, where Swoboda ran it down in foul territory. Koosman went up the ladder to strike Etchebarren out with a letter-high fastball.

With two outs, Mark Belanger came up. Having hit a career-high .287 during the season, Belanger had a short swing and specialized in punching the ball to right. You don't want to get too cute with bottom-of-the-order hitters. Koosman was a young, hard thrower, and he went at Belanger with gas on three straight pitches, the last of them producing a grounder to Bud Harrelson. It was an eight-pitch inning for Koosman. Pitchers love those, especially late in tight games.

Koosman was getting stronger the longer the game went on, which made for another difficult decision for Hodges since Koosman was due up second in the bottom of the seventh, after Al Weis. Hodges wanted to keep Koosman in the game, but with his team down a run and only nine outs remaining, he wasn't sure he could afford to. Tug McGraw was warming in the bull pen. Hodges talked it through with Rube Walker. The manager decided that if Weis didn't get on, he would pinch-hit for Koosman.

• • •

STEVE APTHEKER, THE Canarsie kid who had shown up at the Polo Grounds with three pals and a bedsheet that read LET'S GO METS seven years earlier, wished he could've been at Shea for the World Series. But the US Army had other plans. After graduating from the University of Florida in June, Aptheker, an ROTC student, was drafted and sent to the Armor Basic Officer Leaders Course in Fort Knox, Kentucky.

The timing wasn't ideal. "The Mets were in the World Series, and I was in Fort Knox," he said.

A second lieutenant, Aptheker specialized in military intelligence. A year later, he would be sent to Vietnam, where he would earn a Bronze Star for his role in relocating a base from a very dangerous area to a safer one.

On the afternoon of October 16, 1969, Aptheker was in the field at Fort Knox, presiding over tank exercises. Somebody brought a tiny black-and-white television with rabbit-ear antennae and a generator to plug it into, and put it on the tailgate of a flatbed truck. Aptheker and his men gathered round as Weis walked to the plate, listening to Mets fans chanting the slogan that Lieutenant Aptheker and his friends had kick-started the year the Mets were born.

Weis had been a pest to the Orioles the whole Series, with an on-base percentage approaching .600. He had the game-winning hit in game two and would finish the Series with a 1.290 OPS. Smart, versatile, and gritty, he was the embodiment of a Hodges-type player, no matter what the numbers on the back of his baseball card said. All of Hodges's years on pennant-winning (and, in 1955, World Series–winning) teams had reinforced his belief that often it is the lesser-known players who make the difference between winning and losing. Weis had a knack for delivering in the clutch; just ask the fans at Wrigley Field, where he hit his only two home runs of the year. He wasn't a player bound for Cooperstown, but he was an eminently reliable pro.

McNally started Weis off with a sweeping curveball that dropped in for a strike. Weis swiped at the dirt with his spikes and stayed in the box, his stance slightly closed, his lean, 160-pound body bent a little at the waist, his bat pointing straight up to the sky. The bat was 35 inches long and 33 ounces in weight, and it was made by Adirondack. Weis had had no plans to use anything other than a Louisville Slugger, the company he was under contract to, in the Series, but before game one in Baltimore, Louisville Slugger had delivered a shipment of commemorative World Series bats. The only problem was that they were souvenir bats, not the kind you use against big-league pitchers. Adirondack had also shipped commemorative bats, but theirs were full size and game ready. Weis found a 35-33 Adirondack model, tried it out in batting practice, and liked it so much he decided to use it in the Series. When the Louisville Slugger sales rep, a fellow named Frank, found out, he said, "Al, you can't use that bat. You are under contract with us."

"Frank, I'm sorry. It feels good, and I'm going to use it," Weis said.

Frank knew he wasn't winning this argument. He asked Weis for one favor. The Adirondack bats had a distinctive blue ring about a third of the way up the handle. "Take some pine tar and wipe out the blue ring," he said.

Weis complied, gobbing up his bat with pine tar and obliterating the ring. He was hitting .444 in the Series (4 for 9) with his new bat as he came to the plate. Weis may have had a bigger cheering section at Shea than any other Met; his family was from nearby Farmingdale, Long Island, the game-five entourage including his parents and his wife, Barbara, and son, Daniel, who was celebrating his sixth birthday that day. The Weises rode to the park with Sharon Grote, Jerry's wife.

"My dad's going to hit a home run for my birthday," Daniel announced in the car. (Daniel's dad was in the Mets' clubhouse, unaware of his son's forecast.)

McNally bent down, picked up the rosin bag for a second, and put it back down. All Weis was thinking about was getting on base any way he could. He had gotten his game-winning hit off of a high slider from McNally in game two and figured McNally wasn't going to go that route again.

Behind third base, Ehrhardt held up a sign that read BELIEVE IN MIRACLES? Then he answered his own question with another sign: WE BELIEVE.

McNally wound and delivered, a fastball this time. It was a little over belt high, in the middle of the plate. When Hodges had converted Weis from a switch-hitter to a right-handed hitter, one of the manager's suggestions had been for Weis to hold his hands farther back and take a more robust cut at the ball. When the pitch came in, Weis stepped into it and brought his ringless, 33-ounce bat around. He met the ball squarely, powering it to left-center.

McNally did not even turn to look. Buford ran back to the 371 sign and then had no more room to run.

Al Weis had tied the score 3–3 and made Steve Aptheker the happiest second lieutenant at Fort Knox. Weis had been to the plate 230 times at Shea Stadium in his two seasons with the Mets. He had never hit a home run at home until now. His blast flew over the temporary bleachers in left-center field. It was the seventh homer of his career, his second off McNally.

"When you only have seven, you don't forget when two of them are off of the same pitcher," Weis said.

Apart from getting the Mets even, Weis's clout kept Koosman in the game and got Dick Hall up again in the Orioles' bull pen. At the plate, Koosman saw nothing but curveballs and went down swinging, getting a rousing ovation from the crowd nonetheless. Agee fought McNally through a 10-pitch at bat before flying to right, and Harrelson, too, worked the count full. McNally came inside with a fastball, and Harrelson drilled it on a low line to third, but Brooks Robinson snagged it at his shoe tops.

Due up first in the eighth, McNally was lifted in favor of Curt Motton, a diminutive outfielder making his first World Series appearance. Motton (pronounced MOE-ton) had his name mispronounced by Shea public address announcer Jack Lightcap (whose version rhymed with *cotton*), then bounced out to Harrelson on the only pitch he saw. Koosman got Buford on a fly to center, before starting off Blair with a slo-mo breaking ball that tumbled low. Koosman came back with another curve, which Blair bashed off the facing of the mezzanine in left field, very deep and very foul. The huge crowd let out a collective gasp. Off the bat, it sounded scary.

Koosman followed the flight of Blair's shot, then got a new ball from DiMuro and got right back onto the rubber. After missing with two fastballs up and away, he went with another fastball, Blair smashing a hard grounder in the hole between third and short. Harrelson ran it down, planted, and rocketed a perfect throw to nail the fleet Blair by a half step.

The new Orioles pitcher in the bottom of the eighth was Eddie Watt, who only had the Orioles' whole season riding on his performance. With the game tied at three, he needed to keep the Mets off the board and count on the Baltimore hitters to come through with some late thunder. The Orioles had the right man on the mound. Watt's 1.65 ERA was the second best in the entire American League. He had allowed just 49 hits in 71 innings. He had thrown nothing but strikes in his first inning of work the day before in game four and was hoping for the same command now, starting with Cleon Jones, the Mets' first hitter in the bottom of the eighth.

Jane Jarvis led the crowd with a high-speed, organ-backed rendition of a "Let's go, Mets!" chant. Jones picked up dirt and rubbed it on his hands. It was his first at bat since the shoe-polish play to lead off the sixth. Watt started him off with a sidearm fastball that ran outside. He came back with another fastball, this time low. After he missed again with a fastball outside, he took a moment, reset his hat, and got his 3-0 pitch over, Jones taking all the way. Watt had thrown Jones nothing but fastballs. Jones stepped out briefly and got some more dirt for his left hand. Watt had his customary wad of tobacco bulging in his left cheek. His 3-1 offering was still another fastball, out over the plate, thigh high.

Jones was all over it, driving it deep to left-center. Blair chased it as fast as he could go, sprinting toward the precise spot where Agee had made his catch against Elrod Hendricks in game three. Blair had no chance; the ball hit well up on the wall. He played the carom perfectly, but Jones still cruised into second with a double.

Looking to get Jones to third so he could score on a sacrifice fly, Hodges had Clendenon bunt. He made two awkward attempts, fouling the ball off both times, then swung away and served an outside pitch to the right-field corner, the ball just slicing foul. Watt came back to get Clendenon on a ground ball to Brooks Robinson, Jones holding second.

Up stepped Ron Swoboda. After an inauspicious beginning to his World Series—not making the best play on Buford's leadoff homer in game one—he had been one of the best players on either team, with his bat *and* his glove.

Watt began with a curveball—no surprise since Swoboda was a notorious fastball hitter. The pitch came knee high, by the outside corner. DiMuro called it a ball. Watt wanted the call badly. He held his glove up as if he were posing for a statue upon receiving Etchebarren's throw, just to make sure DiMuro knew how he felt.

Watt went back to the rubber, got the sign, and came to the set position. Jones edged off second, checking on the whereabouts of Belanger and Johnson. Watt turned and looked at Jones and then came home, another curveball, this one up and hanging over the plate.

Swoboda swung, ripping a ball down the left-field line, inches from the warning track, maybe 10 feet inside the line. Buford's first steps appeared tentative, and he didn't take the shortest route to the ball. He went as hard as he could on his balky leg and stretched out his glove but could only manage to play the ball on a half hop.

Jones, reading the play perfectly, could see that Buford had a remote chance of catching up to it. He held up before he turned third just in case. When the ball bounced, coach Eddie Yost furiously waved Jones home. Buford made an off-balance, desperate throw that landed near Yost's coaching box, Jones scoring easily and

Swoboda taking second. It was Swoboda's second hit of the day and sixth of the Series, the most of any player.

More than 57,000 fans were up and screaming in delight, Shea Stadium almost quaking. With two in the sixth, one in the seventh, and another one here in the bottom of the eighth, the Mets had taken a 4–3 lead.

• • •

NEITHER ETCHEBARREN nor George Bamberger nor Weaver went out to talk to Watt, who had faced three hitters and given up two rockets. A brilliant reliever all year, he didn't have much bite on his curveball or much command of his fastball. He got Charles on a short fly to Buford for the second out, bringing up Grote. Sacca, in his batboy circle, had made sure Grote had all the pine tar he wanted; Grote used more of it than any other Met.

After throwing two breaking balls up in the zone—one ball and one fouled off—Watt went to the grass behind the mound, a mental health break before they called it that. He went to his mouth and rubbed up the ball with both hands, giving it a good going-over, then climbed back onto the mound, took a little rosin, and went back to work.

Watt fired a fastball on the outer half, and Grote went with it, socking a hard one-hop grounder at Powell. Powell did well to block it and keep it in front of him, but Watt was late covering. Powell's underhanded throw to Watt was a bit high. Grote, busting it out of the box, beat Watt by a couple of steps to the bag, and when the pitcher dropped Powell's throw, Swoboda came all the way around to score. Koosman, in his blue jacket, was first out of the dugout to greet him. Sacca ran to pick up Grote's pine tar–covered bat. Grote was Sacca's catching mentor and always had time for a nice word or a helpful tip. Sacca loved Grote's intensity, how he assumed nothing and ran all out from the moment he hit the ball.

Now it was 5–3, and Shea was complete bedlam. In the Baltimore dugout, Weaver and Bamberger sat side by side, looking almost catatonic. Watt caught Weis looking with a curveball, but the roar in Shea went on.

The Mets were three outs away.

They took the field for the top of the ninth, Koosman throwing his warm-up tosses, still making good on his promise. The heart of the Orioles' order—Frank Robinson, Boog Powell, and Brooks Robinson—awaited him. Another "Let's go, Mets!" chant got going, as if the fans had no idea what to do with their excitement and anticipation. Hodges reached into his pocket and pulled out a fresh stick of gum.

Koosman had retired 16 of his last 17 hitters. He missed with a curveball on the outside to Robinson and missed again with a fastball on the inside to fall behind 2-0. DiMuro called for time when an overzealous Mets fan in a beige turtleneck jumped the railing to spend some time with Clendenon at first. He was escorted off without incident. Ron Taylor and Tug McGraw were warming in case Koosman got into trouble.

Koosman delivered a fastball for 2-1 but missed with two more fastballs to put Frank Robinson on. It was Koosman's first walk of the game and a terrible time for it. The tying run was at the plate. Charles and Clendenon, the veterans who had started the game with a little pep talk for their young pitcher, both went to the mound again.

Hodges never budged from the bench. He was sticking with Koosman.

Big Boog Powell came up, one long ball away from tying the game. Koosman fell behind again 2-1, missing with a breaking pitch. He got his sign from Grote and fired a fastball. Powell hit a chopping ball to Weis at second. Weis double-clutched for an instant and then whipped a throw to Harrelson. Robinson came in hard and slid hard, right on top of Harrelson, who never blinked, hanging in, taking the throw, then spinning his right leg out of harm's way as Robinson rolled across the bag.

The crowd booed Robinson, but Harrelson didn't complain and

neither did any other Met. It was clean, hard baseball. It was close, but the Mets had gotten their force-out.

Chico Salmon came on to run for Powell at first as Brooks Robinson stepped to the plate. Robinson had slumped the whole Series— his best hit had ended up in Ron Swoboda's glove a day earlier—but here was a fresh chance for the future Hall of Famer to make an impact at last. Koosman quickly got up 0-2. Robinson fouled off a high fastball to stay alive, and then Koosman switched it up, attacking him with a curveball on the outside.

Robinson popped up to Swoboda in right.

Two outs.

Now it was up to Dave Johnson, the Orioles' talented young second baseman. Koosman wiped his face with his right sleeve and looked in for the sign, his face betraying nothing about the circumstances. Grote pounded his glove three times and set his target. Koosman threw a fastball outside for ball one. When he got the ball back, he wriggled his shoulders a bit, touched his hat, and was immediately back in the set position, feet shoulder width apart, hands together just above his belt. Get the ball, throw the ball: it had long been Koosman's pitching mantra, and he wasn't changing it now. He fired a fastball on the outside corner to even the count. He was two strikes away now. Koosman touched his hat again, got the sign, then checked Salmon leading off first. He came with a curveball that stayed outside to put Johnson up 2-1. Grote threw the ball back and simulated the curveball motion to Koosman, telling him to finish the pitch, bring it down. Grote called for a fastball, then pulled his left hand out of the glove and swiped it in the dirt. He pounded his glove a few more times. Koosman's countenance remained completely impassive, all business, his focus fixed on Grote's target. Salmon took a lead off first, Clendenon playing behind him.

Just make sure you throw your best fastball, Koosman told himself. *Don't hold back. Bring it hard.*

Koosman wound and delivered the pitch about belt high, on the outside part of the plate.

Johnson swung. He made decent contact, sending a fly ball to left field.

Cleon Jones, playing deep, retreated a few steps, to the edge of the warning track. As the ball came down, he pounded his glove, Agee-like, once and then again. "Come on down, baby," he told the ball.

Jones had both hands up, in front of his eyes. This was a ball he was going to follow all the way into the glove and a catch he was going to make with two hands. On the mound, Koosman had a pretty good idea he had thrown his last pitch. Only later did he think back to Pearl Bailey's premonition of the number eight.

The scoreboard read: Mets 5, Orioles 3.

As the ball descended into his glove, Jones kept his hands together, then brought his arms straight down as he dropped to his left knee. It was 3:16 p.m.

The World Series was over. The New York Mets were the champions of baseball. Jerry Grote rushed the mound and jumped into Jerry Koosman's arms, Ed Charles joined them from third base, and then the party was on, the Mets fleeing for the safety of their clubhouse as the field was overrun by tens of thousands of believers who, for the third time in three weeks, were overcome with euphoria, trying to take in what they had just witnessed, celebrating by carving Shea Stadium up into little pieces. Regrettably, some celebrants did not stop there. As the Orioles filed out of Shea Stadium to their bus a couple of hours later, Boog Powell felt a spray of what he thought was water. He looked up about 20 feet, to an opening on a ramp.

"Four or five people were standing there urinating on us," Powell said. "We were saying 'What the hell?' If there was some way we could've gotten up there . . ."

Bobby Sacca and Bill Curtin scrambled to gather up the equipment as fast as they could, but the barbarians were already inside the gates. One fan snatched the hat off of Sacca's head, and another tried to rip the uniform shirt off his back.

"Shea Stadium was shaking, that's how crazy it was," Sacca said.

"It felt like it was bouncing up and down." Even as he had to fight off people who wanted to disrobe him, he felt such lightness and joy, a thrill beyond anything he'd known. That was absolutely the right feeling, said the Mets third baseman and resident poet, Ed Charles, who had worshipped Jackie Robinson as a kid in Daytona, Florida, fought through hatred and injustice and discrimination, and still kept believing that anything was possible in this country.

And now, at the close of his 18 years in professional baseball, he found out that he was right.

"This is the summit," Ed Charles said. "We're number one in the world, and you just can't get any bigger than this."

EPILOGUE

Please Don't Use the M-Word

THE *OXFORD ENGLISH DICTIONARY* DEFINES A MIRACLE AS "AN extraordinary and welcome event that is not explicable by natural or scientific laws and is therefore attributed to a divine agency." It is a perfectly appropriate word to use to describe the parting of the Red Sea or turning water into wine. To a man, the 1969 New York Mets do not believe it is a word that has any applicability to what they did between April 8 and October 16 that season—a 192-day stretch of baseball that turned the most hapless franchise in the game into World Series champions.

Indeed, if you used the term "miracle Mets" in the presence of Jerome Martin Koosman, he might've just drilled you with a fast-ball, the same way he had Ron Santo when the Cubs visited Shea Stadium in September. His manager agreed.

"There's nothing miraculous about us," Gil Hodges said as champagne sprayed and Mets hugged in a riotous celebration, the festivities featuring lots of kissing and dancing by the resplendent Broadway sensation Pearl Bailey and pithy proclamations from a resurgent political sensation, Mayor John V. Lindsay. It was the mayor who announced that the Mets' ticker-tape parade would be the coming Monday, when "the number one city in the world will honor the number one baseball team in the world." The mayor also called the victory "a modern miracle," but amid the merriment everybody gave him a pass.

Nineteen days after cavorting in the Shea clubhouse—and four months after his political career had appeared doomed when he lost the Republican primary—John V. Lindsay was reelected mayor of New York City. His margin of victory—over 7½ percent—was bigger than it had been four years earlier. In the biggest upset of all, Lindsay, the Man Who Forgot Queens during the February snowstorm, even won the Mets' home borough.

The bedrock of the Mets' triumph wasn't divine intervention but the quality of the men Hodges sent out to the mound. No less a baseball sage than Casey Stengel said as much after watching the Mets' pitchers limit the Orioles to nine runs in five games and a .146 average.

"You can't be lucky every day, but you can if you get good pitching," he said.

The Mets' pitching was so good, he went on, that "we don't even know who the best six are." Indeed, when pitchers as good as Tug McGraw and Jim McAndrew never throw so much as a single pitch in the five games of the World Series, it shows you what Stengel was getting at. McAndrew had a 2.28 ERA for the year, and was a lockdown starter as the Mets made their charge. The club's most dominant reliever, McGraw finished the year 9-3 and had an ERA of 0.84 after the All-Star break, finishing 17 games and saving 12. It wasn't his fault that the Mets' starters had an annoying habit of pitching complete games (51) and throwing shutouts (a league-leading 16).

Apart from their abundance of quality arms and a red-ass catcher, Jerry Grote, who handled them brilliantly, the Mets' most defining quality may have been their collective belief—in each other and in what they were capable of doing as a club.

"We started out as a lot of young guys not really knowing what we could do against all those great teams out there," Koosman said. Then the Mets started to win, and their confidence began to swell like a stream in spring. Before long Hodges's spring training prediction of 85 victories didn't seem so laughable at all. It turned out that the Mets won their 85th game on September 11, Gary Gentry shutting out the Montreal Expos and Cleon Jones reaching base three times and hiking his average to .347. The Mets may have had a roster full of guys hitting over 100 points below Jones, but by the time October arrived, it somehow didn't matter.

"Man for man, [the Orioles] may have been better on paper, but we had the unity, the togetherness," Jones said.

Hodges didn't just believe in his players; he refused to let them wander into the abyss of low expectations. From the day he became the Mets manager, Hodges wouldn't accept anything but his players' sharpest focus and best effort. In early June, Koosman was throwing a shutout against the Padres in San Diego with two outs in the ninth. The Mets were up 4–0. The Padres had a runner on first when Ed Spiezio, their third baseman, came up. Grote called for a curveball.

Strike one.

Grote called for another curveball.

Spiezio swung and missed again. Strike two.

Koosman was one strike away from a shutout. Grote switched it up and called for a fastball. Spiezio socked it off the center-field wall. Koosman got the final out, and the Mets filed happily into the clubhouse. Hodges immediately summoned his pitcher and catcher into his office.

"You never wanted to get called into Gil's office," Koosman said.

Hodges asked Grote, "What was your thinking on the 0-2 pitch to Spiezio in the ninth?"

"Well," Grote said, "we had just thrown two curveballs to him and he looked like shit on them. He's got to be looking for another one. So I thought we could fool him with a fastball."

Hodges turned to Koosman.

"What was your thinking?"

"I agree with Grote."

Hodges paused a moment. His face reddened and he started to holler. "You two dumb sons of bitches! Don't you know he can't hit a curveball?"

Said Koosman, "Those were the teaching lessons that Gil would give you. He just wanted you to know more, watch the hitter more. He wanted your best. He said, 'Don't get into a situation where you are outthinking yourself, when the hitter is showing you he can't hit a pitch.' Managers today would never do that. They'll come in and say, 'Hey, nice going. Good job out there.'"

• • •

HODGES CULTIVATED a culture that brought everyone on the club to-gether. He played no favorites and, if anything, nurtured the lesser-known players more than he did his stars. He wanted players to own their mistakes, look after one another, and stick together no matter what.

Ed Charles and many other Mets believed that Hodges's genius had little to do with knowing when to double-switch or put on a hit-and-run. Yes, he was a superb strategist who was able to think innings, and sometimes even games, ahead, but what set him apart was his even-handed treatment of everyone on the club and the spirit of inclusion that he fed and watered every day, like a master gardener. He forged a winning environment by defining roles and not surprising players, by putting players in positions where they could succeed, and by believing in his players and transmitting that belief to them every day.

Al Weis had spent most of his career being pinch-hit for. Hodges not only got him to scrap switch-hitting, he got him to go up to the plate in a more positive frame of mind. Sure, Weis hit .215 in 1969. The Mets also probably do not hoist that flag without him.

"I have to give Gil a lot of credit," Weis said. "He instilled a world of confidence in me by not taking me out at times when a lot of other managers would have."

After Donn Clendenon was named World Series MVP and won a car, a reporter asked Hodges who he thought should be MVP. "That's not my job," he said. "I think all twenty-five of them—and four coaches. Let's see. That's twenty-nine."

"What about the manager?" the reporter followed up.

"No, not the manager. The manager already has a car," Hodges said.

• • •

ED CHARLES'S OFFENSIVE production dropped off sharply in 1969, but Hodges understood that Charles's value far transcended a string of digits. It was his leadership skills and mental makeup, his substance, that prompted Hodges to play him in four of the five World Series games. In Charles's two years under Hodges, he was pinch-hit for only one time. Charles took great pride in being a clutch hitter, and the one time Hodges called him back, he was so unhappy that he slammed his bat into the bat rack.

It was almost unheard of for Charles to act out that way.

Hodges was sitting right there. He saw it all, said nothing. Charles took his role as a mentor to the young players seriously. He thought about his outburst after the game. He felt terrible about it.

The next day, he knocked on Hodges's office door.

"Come in," the manager said.

"I just want to apologize for yesterday," Charles told him. "I wanted to get up and knock those runs in, but I shouldn't have done that. That's no kind of example for the young guys like Garrett and Boswell, and I already told them that. I told them, 'You saw my display yesterday? I was wrong. You shouldn't do that.'"

Hodges waited for Charles to finish.

"I knew you would be coming in," Hodges said with a smile.

Hodges was a superb judge of character. When Herb Brooks was selecting his 1980 US Olympic hockey team, he famously said that he didn't want the best players. He wanted the right players. So it was with Gil Hodges. Perhaps because of his background with the Jackie Robinson Dodgers, Hodges succeeded in building as close, and as color-blind, a clubhouse as it was possible to have—a remarkable achievement in an era not far removed from baseball's integration and one in which race remained a flash point in the culture at large. Ed Charles considered his Mets teammates brothers, and it started with the values of the man in the manager's office. "It was a privilege playing with such a great bunch of guys—guys who all had a [team-first] attitude," Charles said. "You knew every guy would have your back." In his autobiography, Robinson wrote about how much he admired and respected Hodges. Rachel Robinson, Jackie's wife, said that Gil Hodges was one of the few Dodgers teammates they socialized with away from the ballpark.

"He was quiet, friendly, warm—you could count on him," Rachel Robinson told author Mort Zachter. "And you didn't have to ask for help from Gil—he anticipated what you needed and was there for you."

The core of the Mets included four African-American players—Tommie Agee, Cleon Jones, Donn Clendenon, and Ed Charles—who had grown up deep in the Jim Crow South, living in a very separate and very unequal world, beaten up by the daily affronts and injustices that were as much a staple of southern life as cotton fields. The affronts and injustices continued as they made their way in professional baseball, second-generation heirs of Jackie Robinson's legacy, a role that each of them embraced in his own way. Clendenon joined his Morehouse big brother, Dr. Martin Luther King, Jr., on several civil rights marches, and Dr. King took the opportunity to remind Clendenon that responsibility came with his stature as a big-league ballplayer: "Donn, you have a forum to enact change in your own way. You need to lead by example, to show our youth that they can achieve great things in the face of adversity."

"I know my father took those words seriously," Donn Clendenon, Jr., said, "because he drilled them into me over and over again."

It would be absurd to give Hodges credit for the moral fiber of his players, but he was a man of deep integrity, and without being preachy about it, he set a powerful example, one that was admired even by the one—and only—player Hodges publicly called out that year: Cleon Jones.

As much as any other Met, Jones felt, and feels to this day, a profound connection to his roots, a yearning to honor those who came before him. It's what took Jones back to Africatown as soon as the baseball season ended and that keeps him there still. If the most notable citizen in the history of Africatown was Cudjo Lewis, the 19-year-old who was captured on the West African coast in the region that is now Benin, herded onto the *Clotilda*, and sold along with more than a hundred others to an Alabama slave trader, Cleon Jones is not far behind.

When Lewis died in 1935 at the age of 94—the last surviving former slave in the United States—he was buried in the Africatown cemetery, where all the graves face east—in the direction of West Africa. Some descendants of *Clotilda* passengers still live in the area, and they are working with community activists, including Cleon Jones, to revitalize the region and hope to one day establish a museum to honor the history of Africatown. Hundreds of artifacts—photos, letters, artworks, religious symbols, and musical instruments—are arrayed in a former school gymnasium in Africatown, awaiting a permanent home.

"I get chills to the bone every time I think about it," said Donna Mitchell, a former assistant to the mayor of Mobile and a leading advocate for Africatown. "I am an African-American. I've tried to figure out where my people came from, but in this small community on the Gulf Coast of Alabama, people can actually say, 'I know where I came from. My people came from West Africa on that ship.'"

One of those people is Lorna Woods, who is a great-great-great-granddaughter of Charlie Lewis, Cudjo's brother. She is 70 years old and lives not far from where she grew up in Africatown, a place she believes embodies the best qualities humanity has to offer. Woods grew up in a shotgun house with no running water, an outhouse, and 11 kids squeezed into two bedrooms. It was similar to the house that Cleon Jones was raised in.

"We were poor and didn't have things other people had, but we didn't know that," she said. "You can make your life as good as you want. You don't give in to hate and meanness. You go through what you have to go through, and you keep looking up. You stay on the battlefield. You have to be persistent. If you do that, you show the way for the people who are coming up behind you."

In the spring of 2018, those people included Lorna Woods's grandson and niece, both of whom graduated from college, as well as a nephew who graduated from law school. She celebrated them all, the same way she still celebrates Cleon Jones, whom she followed by a few years in Mobile County Training School.

"Cleon was a great inspiration to so many young men, making it to the major leagues and the World Series," Woods said. "He showed them it could be done. He didn't have it easy. There were no stadiums, no training programs, no coaches. He had to walk everywhere. It was persistence that made it possible."

Jones traveled the country as a ballplayer, stayed in the finest hotels, became a star in the media capital of the world, but home always remained Africatown.

"I can't imagine being anyplace else," he said.

Jones is now the president of the board of the Africatown Community Development Corporation. His advocacy includes everything from clearing fields with his tractor to meeting with local business groups and government officials about getting funding for the museum and other developmental initiatives, according to Donna Mitchell.

"He's one of those people who never stops," she said. "He's humble. He's dedicated. It's never about him. It's about Africatown and its history. I don't think Africatown could've been blessed with a kinder soul."

· · ·

THE BEAUTY OF the '69 Mets went so much deeper than Tom Seaver, the wonder-boy pitcher and face of the franchise, and his left-handed sidekick, Jerry Koosman; than their dazzling defenders up the middle—Tommie Agee, Bud Harrelson, and Jerry Grote—and their world-class hitter in left field, Cleon Jones. It went beyond the savvy move by general manager Johnny Murphy to get Donn Clendenon, an outsized hitter and personality, at the trading deadline, and the season-long relief work by the bookish Ron Taylor and the irrepressible Tug McGraw. It was Seaver himself who called the Mets' triumph "the greatest collective victory by any team in sports," an observation as brilliantly on target as any knee-high curveball on the outside corner that he threw all season.

So much of the magic of this club came from the periphery, from the least expected sources. It was Jack DiLauro starting the first game of his career in Dodger Stadium and pitching nine shutout innings. It was Al Weis, the Mighty Mite, hitting home runs in back-to-back games in Chicago, and hitting his first-ever Shea Stadium home run to tie the score in game five of the World Series. It was J. C. Martin using his knowledge of the knuckleball to get a huge pinch hit in the NLCS, dropping down a perfect bunt on the play that ended game four against the Orioles; Don Cardwell pitching the best baseball of his life down the stretch; and Nolan Ryan turning in his epic relief effort to close out the Braves.

It was Ed Kranepool's gutty, if looping, opposite-field single to beat Ferguson Jenkins and the Cubs in a massive game in July, and it was the youngest of the Mets, Wayne Garrett, who wasn't even supposed to be in the major leagues, slamming a huge home run against the Braves in the final game of the NLCS. It was Bobby Pfeil filling in all over the infield and winning a game in Montreal with a bunt single that hit the third-base bag, and it was the unstinting work ethic of the glove-challenged Ron Swoboda, who hit two home runs to beat Steve Carlton on a night Carlton struck out a record 19 hitters and then made the catch of ten lifetimes to save game four.

More than anything, in the same summer that two men walked on the moon, 400,000 men and women descended on a farm in the Catskill Mountains, and millions more all over the country were embroiled in conflict about the war in Vietnam, the Mets embodied hope. They embodied possibility—a belief that things could get better and would get better. It was, and is, a wonderful thing to hold on to, even if the afterglow of the Mets' remarkable achievement was much shorter lived than anybody ever imagined it would be.

Johnny Murphy, the general manager who played a huge role in assembling the championship Mets, died of a heart attack at the age of 61, not even three months after the final out of the World Series. It was a devastating loss to the organization, and an even more devastating loss followed some 26 months later, on April 2, 1972, days before the start of a new season. It was Easter Sunday, and Gil Hodges, a devout Catholic, attended services at St. Ann's Church in West Palm Beach, then played 27 holes of golf with his coaching staff—Eddie Yost, Joe Pignatano, and Rube Walker—at the Palm Beach Lake golf course. The foursome came off the course at about 5:15 p.m. and were on a walkway, steps from their hotel rooms in the Ramada Inn, when they stopped to make plans for dinner. Pignatano asked what time they should meet.

"Seven-thirty," Hodges said.

Then Hodges suddenly fell backward, collapsing onto the asphalt, hitting his head on a curb. He had been stricken with a heart attack. "He went down like a fallen tree," remembered Arthur Friedman, the Mets' statistician, who had met the group as they came off the course. Hodges was rushed to the hospital. The coaches, Friedman, and a few other team officials followed. Despite efforts to revive him, Hodges was unresponsive and was pronounced dead a short time before 6 p.m. He was 47 years old, two days short of his forty-eighth birthday. Gil Jr. heard the news on the car radio.

It can't be my father. It must be another Gil Hodges, he thought.

The following day, the Mets, Yankees, and the body of Gil Hodges flew back to New York in a charter airplane. The funeral Mass was held three days later, on the morning of April 6, at Our Lady Help of Christians, a small brick church in Brooklyn, a few blocks from the Hodges home on Bedford Avenue. St. Patrick's Cathedral on Fifth Avenue had been offered to the Hodges family by the archbishop of New York, Terence Cardinal Cooke, but Joan Hodges knew that her husband, the ex-Marine from Princeton, Indiana, would've wanted the service to be in their neighborhood parish. It was where he attended Mass every Sunday, after all, and where he'd never skip out early to avoid the autograph seekers. He would sign every one.

"Gil was a hero—one to look up to and imitate," said Reverend Charles E. Curley, who gave the homily.

"All I can say is that there was no finer man in baseball than this gentleman," Walter Alston, Hodges's manager with the Brooklyn Dodgers, said.

The old Dodgers—Jackie Robinson, Sandy Koufax, Pee Wee Reese, and Ralph Branca among them—showed up in big numbers to pay their respects, as did the young Mets and too many celebrities and dignitaries to count. Gilbert Ray Hodges was laid to rest in Holy Cross Cemetery, about two miles from Ebbets Field.

• • •

THE ENSUING YEARS in New York City brought crushing financial problems and accompanying gloom, and a seeming vise grip of depravity that included filth, crime, prostitution, squalid subways, and rats so big you could hear them coming. On some nights it seemed that half the Bronx was on fire. The city seemed completely unmanageable, ungovernable, incorrigible.

"The Mets' victory was a magic moment, for sure," said Dr. Joseph Viteritti, the Hunter College professor who had grown up riding his bike to Brooklyn Dodgers games. "But it occurred in the midst of a rapidly changing city characterized by racial unrest, antiwar protests, rising crime, vacant buildings, an exodus of middle-class families, and a quick abandonment by revenue-producing businesses. All of this would culminate with the 1975 fiscal crisis, when the city went bust and literally could not pay its bills. The 1969 World Series was in many ways the last hurrah of a more innocent age."

The unrelenting grimness in the city in the years that followed somehow made the halcyon days of October 1969 that much more of a civic elixir. It is the unceasing charm of the underdog story, isn't it? Someone, some entity—a team, a person, even a city—has no chance, no way up, and no way out. They should just give up and go away. But they don't go away. They keep at it, they try their best.

A few good things start to happen, and then they happen more frequently. And then, finally, the unthinkable happens.

Even people who didn't root for the Mets had to admire how they kept defying the odds and finding ways to win. Gil Hodges, Jr., was absolutely right when he compared the statistics of the Orioles and the Mets. It wasn't a fair fight.

Then they started playing ball.

Spontaneous celebrations broke out all over the city, New Yorkers' famously steely street faces punctured by the news from Flushing at 3:16 p.m. The following Monday, the ticker-tape parade through the Canyon of Heroes in lower Manhattan was judged to be the second biggest in history, behind only the parade celebrating V-J Day at the end of World War II. The city's Department of Sanitation swept up 578 tons of confetti after the Mets had passed through. They hadn't defended our democracy or won a war, but the New York Mets were nonetheless saluted as heroes, every one of them, as they headed up Broadway, serenaded as they went with the words Steve Aptheker and his friends wrote on a bedsheet in 1962:

Let's go, Mets.

ACKNOWLEDGMENTS

MOMENTS AFTER Cleon Jones caught Dave Johnson's fly ball to end the 1969 World Series, the happy hordes busted loose once more from the Shea Stadium seats. They reveled, ransacked, pillaged, plundered—the most benign mayhem Flushing, Queens, has ever witnessed. I speak from firsthand knowledge. I was one of the trespassers. I played hooky that day from my sophomore year at John Glenn High School in East Northport, Long Island. I don't remember whether I called in sick or had a daylong doctor's appointment. I do remember that it was the best Thursday afternoon of my life. I was at the game with my grandfather, my usual companion at Mets games. He was a retired steamfitter who loved going to ball games, especially with his grandchildren. Somehow he got tickets to the biggest game in Mets history, and though it wouldn't have mattered if our seats had been in the section where Tommie Agee had smashed the ball off of Larry Jaster in the third game of the season, we wound up in box seats maybe 20 rows back from the field behind first base, Nancy Seaver's neighborhood.

It made for a short commute to the field.

I was much more of a timid, 15-year-old suburban kid than a committed hooligan, but when the Mets defied all reason and finished off the Orioles, I was overcome.

"I'm going to go out there, Gramps," I said.

"Be careful," my grandfather said.

I ran down the aisle, jumped the railing, and landed on the field. I ventured toward the infield and a few steps in from first base, bent down, pulled up a three-inch-square chunk of world-championship turf, and raced back to the seats to rejoin my grandfather. I planted the Shea sod between two dogwood trees in the backyard of our house in Huntington. I mowed it very carefully.

Our family sold the house seven years later. The new owners negotiated for the washer and dryer and had no idea they had gotten a piece of Shea Stadium at no extra charge.

Having the opportunity to revisit the thrill given to me by Gil Hodges's 1969 Mets has been one of the richest experiences I've had in four decades of writing about sports. This book was nearly three years in the making and would not have been possible without huge contributions from a roster of people that far exceeds baseball's 25-man limit. From the outset, former Mets VPs David Newman and the great Jay Horwitz, a New York Mets icon in his own right, were ardent supporters of the project, as was Ethan Wilson, the club's director of media relations. They referred me to the estimable Lorraine Hamilton, the Mets' executive director of broadcasting and events. Lorraine was indispensable in helping me connect with the 1969 Mets.

When one works on a book about an event that happened a half century earlier, it's a given that primary sources may not be as abundant as an author would like. I had the great fortune to connect with a number of behind-the-scenes people who were extremely generous with their time and recollections. Dennis D'Agostino— author, New York sports historian, and former Mets public relations staffer—couldn't have been more of an ally or a more reliable fact-checking source. Arthur Friedman, who would be in the statisticians' Hall of Fame if such a thing existed, was always at the ready to help, as was Matt Winick. Dr. Joseph Viteritti, professor at Hunter College, offered a wealth of insight into the John V. Lindsay years in New York City and even more insight into what it was like to grow up with the Brooklyn Dodgers. Mort Zachter, who wrote a splendid biography of Gil Hodges, shared his time and expertise willingly. Two lifelong Mets fans from Brooklyn, Steve Aptheker and Steve Zelkowitz, shared their passion and their stories about growing up with the Mets and could not have been more accommodating. The latter Steve can blame his friend Bill Bandon, Princeton class of '83, who was kind enough to connect me with him.

When a writer needs to hunt down obscure stats and little-known facts, Elias Sports Bureau has long been the number one destination. It was no different here. Elias's John Labombarda fielded one query after another, and his fielding percentage was 1.000. John Thorn, the official historian of Major League Baseball, has an encyclopedic knowledge of the game and was always available to share it. Bill Francis is a research icon at the National Baseball Hall of Fame, and if he got tired of hearing from me, he did a good job disguising it. Cassidy Lent of the Hall's research department unearthed more clips than I could ever have hoped for and was full of good cheer even when I emailed her at 4:45 p.m. on Friday afternoons. Craig Muder, communications chief at the Hall, is a consummate pro who was also a major help, as was his colleague John Horne, who kindly helped me sort through the Hall photo archives. John Blundell of the MLB public relations team has assisted me with research needs for years and came up especially big for the 1969 Mets.

A number of books about Mets history have been published over the years, and they provided invaluable background knowledge. William J. Ryczek interviewed more than 100 people in writing *The Amazin' Mets, 1962–1969*, and his spadework shows on every page. Joseph Durso, Mets beat writer for the *New York Times*, turned out *Amazing: The Miracle of the Mets* a year after the Mets won, and it offered a wealth of detail and immediacy, as did Stanley Cohen's *A Magic Summer: The '69 Mets*.

One of the great treasures in any community is the local library, and I was blessed to have the folks at Warner Library in Tarrytown, New York—especially Maureen Petry, director, and Robert Mannion, reference librarian—in my corner for anything and everything. No less a treasure is a local bookstore, and Jennifer Kohn, new proprietor of the Village Bookstore in Pleasantville, New York, runs a gem of one.

Gary Cohen, an all-time-great baseball broadcaster, knows as much about the Mets as any person on earth and has a recall of virtually every Mets thing he saw as a kid growing up in Queens. He helped the cause tremendously, as did another iconic New York voice, Howie Rose, whose gripping account of Tom Seaver's imperfect game on July 9, 1969, made me feel as though I were sitting right there with him. George Vecsey, a man whose prose is something to aspire to, graced the pages of the *New York Times* for decades and covered the Mets from the beginning. He generously shared his insights, because that's how he is. The batboys for the '69 Mets, Bill Curtin and Bobby Sacca, also shared their memories and took me inside the Mets' dugout in the process.

Gil Hodges, Jr., endured the tragic loss of his father as a young man and honored his memory of his dad with every word he said. Joe Agee, Tommie's older brother, is an upholsterer by trade and was the most generous of tour guides, taking me all over greater Mobile, Alabama, and the communities of Whistler and Plateau. Tommie's wife, Maxcine, and daughter J'Nelle were no less gracious. Cleon Jones was on a tractor the first time I reached out to him and never strays too far from it, living in the same house he grew up in in Africatown. He welcomed a visitor from up north, and then he and his wife, Angela, introduced me to their favorite barbecue place for lunch. So many of the '69 Mets were similarly gracious, accommodating me and my unending questions and giving me hours of their time; special shout-outs go to Al Weis, Ed Kranepool, Rod Gaspar, Wayne Garrett, J. C. Martin, Bobby Pfeil, Duffy Dyer, and the ace left-hander Jerry Koosman, whom I met over a two-hour breakfast down the road from his home in Wisconsin. For months afterward, I peppered him with calls and emails. He answered every one.

I had the privilege of spending hours with Ed Charles in his apartment in East Elmhurst, Queens, before his passing, and his passionate soul and gentle spirit were profoundly uplifting. RIP, Glider.

Esther Newberg, my literary agent, and Colin Graham, ICM's sultan of contracts, did their customary yeoman work in representing me. I am lucky to have them, and likewise lucky to have the friendship of Joe DeSantis, who graciously afforded me a writing getaway, as he and his crack staff welcomed me at the wonderful Hampton Inn in Lake George, New York. Kevin Doughten, my editor at Crown, had a clear vision of the narrative from the outset and was a gem to work with throughout. Every one of his edits and suggestions made the book better, and if I didn't understand that completely in the moment, I certainly do now. Jon Darga, Kevin's able assistant, contributed mightily in more ways than I know. We wouldn't have even had a project without an enthusiastic go-ahead from Molly Stern, the publisher of Crown, and Tricia Boczkowski, the editorial director of Crown Archetype. Nearly fifteen years ago, I wrote another book for Crown, *The Boys of Winter: The Untold Story of a Coach, a Dream, and the 1980 U.S. Olympic Hockey Team*, and was blessed to have a first-rate group of professionals behind me, and it's no different this go-round. Special thanks to Ellen Folan for her unstinting publicity work and Kathleen Quinlan for the same in the marketing realm. Patricia Shaw and Phil Leung ably oversaw the whole production process, and the book would not be in your hands without them.

For well over a year, my go-to readers were my brother, Frank Coffey, who taught me to love baseball and words, and my friend Jordan Becker, a lawyer, music blogger, and accomplished chef who was more or less on 24-hour call, except when there was a Princeton reunion going on. If I were handing out MVPs for behind-the-scenes contributions, Frank and Jordan would both get one.

My home team—Denise Willi, my wife of 30 years, and our children, Alexandra, Sean, and Samantha—have long been my anchors, my greatest source of love and support. It has been a time of loss and challenge in our family, and having all of them around me has been a blessing beyond words because of the kind of people they are and the kind of hearts they have. I love you all more than you know. I don't tell you that nearly often enough.

WAYNE COFFEY is one of the country's most acclaimed sports journalists. A former writer for the New York *Daily News,* he co-wrote R. A. Dickey's bestselling *Wherever I Wind Up* and Carli Lloyd's bestselling *When Nobody Was Watching,* and is the author of the *New York Times* bestseller *The Boys of Winter.*

waynecoffeyauthor.com
Twitter: @wr_coffey
Find Wayne Coffey on Facebook

Also from the award-winning sportswriter

WAYNE COFFEY,

the *New York Times* bestselling book

The Boys of Winter

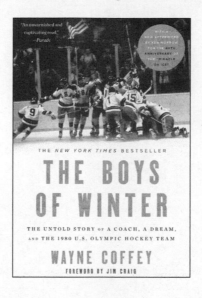

"Wayne Coffey brilliantly weaves the behind-the-scenes
story that amplifies how improbable this 'miracle' really was."
—PAT LaFONTAINE, NHL Hall of Famer

"First came the Hollywood version of the Miracle on Ice.
Now comes the real story, rich in context and texture,
as only a journalist and author like Wayne Coffey
can report it and tell it."
—HARVEY ARATON, *The New York Times*